DATE DUE

NR 26 03			

DEMCO 38-296

Events That Changed
the World in the
Nineteenth Century

The Greenwood Press "Events That Changed the World" Series

Events That Changed the World in the Twentieth Century
Frank W. Thackeray and John E. Findling, editors

12

Events That Changed the World in the Nineteenth Century

edited by
Frank W. Thackeray
&
John E. Findling

THE GREENWOOD PRESS
"EVENTS THAT CHANGED THE WORLD" SERIES

GREENWOOD PRESS
Westport, Connecticut • London

Library of Congress Cataloging-in-Publication Data

Events that changed the world in the nineteenth century / edited by
    Frank W. Thackeray & John E. Findling.
        p.   cm.—(The Greenwood Press "Events that changed the
    world" series, ISSN 1078–7860)
    Includes bibliographical references (p.   ) and index.
    ISBN 0–313–29076–8 (alk. paper)
    1. History, Modern—19th century.   I. Thackeray, Frank W.
    II. Findling, John E.   III. Series.
    D358.E97   1996
    909.81—dc20   95–53133

British Library Cataloguing in Publication Data is available.

Library of Congress Catalog Card Number: 95–53133
ISBN: 0–313–29076–8
ISSN: 1078–7860

First published in 1996

Greenwood Press, 88 Post Road West, Westport, CT 06881
An imprint of Greenwood Publishing Group, Inc.

Printed in the United States of America

∞™

The paper used in this book complies with the
Permanent Paper Standard issued by the National
Information Standards Organization (Z39.48–1984).

10 9 8 7 6 5 4 3 2 1

Contents

Illustrations

Preface

This volume, which describes and evaluates the global impact of ten of the nineteenth century's most important events, is the second in a multivolume series intended to acquaint readers with the seminal events of modern times. An earlier volume covered the most important world events of the twentieth century. Future volumes will include the most important world events of earlier centuries. There is also a series of volumes specifically addressing the American experience.

Our collective classroom experience provided the inspiration for this project. Having encountered literally thousands of entry-level college students whose knowledge of the world in which they live is sadly deficient, we determined to write a series of books that would concentrate on the most important events affecting those students (and others as well) in the hope that they would better understand their world and how it came to be. Furthermore, we hope these books will stimulate the reader to delve further into the events covered in each volume and to take a greater interest in history in general.

The current volume is designed to serve two purposes. First, the editors have provided an introduction that presents factual material about each event in a clear, concise, chronological order. Second, each introduction is followed by a longer interpretive essay by a recognized authority exploring the ramifications of the event under consideration. Each chapter concludes with an annotated bibliography of the most important works about the event. The chapters are followed by four appendices that give additional information useful to the reader. Appendix A is a glossary of names, events, organizations, treaties, and terms mentioned but not fully explained in the introductions and the essays. Appendix B is a timeline of nineteenth-century events. Appendix C traces the population growth of selected countries during the nineteenth century. Appendix D lists countries colonized during the "Imperial Scramble" (1870–1914).

The events covered in this volume were selected on the basis of our combined teaching and research activities. Colleagues and contributors made suggestions as well, and for this we thank them. Of course, any pair of editors might have arrived at a somewhat different list than we did; but we believe that we have assembled a group of events that truly changed the nineteenth-century world.

As with all published works, numerous people behind the scenes deserve much of the credit for the final product. Barbara Rader, our editor at Greenwood Publishing Group, has consistently lent her support, encouragement, and patience to the project. Our student research assistant, Bob Marshall, worked diligently to fulfill our every request. Special thanks go to Brigette Colligan, who cheerfully, speedily, and efficiently word processed what appeared to be reams of material. As always, Kirk Klaphaak applied his computer-oriented magic to the manuscript with salutary results. We also wish to thank Indiana University Southeast for supplying us with funds to hire our student research assistant. Many thanks to Roger and Amy Baylor and to Kate O'Connell for opening their hearts and their establishment to us, thereby giving us a congenial, enlightened atmosphere for wide-ranging discussions on every conceivable subject, including our manuscript, at the very time when our campus seemed less than enthusiastic about fulfilling that role. Most important, we wish to thank the authors of the book's essays. All were cooperative, and all presented us with insightful, articulate analysis. Without them, there would be no book.

Finally, we wish to express our appreciation to our spouses, Kathy Thackeray and Carol Findling, and to our children, Alex and Max Thackeray and Jamey Findling, who nurtured our dreams, supported our work, tolerated our idiosyncrasies, and overlooked our idiocies as we grappled with our manuscript. For that we are grateful.

Frank W. Thackeray
John E. Findling

Events That Changed the World in the Nineteenth Century

Napoleon salutes his troops. Napoleon's seemingly invincible army ranged freely across Europe until its disastrous invasion of Russia in 1812. (Reproduced from the Collections of the Library of Congress)

1 _____

The Napoleonic Era, 1799–1815

INTRODUCTION

Napoleon Bonaparte was one of those rare figures who made history rather than being made by history. He shaped events, frequently forcing the world to conform to his expectations; and those expectations were revolutionary in nature. Although Napoleon ultimately failed, he left an indelible mark on the modern world.

Napoleon Bonaparte was born in 1769 on Corsica, a rather remote Mediterranean island that France had only recently acquired. As the Bonapartes were minor nobility, Napoleon qualified for admission to a military academy. Commissioned a lieutenant in the royal army, Napoleon managed to keep his head during the turbulent days of the French Revolution. In 1793 he helped to drive the British from the French port of Toulon, and in 1795 he gained some fame when he broke up a Paris demonstration with "a whiff of grapeshot." Eventually, Napoleon emerged as a general under the Directory, a weak and corrupt French government formed in 1795.

In 1797 Napoleon took command of France's Army of Italy. He scored several significant military successes in northern Italy and in October imposed the Treaty of Campo Formio on Austria. In the course of his

Italian campaigns, Napoleon demonstrated not only military prowess but also a unique facility for self-promotion. He was fast becoming a well-known figure in France.

In 1798 Napoleon led an expedition to Egypt in order to threaten the British position in India and the eastern Mediterranean. Although his troops were cut off in August when the British fleet under Horatio Nelson defeated the French navy at the Battle of the Nile, or Aboukir Bay, French public opinion regarded the young general as a hero. Sensing that the time was right to further his ambitions, Napoleon abandoned his army in Egypt, returned to France, and joined a group of conspirators who plotted to overthrow the Directory and needed a military figure to give their scheme credibility. On November 9, 1799, the conspirators ousted the Directory, replacing it with a new government called the Consulate. Although the Consulate consisted of three consuls, Napoleon soon emerged as first among equals and dominated the new regime as First Consul.

By December 1804, Napoleon had turned the Consulate into an empire with himself at its head. Napoleon's imperial state proved to be quite impressive, so much so that many subsequent rulers patterned their governments after his. A key feature was its centralized bureaucracy. The emperor exercised a monopoly on all power, and he used a dedicated, intelligent, and omnipresent administration to rule the country. Although for a time there existed on paper a number of representative institutions, this was a sham. The most important legislative body was the Council of State, an appointed group filled with technocrats who crafted laws according to the emperor's desires. Furthermore, Napoleon virtually did away with local government; Paris made practically all local appointments.

Although Napoleon did not institute a democracy, he did establish a meritocracy. France became a state where "careers were open to talent." Napoleon did not care about one's social background as long as one was competent and loyal. Perhaps Napoleon said it best when he remarked that every army recruit potentially carried a marshal's baton in his knapsack; and, in fact, common soldiers did become generals under the empire. The upper ranks of the Napoleonic administration were filled with people ranging from former aristocrats to revolutionaries and regicides. Ability and loyalty alone counted; all the rest was inconsequential.

Napoleon also established the rule of law, but it was a curious one in that it buttressed a police state. The Code Napoléon placed all France on a uniform legal basis; it did away once and for all with the legal jumble of the old regime and brought order out of chaos. Simultaneously, however, Napoleon erected an authoritarian superstructure. Centralized, systematic censorship was introduced. Political clubs were banned and the emperor's opponents were deported to the colonies. Both uniformed and plainclothes policemen proliferated, and police spies were everywhere.

The Napoleonic regime also turned its attention to education. Not unexpectedly, it created a large, centralized bureaucracy to oversee instruction in France. In particular, it established a system of *lycées*, or elite secondary schools, where the "best and brightest" were taught to follow the emperor and trained in a variety of subjects that would prove useful to the state.

Napoleon also fashioned a Concordat, or agreement, with the Roman Catholic Church. Relations between revolutionary France and the Vatican had progressively deteriorated, and Napoleon realized that if this enmity continued, his regime would never be secure. Consequently, in 1801 he signed the Concordat, which settled matters on terms favorable to the emperor-to-be. According to the Concordat, the state recognized the obvious, namely, that Roman Catholicism was the religion of most Frenchmen. In an important concession to the Vatican, the Concordat gave Rome greater control over the Church in France. In return, the Vatican recognized the Consulate and surrendered all claims to Church property seized and subsequently sold by the revolutionaries. The Concordat turned over to the Church primary education in France, but the state would now pay clerical salaries and nominate bishops (although their consecration remained in papal hands). Finally, and perhaps most important, the Concordat granted religious freedom to all Frenchmen.

Despite its shortcomings, the Civil Code, renamed the Code Napoléon in 1807, was a great accomplishment. It firmly established the principle of equality under the law and brought legal and judicial uniformity to France. It also guaranteed religious freedom and the right of individuals to enter into contracts and to own property. It was particularly solicitous of property rights. However, the Code also had its downside. Women were clearly subordinated to their fathers and husbands. Trade unions and strikes were outlawed, and workers were placed in an inferior position vis-à-vis their employers. The rights of criminal defendants were diminished and the jury system was abridged.

As spectacular as Napoleon's rule in France was, his nearly successful attempt to conquer Europe overshadowed it. Napoleon had made his mark as a general, and even after he seized power in France, soldiering was never far from his mind and conquest was always dear to his heart.

Shortly after the Consulate was established, hostilities with Austria resumed. In 1800 Napoleon's forces won major victories at Marengo in Italy and at Hohenlinden in Germany, and in February 1801 Austria signed the Treaty of Lunéville. This treaty confirmed the earlier Treaty of Campo Formio by which France annexed Belgium (the Austrian Netherlands), established its northeastern boundary at the Rhine River, and made significant gains in Italy.

After Lunéville, only an isolated and exhausted Great Britain remained at war with France. In March 1802 Britain and France signed the Peace of Amiens; however, in May 1803, hostilities resumed and Great Britain built the Third Coalition against France.

Two earlier coalitions, or alliances, against France had failed, and the third one, consisting of Britain, Austria, and Russia, suffered the same fate. Between 1805 and 1807, Napoleon crafted a series of incredible military triumphs that left him practical master of continental Europe west of the Russian steppes. Victories at Ulm (1805), Austerlitz (1805), Jena (1806), and Auerstädt (1806) rendered Austria and Prussia helpless. A draw at Eylau (1807) and victory at Friedland (1807) humbled Russia and brought the tsar, Alexander I, to the negotiating table. According to the terms of the Treaty of Tilsit (1807), Russia and France became allies, France continued to occupy Berlin, and Prussia lost considerable territory to the Kingdom of Westphalia.

Tilsit marked the high point of Napoleonic hegemony in Europe, but even then Napoleon's domination was not complete. The island nation of Great Britain still opposed the French emperor, and the British had won a pivotal victory in October 1805 when Nelson destroyed the combined French and Spanish fleets at the Battle of Trafalgar. Unable now to invade Great Britain, Napoleon commenced to wage economic war on his rival by implementing the Continental System, which effectively closed Europe to British goods.

In trying to enforce the Continental System, Napoleon experienced his first setback on land. Napoleon marched into Spain in 1808 in order to prevent that nation from trading with Britain. The Spanish resisted Napoleon's scheme to place his brother Joseph on the Spanish throne and resorted to guerrilla warfare. Great Britain encouraged Spain, sending British troops under Arthur Wellesley, later the Duke of Wellington, to aid the Spanish. Napoleon never gained the upper hand in Spain, and the so-called Spanish ulcer dogged him to the end.

Despite another easy victory for Napoleon over Austria in 1809, tensions between Russia and France mounted. Napoleon decided to attack his ally, and in June 1812 he invaded Russia at the head of an army estimated at 500,000. However, even after he seized Moscow, the Russians refused to discuss peace terms with him. Isolated in hostile country, and with a tenuous supply line stretching hundreds of miles, no proper housing for his soldiers, disease rampant, and winter beginning to set in, Napoleon had no alternative but to retreat. The result was disastrous. By the time the French extricated themselves from Russia, about 90 percent of their original force had perished. Napoleon, meanwhile, had abandoned his troops to race back to France to raise another army.

Napoleon's dizzying descent from the heights of power now accelerated. In January 1813 the victorious Russians decided to pursue Napoleon into the heart of Europe. Shortly thereafter, Prussia abandoned Napoleon and sided with Russia. In June 1813 Wellington crossed the Pyrenees Mountains and invaded France from Spain. In August Austria joined the anti-Napoleonic coalition. Finally, in October 1813 this huge coalition defeated Napoleon at the Battle of Leipzig, sometimes called the Battle of the Nations.

Napoleon retreated to France, but his enemies pursued him. In March 1814 coalition troops occupied Paris, and in April Napoleon abdicated and was exiled to Elba, a small Mediterranean island. However, Napoleon was not quite finished. In March 1815 he returned to France for a tumultuous "Hundred Days." Landing in the south of France virtually alone, Napoleon quickly gathered support as he moved toward Paris. In a very short time, Napoleon ousted the restored Bourbon dynasty and regained control of the French army. However, in June 1815 he met an Anglo-Prussian force at Waterloo in Belgium commanded by Wellington and was defeated. This time the victors exiled him to the remote island of St. Helena in the South Atlantic, where he died six years later.

INTERPRETIVE ESSAY
M. B. Biskupski

Napoleon may well be the most consequential actor ever to have appeared on the European scene. The enormous changes associated with his career profoundly affected Europe, and they are still evident. We may best understand Napoleon's influence by concentrating on two questions. The first concerns his career as a conqueror. What did Napoleon do to restructure the traditional European balance of power, how did he use military, diplomatic, economic, and other means to transform the international structure, and what were the consequences of this transformation? This problem is often and mistakenly understood in narrowly military terms, when in reality the focus should be on much larger issues. In other words, we must regard Napoleon in geostrategic terms.

The second question requires us to enter the world of ideas. Napoleon spread the ideas of the French Revolution—popular sovereignty, legal equality, republican forms, and administrative reorganization along Enlightenment principles—dramatically and disruptively across Europe. Furthermore, the remaking of France, which emphasized the sovereignty of the French people, greatly stimulated the notion of political nationalism, or the right of each national community to unfettered self-expression free from foreign control. Nationalism is arguably the most powerful political force in the modern world. Napoleon, and the era he did so much to shape, had an enormous effect on the emergence of nationalism and the movement for national unity within Europe. In this context we are concerned with the most controversial question regarding the Napoleonic era, namely, Did Napoleon really spread the ideas of the French Revolution, and thus act as a revolutionary force in history, or did his dictatorial form of government "betray the revolution"?

The French Revolution aroused monarchical and conservative opposition throughout Europe. War against Prussia and Austria began as early as 1792. In the same year the French government declared itself a republic and offered aid to any people that rose up in opposition to monarchy. This was a declaration of war against the European political structure. France not only repulsed the Austro-Prussian invasion, but advanced boldly along the Dutch coast. This established France as a threat to the prevailing strategic balance. The powers of Europe saw clearly what was at stake. The French were threatening to dominate northwestern Europe, thus reviving an aggressive strategy reminiscent of the wars of Louis XIV a century earlier. Now, however, the French threat was double: their armies were moving borders, while the Revolution's republican ideas were threatening to destroy the internal cohesion of their enemies. Most of Europe united in the face of the threat.

The First Coalition brought enormous though uncoordinated forces into play against France, with mixed results. By early 1796 French forces were successful in the north, defeating and occupying Holland and forcing Prussia to accept peace. Imperial Austria, however, proved resilient and intractable, and French troops in the south, on the Italian front, were on the defensive. At the age of twenty-six, Napoleon was already a well-known general when the Directory sent him to command the ragtag and demoralized French army in Italy. There he engineered a dazzling series of victories over the Austrians. In these campaigns one sees for the first time many of the features that were to epitomize the Napoleonic art of war. First, Napoleon transformed the supply system, insisting that his army live off the land. This not only freed it from long and tenuous supply lines, but it also gave it much greater maneuverability than his enemies' more traditionally maintained forces. Second, Napoleon emphasized speed, maneuver, and numerical superiority at the point of attack (even if he was outnumbered overall). In turn this required his troops to adopt an exclusively offensive mentality, attacking almost ceaselessly, and relying on surprise and enthusiasm to overcome the enemy. Napoleon has been criticized for his offensive-mindedness, but in Italy as elsewhere this did much to demoralize his opponents and contributed to what was the third, and perhaps greatest, aspect of the Napoleonic military system, namely, the enormous confidence and almost fanatical belief his troops had in Napoleon's abilities. Napoleon's famous adversary at Waterloo, the Duke of Wellington, once remarked that Napoleon's charisma was worth 60,000 troops to the French.

By 1797 Napoleon had beaten the Austrians, knocked Sardinia out of the war, taken a brief expedition south forcing Naples and the pope to terms, and was crossing the Alps for a final assault on Austria proper. Hence was born the Treaty of Campo Formio (1797), which made Napoleon a national hero, removed Austria from the war, brought all of Italy and Switzerland into French hands, and shattered the anti-French coalition. France dominated western Europe. Only Britain, due to its insular position, had been able to survive the French juggernaut.

British naval power precluded direct French attacks on the island kingdom. It also allowed the British to intervene on the Continent at will, thus preventing the French from stabilizing their position. To counter the British threat, Napoleon devised a strategy that would weaken and distract them. This explains his seemingly quixotic Egyptian campaign. Often presented as a strange episode, the Napoleonic invasion of Egypt demonstrated a broad grasp of strategic issues. By capturing Egypt (nominally under Turkish suzerainty, but really dependent upon the British), the French would accomplish many things: drive the British from the Mediterranean, thus damaging their overall maritime position (the key to British power); sever British communications with India, the heart of the empire; and degrade British trade worldwide. Unfortunately for Napoleon, the French success in Egypt was nullified when British admiral Horatio Nelson destroyed the French fleet at Aboukir (August 1798), thereby stranding the French field forces. Realizing his campaign had been a failure, Napoleon ruthlessly abandoned his men and returned to Europe. The significance of naval power, the command of the seas, was demonstrated.

Napoleon returned to a France now gravely threatened by the Second Coalition, which had been provoked by the Egyptian campaign and encouraged by its failure. Austria again took the field, now joined by Russia, which had been especially unhappy about French efforts in the eastern Mediterranean, an area where it had its own designs to pursue. Minor allies included Naples, Portugal, and Turkey. By the time Napoleon returned from Egypt, an Austro-Russian army was operating in northern Italy and Switzerland. Soon, however, Austro-Russian unity disappeared, and by 1799 Austria faced France alone. Napoleon, now virtual dictator of France, defeated the Austrians at Marengo, while other French units crushed them at Hohenlinden. After these double defeats, the Austrians agreed to the Treaty of Lunéville (1801). The British, without allies, war-weary, and financially hard-pressed, accepted the Treaty of Amiens (1802), bringing general peace to Europe for the first time in a decade; but it was a Europe in which France had demonstrated its military mastery.

The incompatibility of French domination of western Europe with British national interests made the 1802 peace precarious. The British were especially concerned about Napoleon's efforts to consolidate central Europe under French hegemony. Worse, there were indications that Napoleon wished to reassert French influence in the Western Hemisphere. A series of minor provocations led London to renew the war in 1803. Napoleon assembled an armada, but the French concentration in the northern coastal regions almost invited the Austrians to act in the east. Consequently, under the able leadership of Prime Minister William Pitt the Younger, Great Britain cobbled together the Third Coalition, with Austria and Russia again combining to attack French positions in northern Italy.

The Russo-Austrian alliance intended to sweep lightly defended northern Italy, then move west across the Rhine River into France itself. Napoleon, learning of his enemies' strategy, moved at once, virtually surrounding the utterly confounded Austrians at Ulm (October 1805). The result was one of history's most decisive battles; indeed, it was not a battle, for the Austrians were so completely outmaneuvered that they capitulated without serious resistance.

After the Austrian disaster at Ulm, Napoleon swept aside the Russian attempt to block his path to Vienna, which he occupied in November 1805. The remaining Austrian forces, joined by a considerable Russian army, sought to surround the extended French near Vienna. Instead they were led into an elaborate trap when Napoleon encircled and routed them at Austerlitz (December 1805). The Austrians surrendered unconditionally, signing the Treaty of Pressburg. Distance saved the Russians, who withdrew. Napoleon now held sway over all of central Europe; but this was merely the beginning.

Alarmed by the magnitude of the French victory, Prussia, under vigorous British prompting, belatedly entered the fray. It was a colossal mistake. The Prussian army was completely crushed at the Battle of Jena (October 1806). On the same day the Prussians were also thrashed at Auerstädt. Demoralized and thoroughly beaten, the Prussian army disintegrated. Napoleon pursued the remnants of the Prussian forces and their Russian allies. Berlin was occupied, and the Prussian king sought refuge with the Russians. During early 1807 Napoleon chased the Russians along the Baltic coast, falling upon them at Eylau. Shortly thereafter Danzig fell to the French, setting up the decisive Battle of Friedland (June 1807), where Napoleon smashed the Russians, inflicting huge casualties and driving the rest into disordered retreat. The Russians asked for a truce, formalized at the Treaty of Tilsit in July 1807. Napoleon was the master of Europe.

Only one failure marked the French triumph over the Third Coalition, and this was a major failure indeed. In October 1805 Nelson annihilated the luckless French navy and their Spanish allies at the Battle of Trafalgar. The result was arguably the most decisive naval battle of all history. It ended the war at sea, secured the British maritime position, left Napoleon no serious naval weapon, and made Britain invulnerable to attack. Napoleon's inability to match the British at sea demonstrated the futility of merely successful land operations in grand strategy. This was a problem Napoleon understood but could not solve.

His continental victories allowed Napoleon to redraw the map of Europe. Tilsit forced Russian cooperation in a de facto division of the Continent. Prussia was radically reshaped. It was made to disgorge what it had taken in the partitions of Poland, a territory now reconstituted as the Grand Duchy of Warsaw, a French strategic outpost in eastern Europe. Prussia's western territories between the Rhine and the Elbe Rivers were surrendered outright. A French army of occupation settled in until a large indemnity was paid. Napoleon also created the Confederation of the Rhine, a loose grouping of German states under French influence that replaced the defunct Holy Roman Empire, whose imperial dynasty was now restyled as emperors of Austria. Napoleon's reworking of the boundaries of central Europe underscored the importance of German territory for the mastery of Europe. Although Napoleon destroyed the Holy Roman Empire, he could not maintain French control over the result. Ultimately this prepared the way for a new reorganization in central Europe—a powerful unified Germany.

The short-lived French imperium in Europe consisted of a series of concentric rings. At the core was France itself, bloated by territorial acquisitions, especially in Italy and along the North Sea coast. Beyond lay several French dependencies like the Confederation of the Rhine, Spain (which Napoleon managed to win for his brother Joseph in 1808), and the Kingdom of Naples, ruled by Napoleon's brother-in-law Joachim Murat. Still farther distant lay cowed Prussia and beaten Austria, both with the French outpost of the Duchy of Warsaw on their flank. In 1809 the hapless Austrians once again tried to rise against French control, only to be defeated at Wagram. An Austrian effort to undermine the French position in the east was similarly foiled when Polish troops drove them from the Duchy of Warsaw. The resulting Treaty of Schönbrunn (1809) brought France's curious annexation of the so-called Illyrian Provinces, an irregular strip of land along the Adriatic coast comprising much of today's Slovenia and Croatia. Only Russia in the distant east and insular Britain lay beyond French grasp.

Regarding Britain, Napoleon had made provision. He had forced both Russia and Prussia to agree to participate in the Continental System, a vast economic scheme to prevent British trade with the Continent in order to cripple England economically. However, this project proved impossibly difficult to enforce and thus failed. The Continental System was another example of the same strategic thinking that lay behind the earlier Egyptian campaign. Both arose from the French lack of adequate naval strength to engage the British directly. This, in turn, forced them to consider indirect means of damaging the commerce that supported English economic and military power. In both cases British sea power proved superior, thus demonstrating the overall strategic significance of naval strength for success in war.

Although Napoleon had conquered much of Europe and built an elaborate structure to maintain France's predominance, continental stability still eluded him, since Russia was resentful and Britain invulnerable. This explains Napoleon's controversial 1812 invasion of Russia. After 1807 Europe obviously refused to stabilize under French control. Although Napoleon conquered both Spain and Portugal, he could not hold Iberia securely. For years Spanish irregulars and a British invasion force tied down hundreds of thousands of French troops. The hemorrhage in the west was compounded by perpetual Austrian efforts at reasserting itself in the east. Napoleon's fear of a clash with distant Russia loomed over all. Tsar Alexander I resented the ruinous effects of the Continental System for his economy and in 1812 denounced it, thus openly defying Napoleon. With England unbroken, Russia emerging from its obedience to Tilsit, Austria ever restive, and Spain constantly draining his resources, it was clear to Napoleon that French security in Europe rested on shaky foundations. Having decided to act—characteristic of Napoleon, who always preferred action even if the risks were high—the question became where? Britain was unassailable, but Russia was another matter. The French had bested the Russians before and were confident of their military superiority. A defeat for Russia would ensure French prestige in central and eastern Europe, return the Russians to the Continental System, and convince recalcitrant powers like Austria that French supremacy was permanent. Hence, the 1812 campaign.

It is an oft-repeated mistake to regard 1812 as Napoleon's effort to conquer Russia; actually, his ambitions were relatively modest. The massive army marshaled to invade Russia was the greatest ever assembled; however, only 200,000 of the approximately 500,000 troops were French. The remainder—Germans, Italians, and Austrians—were unwilling and not particularly reliable. Only the Polish units, who viewed Napoleon as the champion of a restored Poland, were fanatically loyal.

Beginning in June 1812, Napoleon marched eastward. He defeated the Russians in several battles, but none was decisive. At the Battle of Borodino, Napoleon's health unexpectedly failed him. The Russians were again defeated, but Napoleon's illness prevented him from rapidly pursuing them. By September Napoleon was in Moscow, and the Russians continued to retreat with the exhausted French in pursuit. However, bad weather, declining morale, and frustration at being unable to end the campaign successfully caused Napoleon to abandon Moscow in October. The lengthy withdrawal became a disaster as the weather turned foul, the supply system broke down completely, and the Russians harassed Napoleon's retreating army. By the end of the year, the invasion force lay in ruins and Napoleon left the remnants to rush to Paris to raise fresh forces.

With Napoleon's situation desperate, the Prussians and the Austrians betrayed their French allies and turned on them. Throwing fresh but inexperienced troops into the fray, Napoleon faced a galaxy of enemies who, following his retreat from Russia, no longer believed in the mystique of Napoleonic invincibility. By late summer 1813, Austrian manpower and British money made the French situation yet more precarious. However, despite a 50 percent numerical superiority, the allied troops refused to attack French units commanded by Napoleon personally, concentrating instead on his subordinates. Defeat of his lieutenants weakened Napoleon's forces, and the desertion of his German allies was disastrous. By October Napoleon was forced to fight at Leipzig, virtually surrounded by Russians, Austrians, and Prussians. The French were defeated, but allied incompetence let Napoleon escape to France, where the allies pursued him. Ironically, Napoleon's tactical virtuosity now shone at its brightest; in February 1814, he repeatedly bested the Prussians and also defeated large Austrian and Russian units. Despite this, the enemy coalition forced the French to surrender Paris before Napoleon could reach the city with relief. The capital fallen, enemy troops everywhere, and the country exhausted, Napoleon agreed to abdicate. Fittingly, the French defeat before Paris was almost simultaneous with the ignominious end to France's Spanish campaign.

Napoleon's "retirement" to Elba proved brief. He returned to France in March 1815, resumed power, and planned a typically bold campaign to smash his enemies before they could combine against him. However, a series of errors and ill luck, including Napoleon's own hesitation when he had Wellington beaten in the opening phase of the decisive Battle of Waterloo, destroyed French efforts. Napoleon very nearly turned overwhelming defeat into another victory, but this time history's greatest soldier had risked long odds once too often.

The Napoleonic conquests gave France an ephemeral greatness, but Napoleon's consequences for Europe endured long after his empire disappeared. This is because Napoleon's conquests were not just military victories, but fundamental reorganizations of Europe's political and social order. Whether one regards Napoleon as exemplifying the liberal and republican ideals of the French Revolution or sees him as a cynical conqueror exploiting these sentiments for his own purposes is, in many ways, inconsequential. Regardless of his intentions, Napoleon remolded Europe's structure and political culture. Initially, he destroyed the established political order—whether it be the Holy Roman Empire, the medieval fragmentation of Italy, or the Partitions of Poland. The fact that he smashed these structures in the name of republican ideals, popular sovereignty, and the right of nationalities to self-expression is yet more important. Whether he wished or not, Napoleon was seen as the bearer of the new political culture; he was the symbol of an era fundamentally opposed to traditional monarchy and committed to recasting borders and polities. Hence Napoleon's conquests have a double effect. Outwardly he overturned established states, redrew borders, and redistributed populations, often cynically and capriciously. At the same time, he represented a principle of reorganization within these newly reshaped territories that forced their inhabitants to address the most fundamental political questions of all: Who are we? What are our people? To whom ought we belong? What is the ultimate locus of sovereignty in our land?

It may well be true that it was the French Revolution and not Napoleon that initiated the political reordering of Europe. But that is to miss the obvious, for without Napoleon's military genius the ideas of the Revolution would have remained local curiosities, devoid of the power and prestige naturally attached to victorious armies and charismatic captains. Napoleon epitomized the ideas of the French Revolution, and by the breadth of his conquests and the overpowering force of his armies he brought these ideas into all parts of Europe in a way that guaranteed them a respectful if not receptive audience. In this sense Napoleon resembled U.S. president Woodrow Wilson in the twentieth century, who personified both the power of American military and economic might *and* the allure of new and attractive ideals. The fact that Wilson was devoid of originality, that his political ideas were derivative, ill-formed, and contradictory, was of no more significance than the fact that Napoleon may not have been a true believer in the ideals of republicanism represented by the French Revolution.

Perhaps the most striking way to demonstrate Napoleon's significance is to consider the consequences of his dramatic conquests. Napoleon permanently reorganized central Europe. The medieval, ramshackle Holy Roman Empire was unable to defend central Europe against French aggression, and Prussia almost vanished from the map after repeated drubbings at the hands of the French. As a result, the powers of Europe realized that a fundamental reorganization of central Europe was necessary. Hence, Napoleon promoted the consolidation of central Europe by laying the strategic groundwork for the emergence of a unified Germany.

But Napoleon's influence in the region proved more profound than this would suggest. Repeated French triumphs had manifold effects on the German population. To a rising generation of young Germans, the French victories demonstrated the superiority of national unification (France) over disunity, thus providing an object lesson of the advantages to be found in creating a German national state. Prussia, beaten and disgraced by France, underwent a fundamental reorganization that eventually brought it to dominate central Europe in Bismarck's era. Napoleon's France became the model for many Germans, and it would remain so until Bismarck's united Germany, also extolling national unity and military efficiency, eclipsed France as the leading continental power.

For the Poles, Napoleon represented the possibility of undoing the partitions that had removed their ancient state from Europe's map at the close of the eighteenth century. Flocking to Napoleon's banner, the Poles fought with the French, but for Poland. Napoleon never succeeded in recreating Poland, and he probably never sincerely tried to; yet his victories over the partitioning powers Austria, Prussia, and Russia, the brief life of the Duchy of Warsaw, and the heroic Polish efforts as France's ally demonstrated both to the world and to the Poles themselves that Poland was not a lost cause. It is little wonder that Polish Romanticism, the cultlike dedication to restore Poland to the map, rose from the wreckage of Napoleon's defeats. The Napoleonic era in Polish history is the direct prelude to the powerful Polish Question in European politics.

Napoleon's campaigns in Italy swept aside the complex and fragmented eighteenth-century structure that characterized the Italian peninsula. Although Napoleon never created a united Italy, just as he never created a united Poland, he did experiment with several larger groupings. Hence Napoleon's major effect was to clear the way for the national movement that swept over Italy during the next generation. Efforts by the Congress of Vienna to restore Italy's pre-Napoleonic divisions proved futile, and the Risorgimento grew rapidly in strength.

There is no more dramatic demonstration of the power and dimension of Napoleon's influence than the example of his Illyrian Provinces. Formed from territory wrung from Austria at the Treaty of Schönbrunn, Illyria became the conduit for French ideas into southeastern Europe. The French incorporated the area directly into France, ended serfdom, introduced the Code Napoléon, and in general awakened the area from its medieval torpor. Yet more important, the example of the Illyrian Provinces stimulated the idea of south-Slav unity. Thus there emerged the "Illyrian Movement," which pursued the goal of a south-Slav state, or Yugoslavia.

However, Napoleon's influence reached beyond the Illyrian Provinces proper and penetrated the Balkans with its message of political reform and national unity. Greeks, Romanians, Bulgarians, and Serbs all looked to the Napoleonic example to stimulate their nascent national movements. It is no coincidence that the Serbian Rising (1804) and the Greek War of Independence (1821) bracket the Napoleonic era. In the eyes of the Balkan peoples, Napoleon represented liberation from foreign domination and sociopolitical backwardness, both exemplified by the Ottoman Turkish Empire that ruled them. Hence Napoleon's role in the emergence of the Balkans' modern national states is direct and considerable.

Even inadvertently, Napoleon influenced national movements. In 1809 Russia, Napoleon's ally after Tilsit, invaded Sweden—ostensibly because of Sweden's pro-British orientation. The tsar grabbed the Swedish province of Finland for his efforts. The result was that the Finns now found themselves in quite another world. In the words of a Finnish patriot, "Swedes we are no longer; Russians we cannot be; therefore we must become Finns."

Thanks to Napoleon, France was given a brief period of mastery over Europe. Ironically, this occurred at just the moment when the Industrial Revolution was making mineral-poor and demographically weak France an unlikely candidate for continental supremacy. Unintentionally, Napoleon condemned France to a frustrating recollection of an unobtainable greatness, thereby making it difficult if not impossible for France to accept a lesser status more befitting its capacities. This led directly to France's overplaying its role in the post-1815 world, with dubious consequences.

For Great Britain and Russia, the two powers which did so much to bring Napoleon low, their part in his defeat has played an enormous role in their self-definition. It not only demonstrated their military prowess—the invincible Royal Navy for the British and the implacable defensive capacities of the Russians—but, by presenting Napoleon as the demonic destroyer of civilization, both these nations included a special status, defenders of civilization, as a defining element of their political culture. The result, be it Russian sense of mission or British disdain for mere Continentals, has been a problematic inheritance for the West.

But Napoleon was neither Satan nor St. George, and the analogies to other conquerors, most notably Hitler, are misleading and, in Hitler's case, repulsive. Napoleon's military efforts were not the result of technical innovation or original theory; rather, they proceeded from a bold and inspired use of existing instruments. And while he was successful on land, he was a failure at sea, thereby revealing both his conceptual and technical limitations. Napoleon's strategic thinking—notably his various efforts to weaken England—shows a powerful and subtle mind; but he was far from genius. The Egyptian campaign, despite its sound goals, did not carefully reckon with French naval weakness in the Mediterranean, and the Russian campaign was clearly beyond French capabilities. However, the Continental System, despite its ultimate failure, is decidedly modern in its goals and means. Here French capacities and the technological limitations of the age thwarted Napoleon's ambitions. Furthermore, the various reconfigurations in Italy and Germany, the musings about Poland, and especially the grotesque nepotism of the imperial empire are hardly examples of profound and clear geostrategic vision. Nonetheless, his shortcomings aside, Napoleon dominated Europe. He was a revolutionary force, both in unmaking the Europe of his day and in spreading the ideas that would shape the Continent's future. His ability to wage war was perhaps unrivaled in history, and this alone makes him a figure of enormous, indeed awesome, interest.

SELECTED BIBLIOGRAPHY

Bergeron, L. *France under Napoleon.* Translated by R. R. Palmer. Princeton, NJ: Princeton University Press, 1981. An in-depth study of domestic administration.

Chandler, David G. *The Campaigns of Napoleon.* New York: Macmillan, 1966. The best synthetic account of all the campaigns.

———. *Dictionary of the Napoleonic Wars.* New York: Macmillan, 1979. An indispensable reference work.

Connelly, Owen. *Blundering to Glory: Napoleon's Military Campaigns.* Wilmington, DE: Scholarly Resources, 1987. A provocative and stimulating reevaluation of the Napoleonic military record.

———. *Napoleon's Satellite Kingdoms.* New York: Free Press, 1965. A leading contemporary specialist on Napoleon looks at an important though frequently overlooked topic.

Delderfield, R. F. *Napoleon's Marshals.* Philadelphia: Chilton Books, 1966. Engagingly written discussion of Napoleon's military lieutenants.

Ellis, Geoffrey. *Napoleon's Continental Blockade.* New York: Oxford University Press, 1981. A reliable account of an important aspect of the Napoleonic strategy against England.

Esposito, Vincent J., and John R. Elting. *A Military History and Atlas of the Napoleonic Wars.* New York: Praeger, 1964. The standard reference work.

Gates, David. *The Spanish Ulcer: A History of the Peninsular War.* New York: Norton, 1986. Probably the standard English-language account of the topic.

Geyl, Pieter. *Napoleon: For and Against.* Translated by Olive Renier. New Haven, CT: Yale University Press, 1949. A famous work posing a series of interpretive questions about the "meaning" of Napoleon.

Glover, Michael. *The Peninsular War, 1807–1814: A Concise Military History.* Hamden, CT: Archon Books, 1974. A first-rate treatment of Napoleon's distracting and draining Spanish problem.

Hamilton-Williams, David. *Waterloo: New Perspectives: The Great Battle Reappraised.* New York: J. Wiley and Sons, 1994. An important and controversial reexamination of the climatic battle based on careful reconsideration of the evidence.

Haythornthwaite, Philip J. *The Napoleonic Source Book.* New York: Facts on File, 1990. A very valuable collection of materials.

Holtman, Robert B. *The Napoleonic Revolution.* Philadelphia: Lippincott, 1967. Concerned with institutional and administrative changes.

Lachouque, Henry. *The Last Days of Napoleon's Empire: From Waterloo to St. Helena.* Translated by Lovett F. Edwards. London: Allen and Unwin, 1966. An important work on the last period of Napoleon's career.

Lefebvre, Georges. *Napoleon from 18 Brumaire to Tilsit, 1799–1807.* Translated by Henry F. Stockhold. New York: Columbia University Press, 1969. The first part of an outstanding full-scale biography.

———. *Napoleon from Tilsit to Waterloo, 1807–1815.* Translated by J. E. Anderson. New York: Columbia University Press, 1969. Part two of the most comprehensive biography; translated from the French.

Lewis, Bernard. "The Impact of the French Revolution on Turkey." *Journal of World History 1* (July 1953): 105–25. Important essay, based on Turkish sources, demonstrating the far-flung influence of the Revolution and Napoleon.

Markham, Felix. *Napoleon and the Awakening of Europe.* London: English Universities Press, 1954. Now somewhat dated, this is still useful for its stress on the linkage between Napoleon and the upsurge in European nationalism.

Puryear, Vernon J. *Napoleon and the Dardanelles.* Berkeley: University of California Press, 1951. The best overall account of Napoleon's involvement in the Balkans and the Near East.

Rothenberg, Gunther E. *The Art of Warfare in the Age of Napoleon.* Bloomington: Indiana University Press, 1978. An important introduction to a subject near and dear to Napoleon.

———. *Napoleon's Great Adversaries: The Archduke Charles and the Austrian Army, 1792–1814.* Bloomington: Indiana University Press, 1982. A specialist on military history examines the oft-defeated Austrian army.

Thompson, J. M. *Napoleon Bonaparte: His Rise and Fall.* Oxford: B. Blackwell, 1952. Now a bit dated, but still widely regarded as the best one-volume biography of Napoleon.

Simón Bolívar (1783–1830), the "father of Latin American independence." Bolívar, José de San Martín, and others led a series of revolutions during the early nineteenth century that toppled the Spanish Empire in America. (Reproduced from the Collections of the Library of Congress)

2

The Latin American Wars of Independence, 1808–1826

INTRODUCTION

From the time of Christopher Columbus, European nations had colonized the New World. Many European countries including England, France, Holland, and Portugal built American empires, but Spain's empire was by far the largest. Stretching from the Atlantic Ocean to the Pacific Ocean, and from California in the north to Cape Horn in the south, at its height the Spanish empire in America spread over several million square miles and included a population of perhaps 15 million. There were millions of natives, that is, Indians; but after the Europeans arrived, many perished due to disease and forced labor. In order to replace the depleted labor supply, the Spanish imported a large number of African slaves. There were also mestizos, or people of mixed European and Indian descent, and Creoles, or pure-blooded Europeans born in the colonies.

By the start of the nineteenth century, signs of discontent had begun to appear in Spain's American empire. Increasingly, the Creoles objected to Spain's policy of sending officials from the mother country, called *peninsulares,* to administer the colonies in an authoritarian fashion. The Creoles sought an expanded role for themselves in the governing of the colonies which—if the Creoles were to have their way—would soon enjoy a significant degree of autonomy if not quite independence. Spain's trading policy also generated opposition. Madrid insisted that the colonies adhere to mercantilism, a trade policy that benefited the mother country, often at the expense of the colonies. Colonial merchants favored free trade, or the right to trade with whomever they wished whenever they wished without undue governmental interference or regulation.

Eighteenth-century developments in Europe and America also stimulated colonial opposition to Spanish rule. The Enlightenment, with its emphasis on reason, tolerance, and the dignity of man, stood in stark contrast to Spanish traditions, which were often defined by the Roman Catholic Church. As in Europe itself, many literate Spanish colonists during the eighteenth century embraced Enlightenment ideals and worked to reform their lands. The American Revolution and the French Revolution provided them with concrete examples to emulate. Both the Declaration of Independence and the French Declaration of the Rights of Man were translated into Spanish and circulated throughout Latin America.

The ferment caused by discontent on one hand and idealistic visions on the other hand gave rise to increasing incidents of rebellion. In the Spanish-speaking world, perhaps the best example of revolution prior to the onset of the so-called Wars of Independence was Francisco de Miranda's unsuccessful attempt in 1806 to overthrow the Spanish authorities in Venezuela. Sailing from the United States, where he had recruited a number of enthusiasts, Miranda found a country not quite ready to follow him in revolution, and his force was easily dispersed. While Miranda failed, the Creoles of the Rio de la Plata viceroyalty (comprised chiefly of present-day Argentina) achieved a large degree of autonomy. When the royal authorities fled in the face of a British attack on Buenos Aires in 1806, local leaders seized control and drove off the invaders. Henceforth, La Plata remained beyond Spain's firm grasp. However, only the western portion of the island of Santo Domingo (Saint Domingue), which afterwards took the name Haiti, achieved true independence. There a slave rebellion under the leadership of Toussaint L'Ouverture expelled the French and established an independent if unstable state.

The rise of Napoleon Bonaparte in Europe sparked the Latin American Wars of Independence. In 1808 Napoleon secured the abdication of the Spanish king, Charles IV, and his son, Ferdinand. In their place he set his brother, Joseph Bonaparte, on the throne. This action provoked resistance among Spanish patriots who opposed Napoleon. Resistance to

Napoleon also surfaced in Spain's American colonies; however, unlike the European opposition to the French emperor, the American resistance movement was divided between those who truly wished to see the deposed Bourbons restored to the Spanish throne and those who wanted to use the movement as a vehicle to secure independence from Spain for the American colonies. While those seeking independence gained strength, the loyalists remained in control. The result was a series of premature declarations of independence between 1808 and 1816, such as that issued by Father Miguel Hidalgo in Mexico. Hidalgo's proclamation of independence, like others, failed as forces loyal to Spain defeated the revolutionaries.

Revolutions began and ended unsuccessfully in Quito (1809–1810), Charcas (Bolivia) (1809–1810), New Granada (1810–1816), Chile (1810–1814), and Guatemala (1811–1814). Venezuela was the site of a major revolt. In 1808 Venezuela defied Napoleon and declared its loyalty to the deposed Spanish rulers. Two years later, however, the Venezuelans declared their independence. The failed revolutionary Francisco de Miranda returned to Venezuela from exile. There he was joined by a young rebel named Simón Bolívar. However, Miranda's forces could not resist loyalist Spanish troops, and he was defeated in 1812. Bolívar managed to escape and to continue the revolutionary struggle, but by the end of 1814 he was forced to flee for his life.

The one qualified success story during this time of revolutionary failure occurred in the Rio de la Plata viceroyalty. After driving out the British, the Creoles controlled the viceroyalty until loyalist elements staged a comeback in 1809. However, the loyalist renaissance was short-lived. In 1810 independence-minded Creoles regained power, and although they were often at loggerheads with each other, in 1816 they declared independence. However, Charcas, Paraguay, and Banda Oriental (Uruguay), all parts of La Plata, followed separate courses. Moreover, as long as Charcas and Peru remained in loyalist hands and thus convenient avenues for invasion, the ultimate success of the La Plata revolution remained in question. To counter this threat, the revolutionary authorities called upon José de San Martín.

San Martín and Bolívar are the two names most commonly associated with the successful phase of the Latin American Wars of Independence that began in 1816 and continued until 1825. Although operating in different locales, these two revolutionary commanders expelled Spain from South America and liberated the continent. San Martín was born in La Plata in 1778, the son of a Spanish officer. He attended military school in Spain and served the Spanish crown for twenty years during the Napoleonic Wars. In 1812 he returned to La Plata and offered his services to the revolutionary government.

The revolutionaries sent San Martín to the town of Mendoza in the Andean foothills, where he spent several years raising an army to conquer Peru and thus end the threat to La Plata's independent existence. His plan was a bold one. He proposed to move his army over the Andes Mountains through passes at 12,000 to 14,000 feet in order to defeat the loyalists in Chile. Having secured Chile, he then moved northward by sea to Peru. San Martín was ably assisted in this risky venture by Bernardo O'Higgins, who had earlier participated in the failed Chilean uprising.

Early in 1817, San Martín crossed the Andes and began military operations in Chile. He defeated Spanish forces at Chacabuco and Maipú, and Chile declared its independence in 1818. Having cleared Chile of loyalist forces, San Martín now turned his attention to Peru. He enlisted Lord Thomas Cochrane, formerly a British naval officer, to gather a flotilla for the invasion of Peru, and in 1820 Cochrane undertook a naval blockade of the Peruvian coast. Landing in southern Peru, San Martín played a waiting game. His efforts mainly consisted of disseminating propaganda in order to radicalize the Peruvian Creoles and mestizos. Eventually the loyalist hold on Lima weakened, and San Martín entered the city without incident in July 1821. Peru then declared its independence. However, significant numbers of Spanish forces had retreated into the Peruvian interior, and San Martín was too weak to challenge them without help.

Help soon appeared in the form of the victorious "Liberator of the North," Simón Bolívar. Bolívar was born in 1783, the son of a wealthy landowner. Orphaned at an early age, Bolívar imbibed liberal doctrines from his tutors and from his extensive travels throughout Europe as a young man. By the time he returned permanently to Venezuela in 1807, he had dedicated himself to his homeland's liberation.

After the first stages of the revolution in Venezuela failed, Bolívar fled to exile in Jamaica. Later he moved to Haiti, where the revolutionary government welcomed him and helped him prepare for an invasion of Venezuela in 1816. Initially, Bolívar's new attempt to liberate his homeland went poorly. Spanish forces defeated Bolívar and forced him to regroup in the isolated Orinoco River valley, where he established his headquarters at Angostura (later Ciudad Bolívar).

Bolívar, however, was not finished. Gathering a ragtag collection of local volunteers augmented by a number of devoted idealists, unemployed soldiers, and fortune seekers from Europe and the United States, Bolívar slowly built an army. Moreover, he devised a daring scheme to lead his army across Venezuela's steamy interior and then over the Andes in order to attack the Spanish headquarters at Bogotá. In May 1819 Bolívar set out on this precarious journey. Despite losing perhaps one-third of his forces during the march, Bolívar successfully crossed the Andes and defeated the loyalists at the Battle of Boyaca. On August 10, 1819, he triumphantly entered Bogotá. Two years later, Bolívar defeated the Spanish at the Battle of Carabobo in Venezuela, thereby clearing the Spanish from the northern part of the continent and securing independence.

Following his victories in the north, Bolívar turned southward. Already, Bolivar's lieutenant, José Antonio de Sucre, had taken the important town of Guayaquil. Sucre next defeated the Spanish in May 1822 at the Battle of Pichincha, where his troops were bolstered by a contingent of San Martín's army that had moved north from Peru. After his victory, Sucre occupied Quito, where Bolívar arrived in June.

With San Martín victorious in the south and Bolivar triumphant in the north, the two liberators met at Guayaquil in July 1822. Apparently their meeting went poorly. Not only did their personalities clash, but the liberators envisioned different futures for South America. San Martín, the more conservative of the two, believed that South America should be divided into sovereign nations ruled over by constitutional monarchs imported from Europe. Bolívar rejected monarchy and, instead, endorsed the republican form of government. He also foresaw the eventual unification of South America on the basis of federalism. In the wake of their meeting, San Martín took his leave and retired from public life. He returned to Europe, where he remained until his death in 1850.

With his rival's retirement, Bolívar now turned his attention to Peru. Although San Martín had conquered the coastal regions, a strong Spanish force controlled the interior. Bolívar determined to defeat this last remnant of Spanish power. In 1824 Bolívar and Sucre mounted an attack. They defeated the Spanish at the Battle of Junin in August, and several months later Sucre won a decisive victory that spelled the end of Spain in South America. Sucre later liberated Charcas, renaming it Bolivia in honor of Bolívar. In 1826 the last Spanish soldiers left South America.

Still, Bolívar's dream remained unfulfilled. The victors now squabbled among themselves. Bolívar lost heart and, worn out at the age of forty-seven, died in 1830. Shortly before his death he wrote: "America is ungovernable. He who serves a revolution ploughs the sea."

INTERPRETIVE ESSAY
J. Burton Kirkwood

With the victory of independence behind them, the Latin American nations faced the reality of governing themselves. What followed was a long struggle to establish stable governments and economic institutions, address social issues arising from independence, and assess the new relationships in the international arena where Latin America was no longer a colonial entity. The struggle to attain the ideals of the Enlightenment, liberalism, and independence quickly fostered a sense of disillusionment and frustration. Simón Bolívar captured this disappointment when he stated: "There is no good faith in America, nor among the nations of America. Treaties are scraps of paper; constitutions printed matter; elections, battles; freedom, anarchy; and life, a torment."

A synthesis of Latin American politics, economic systems, social structures, and international relations is a difficult undertaking. Such an analysis must take into account the regional differences in politics, ethnic makeup, geography, colonial experience, and the power of the Roman Catholic Church. These conditions created broad differences in the outlook on race, the role of the Church, and the type of government created.

Following independence, Latin American nations attempted to establish constitutional governments featuring democratic institutions. With the exception of Brazil, these nations were republics. Under constitutional rule, the state guaranteed individual rights and ensured that governmental transitions occurred through free elections. However, in the post-independence period problems developed as constitutional governments clashed with traditional practices whereby power had been concentrated in a monarchy that often worked hand in glove with the Church's authoritarian control. Although monarchs had been ousted, many Latin American nations found their governments dominated by *caudillos,* or military leaders, and their immediate supporters.

Difficulties beset the Latin American countries from the beginning. Constitutions proved weak and incapable of guaranteeing the peaceful transfer of power. The problem was twofold. First, individuals in power violated basic constitutional provisions to preserve their rule. As the liberal Chilean essayist Francisco Bilbao noted in 1862, such actions demonstrated that the preservation of power was the ultimate goal. Although the rulers violated constitutional provisions, Bilbao argued that governments followed a policy called "preserving the form." Governments allowed, even encouraged, elections to take place, yet they permitted violations of the electoral process to occur. For example, governments abused their power to count votes, appoint electoral inspectors, restrict free speech, and censor the press in order to determine electoral outcomes. Second, those seeking political control believed they could not gain power because the government controlled the electoral process. The opposition, therefore, believed that it could never attain control except by overthrowing the existing order.

Political changes occurred when the government, weakened by economic crisis or military defeat, failed to suppress opposition attempts to gain power. In these conditions violence, not the ballot box, determined the political outcome. As a result of governmental instability, the military decided whether the old government stayed in office or the opposition assumed power. During these struggles for power, *caudillos* rose to positions of authority, not through democratic channels, but typically through military prowess, charisma, and intimidation. As a result of their stature and the uncertain political climate that produced them, these leaders assumed prestige which placed them above the law.

These *caudillos* usually rose through the ranks of the military and eventually seized control of the state. Once in power, they demanded loyalty from their followers. Supported by influential but less powerful regional *caudillos*, they stood above the constitution. In their assumption of authority, they dominated the judicial and legislative branches as well as the electoral process. As a result of the power wielded by the *caudillos*, the opposition concluded that the only way to achieve change was through force.

The role of the military in politics assumed one of two general forms throughout Latin America. In Argentina local *caudillos* controlled the regional military units, which in return received significant support from the urban and landed elite. The *caudillos'* main function was to preserve order, serving the interests of the local elite. Only if necessary did they intervene on the national level. A different form emerged in Mexico and Peru, where the national army upheld the dominant *caudillo* who, for whatever reason, intervened in national politics. Consequently, throughout the nineteenth and well into the twentieth century, the military played a critical role in determining the political direction of many Latin American nations.

During the early years of independence, as the various nations sought to establish governments, political and ideological divisions served to differentiate politicians and political parties. Labels such as "liberal," "conservative," and "federalist" appeared in the political discourse. These characterizations proved more useful as a way to differentiate individuals and their affiliations than to describe strict ideological positions. Latin American leaders such as the Mexican *caudillo* Antonio López de Santa Anna moved from the liberal to the conservative camp and back again whenever it was politically expedient. Despite the ease with which people changed sides, these labels proved divisive and delineated the political framework into the twentieth century.

Attempting to place individuals in one of these political camps is difficult due to the evolving nature of the terms themselves. Furthermore, family and regional loyalties, as well as social and occupational stratification, complicated the establishment of divisions. In many ways the labels divided society along lines previously determined by the caste system. Those who had experienced limited access to political and economic power frequently lined up with the liberals. Liberalism appealed to artisans and shopkeepers, professionals, and provincial landowners. Liberals demanded changes in the existing order, supported individual rights, and called for an end to the special privileges enjoyed by the Church and the military.

The conservative camp usually included large landholders, high-ranking Church officials, merchants, and the military. Most conservatives supported a centralized government, continued privileges for the military, and the Church's dominant role. In the early years, conservatives lamented independence and hoped to restore the monarchy.

Proponents of liberalism or conservatism had two choices: a centralized form of government similar to the political system established by Spain's Constitution of 1812 or a federal system of government advocated by Simón Bolívar. Conservatives identified with a strong centralized government, not unlike a monarchy, while liberals typically supported a federal, representative system. A centralized form of government utilizing Spain's Constitution of 1812 emerged in Gran Colombia (1821), Peru (1823), Chile (1828), and Venezuela (1830). Mexico's Constitution of 1824 had features from both systems; its framework borrowed heavily from the Spanish model, although it created a federal system of states with limited degrees of autonomy.

As the Wars of Independence altered social and political relationships, significant changes occurred in the economic arena. When Spain lost control of trading practices in Spanish America, Great Britain emerged as the region's dominant trading power. Spain's inability to retain commercial control can be traced back to the eighteenth century; but after the French occupation of the Iberian peninsula in 1808, Spain could not protect trade moving in and out of America. Several factors account for Spain's loss of commercial power.

First, French occupation of the Iberian peninsula and the initiation of colonial independence from Spain and Portugal allowed foreign traders and merchants free access to the Latin American economy. Second, Spain lacked the financial resources needed to prevent foreign traders from operating in the Americas. Third, Spanish control was undermined by a rare case of agreement between liberals and conservatives regarding the continuation of free trade. Liberals favored unrestricted trade in keeping with the principles of laissez faire economics. Conservatives also wanted to allow foreigners, particularly Great Britain, the right to trade with Latin America. Facing the need to preserve good relations with Great Britain (Britain and Spain had allied in their mutual opposition to France), conservatives willingly allowed British merchants the right to trade in the region.

The emergence of Great Britain (and later the United States and France) greatly influenced Latin American economic relations. For most of the first half of the nineteenth century, few foreign capitalists invested in Spanish America. Many experts cite political instability as the reason for lack of investment. This was true, but the Industrial Revolution was just beginning in Europe, and many European economies lacked capital for investment outside their internal markets. The destruction caused by warfare in Latin America contributed to the absence of foreign investment and the scarcity of local capital. The Wars of Independence and the subsequent civil wars inflicted damage in the broadest sense. Not only did physical damage occur—the consumption of agricultural goods by invading armies, the seizure of money from public and private sources, and the destruction of mines—but the internal economic, political, judicial, and social systems also suffered. Such instability prevented significant local or foreign investment.

Although the region lacked significant foreign investment, the British did move into Latin America with inexpensive goods produced by their new industrial centers. The arrival of low-cost products weakened the existing Latin American system of production. Cheap, mass-produced clothing undermined the local market and hurt the ability of artisan-produced goods to compete with foreign products. Unable to compete with foreign goods and lacking capital, Latin America's economy turned to the export of agricultural goods. In Mexico the principal exports consisted of henequen (a plant from which rope and twine are produced), tobacco, coffee, and vanilla. Coffee in Venezuela, sugar in Cuba and Brazil, and cattle in Argentina became important export items for these countries, which did not have an industrial infrastructure capable of competing with Britain or the United States. The reliance upon the export of raw materials fostered a dependency in Spanish America upon foreign markets and thwarted the development of an industrial economy.

Independence produced few significant changes in Latin America's social structure, even though social mobility expanded somewhat. While political differences separated liberals and conservatives, they agreed on certain social issues. Both groups remained indifferent to problems facing the Indians and mestizos, or people of mixed blood, whom they continued to regard as backward and ignorant.

In particular, the liberal goals failed to benefit many Indians and mestizos. Literacy tests and property qualifications limited the right of many to vote, and those who could vote were often directed by their patron. After independence, elites faced growing criticism as they attempted to preserve their social position. In the colonial period, the elites utilized the caste system and forms of discrimination against Creoles (Europeans born in the colonies), mixed bloods, and Indians to assure their domination. The Wars of Independence, civil unrest, and liberal ideology removed many obstacles to social mobility. Furthermore, the Wars of Independence provided the opportunity for Creoles and mixed bloods to rise to positions of authority. Agustín de Iturbide, son of a Creole family, briefly held the title Emperor of Mexico. In Peru mestizos such as Andrés de Santa Cruz, Agustín Gamarra, and Ramón Castilla reflected this new social mobility; Santa Cruz even served briefly as Peru's president in 1826.

In the post-independence period, the Creole upper class pursued opportunities that enabled them to move into society's upper echelons. During the colonial period, the Creoles served in the bureaucracy, worked as merchants, and held professional positions, but almost always in second-tier posts. Essentially, a form of de facto discrimination existed which reserved the highest offices in the government, the bureaucracy, and the Church for the *peninsulares* (individuals born in Spain). With changes in the social order, Creoles began to assume positions traditionally held by *peninsulares.*

For mestizos, Indians, and slaves, the changes were less pronounced. Once the Creoles became dominant, they were reluctant to share power. Through the military, mestizos achieved fame and rose to positions of authority and political influence, but the color of their skin worried many. Even Simón Bolívar voiced fear of mestizos or mulattos occupying significant political positions.

Although few reforms occurred in the social order, attitudes regarding the "lower classes" changed with independence. Following the Wars of Independence, a movement developed urging improvement for Indians and slaves in Latin America. In the 1820s a few nations introduced legislation to end slavery. Mexico, Chile, and the Central American countries abolished slavery following independence, but these countries had a relatively small slave population. In countries with greater dependency upon slave labor, abolition received only lip service. For at least two decades after independence, rather than grant total emancipation countries passed laws moving gradually toward abolition. For example, as early as 1810 countries passed laws making the slave trade illegal, while in the early 1820s Chile and Argentina granted freedom for the children of slaves. Emancipation arrived late in Latin America. Proposed in the early 1820s, it was not until the 1840s and 1850s that countries such as Uruguay, Colombia, Argentina, Peru, and Venezuela eliminated slavery. Cuba and Brazil, however, viewed slavery as critical to their agricultural economies and continued the practice until the 1880s. Cuba did not grant freedom to the children of slaves until 1870.

For Indians, independence focused attention on ownership of communal lands. For the first half of the nineteenth century, Indians retained control over their communal lands, although discussions frequently suggested that Indians would be better served by privately owning their lands as individuals. Those who argued for changes in the laws governing Indian lands maintained that communal land ownership violated basic economic laws. Others suggested that a communal society established artificial barriers separating the Indians from the rest of society. Initially, however, little was done to disrupt the Indian communities. Tulio Halperin Donghi, a noted Latin American historian, argued that economic reasons determined the course of action taken regarding Indian lands. He pointed out that weak internal markets and the self-sufficiency

of Indian communities thwarted the acquisition of Indian lands. Furthermore, those with enough capital to consider buying Indian lands
faced greater problems due to political and economic instability in the
first half of the century. As political stability appeared in the second half
of the nineteenth century, Mexico, for example, introduced legislation
undermining Indian claims to their lands. The result was the widespread
removal of Indians from their lands, accompanied by conditions of abject
poverty for the Indians.

While liberals and conservatives might have agreed to move slowly
on the issues of Indian communal lands and ending slavery, they disagreed sharply over the role of the Church. In the colonial period the
Church constituted a powerful independent entity. It obtained considerable wealth through tithes, donations, interest earned on its investments, and ownership of livestock and land. The economic power of the
Church enhanced its prestige, which its separate judicial system further
reinforced.

For liberals, the Church's position clashed with their reformist views.
The Church's tremendous wealth and tax-exempt status angered many,
who saw the state thereby deprived of a substantial income. The
Church's insistence that clerical officials be tried only in ecclesiastical
courts further alienated liberals, who believed that the Church should
not be independent of the state. The Church exercised wide-ranging
powers, reaching far into the social fabric of Latin American society. It
demanded rigid acceptance of its clergy, required its followers to accept
Church guidelines, and extended its control by determining educational
programs, ruling on the acceptability of certain books, restricting some
scientific ideas, and opposing the immigration of non-Catholics.

A wide range of groups defended the Church's privileged position. In
the initial years after independence, the elites allied with the Church
because attacks against the Church's position appeared to threaten their
own interest. Moreover, landowners and merchants saw the Church as
an important source of money. In Mexico's Nueva Galicia, nearly 80
percent of the money loaned from 1721 to 1790 originated from the
Church. As a source of capital, the Church retained important relations
with the traditionally conservative urban merchants and the landed elite
after independence.

The military also supported the Church. Like the Church, the military
played a distinct role in colonial society, receiving a significant propor-
tion of state income and possessing a judicial system separate from the
civil courts. The military's position angered many liberals, who believed

such separation reinforced social inequalities. Perceiving that attacks against the Church could easily be extended to the military, the latter typically allied itself with the Church.

The movement for independence in Latin America did not take place in a vacuum. International relationships both responded to and influenced the separation of the colonies from Spain and Portugal. The Wars of Independence attracted Europe's attention, but European interest in the region went back much further. Soon after Spain established control in the Western Hemisphere, other European nations attempted to move into the region. In many ways the various attempts by European countries to involve themselves in the colonies proved a factor in the separation of the colonies from Spain. Spain exhausted its treasury trying to control and protect its colonies. By the early nineteenth century, Spain lacked the finances needed to continue fighting European encroachment.

Europe influenced Latin America in other ways. The Scientific Revolution, the Enlightenment, and the French Revolution introduced radical new ideas. Creoles, upset with the nature of Spanish rule, cited the French Revolution to attract support for independence and sought sympathetic audiences in European cities.

The French Revolution had a specific impact on Spanish America's move for independence. In 1808 Napoleon Bonaparte invaded Spain and placed his brother, Joseph Bonaparte, on the throne. Both *peninsulares* and Creoles opposed French occupation of Spain, and in doing so suggested that the right to govern the colonies rested with the colonists, not France or Spain. Subsequently, colonists assumed leadership positions in their colonies. In Buenos Aires and Venezuela, colonists created provisional governments that ruled in the name of the deposed Spanish king, Ferdinand VII. The success of these governments revealed the crown's shortcomings and demonstrated that the colonists were capable of self-rule. Following the experiment with self-government, some Creoles such as Simón Bolívar began to consider the creation of governments separate from Spain.

Two other countries, Great Britain and the United States, significantly influenced events in Latin America. Following the French invasion of Spain in 1808, Great Britain allied with Spain and supported Madrid's demands for retention of its colonies. When the colonies initiated open hostilities against Spain, Britain negotiated a difficult course between adhering to Spain's desire to retain its colonies and ensuring open markets for British traders. Hoping both to preserve its relationship with Spain and to maintain open avenues of trade, Britain adopted a position of neutrality regarding colonial independence. Britain's neutrality underscored its desire to continue trading with the colonies, but it limited its international commitments. As a result of its neutrality, Britain refused to assist Spain in retaining its colonies.

Following Napoleon's defeat, the victorious European coalition met at the Congress of Vienna in 1815 to restore the governments overturned by the Napoleonic Wars. The Congress implied that the colonies lost during the wars should be restored. However, by 1820 Great Britain, Prussia, Austria, France, and Russia had concluded that Spain faced a losing battle in its attempt to hang onto its colonies given their physical distance from Spain and the overwhelming financial demands. Rather than become involved in a revolution, with its concomitant violence, European leaders suggested that Spain accede to some of the colonists' demands. Such a policy lacked altruistic motives, but rather revealed conservative fears that any instance of revolutionary behavior might encourage similar action against the existing European order.

In 1820 liberals in Spain forced Ferdinand VII to agree to conditions guaranteed by the Constitution of 1812 and to establish a constitutional monarchy. In Latin America clerical officials, military officers, merchants, and landowners panicked at the news. Conservatives feared that independence would threaten the traditional social order. As a result, conservatives in Mexico, Venezuela, Central America, and Peru led movements for independence in order to establish governments identified with their own viewpoints.

By 1822, Spain's only hope of recovering its colonies rested with a European coalition, but British neutrality foreclosed that possibility. Periodically European states discussed returning the colonies to Spain. Subsequently, Austria, Prussia, and Russia talked about assisting Spain, but they lacked naval forces large enough to undertake a transoceanic campaign. Aware of Britain's neutrality, the Europeans in 1823 had to consider President James Monroe's declaration that the United States would view any European attempt to control the region's governments as a hostile act.

While the Monroe Doctrine coincided with Britain's goals, the idea of the United States telling the European nations to stay out of Latin America was not well received. British foreign minister George Canning believed the United States wanted to reduce British influence in the region. Meanwhile, some European governments suspected that the British supported Monroe's declaration so that they could act more independently of the conservative coalition that dominated Europe. Ultimately, problems closer to home, and perhaps an awareness of what the undertaking would require, caused the European powers to refrain from demanding the restoration of Spain's colonies.

As independence became a reality, both the United States and Great Britain negotiated commercial treaties with the new nations, which also served as a de facto form of recognition. The American and British decisions to recognize the Latin American governments caused other European nations to reexamine their positions toward the new countries. Spain, not surprisingly, refused to acknowledge their independence; however, other continental states began to explore the possibility of economic treaties. The European powers, especially Prussia, Austria, and Russia, struggled over whether to recognize the former colonies or to uphold the idea of restoring the colonies to Spain. In the end they accepted colonial independence.

While the commercial agreements led to recognition of the Latin American states, the agreements did not achieve the benefits hoped for by the negotiators. Although Latin American trade increased following independence, it did not reach the level many anticipated. Several reasons explain this. First, the Wars of Independence disrupted Latin American economies, thereby preventing the creation of goods that would sustain a dynamic trade relationship. Second, the political instability that followed independence served to deter serious investors. Third, agriculture had not yet evolved into a substantial export economy, while the mining sector, one of the more lucrative components of Latin American economic life, also suffered from the warfare. Finally, widespread poverty limited the size of the market capable of buying European products.

In the international arena, Latin America moved further away from the orbit of European diplomacy. Economically weakened by the prolonged fighting, struggling for international recognition, and disrupted by contests for political control, the Latin American nations played only a minor role in international diplomacy. Simultaneously, the European nations—faced with more immediate conflicts, threats of revolution, and social friction brought on by industrialization—tended to ignore Latin America. The British and French attempted to influence affairs in Mexico, Buenos Aires, and Rio de la Plata, but learned that their power was limited.

The independence achieved by the Spanish and Portuguese colonies in the early 1820s introduced ideas for social change. After independence, reformers pushed to eradicate slavery, establish public schools, eliminate privileges held by the military and the Church, and end discrimination based on race. But the reality was that much of the old order remained. The Creoles, who led the independence movement, did not desire reforms for the masses; rather, they sought to replace the *peninsulares* in positions of power. The social and economic systems remained intact, allowing the Creoles to occupy the positions they had long desired. For example, agrarian reform did not follow independence; instead, the number of landowners actually decreased after the revolutions, thereby forcing an increasing number of people into a position of subservience to the landed aristocratic elite. The struggle for significant social reform would wait for the twentieth century.

SELECTED BIBLIOGRAPHY

Anna, Timothy. "The Independence of Mexico and Central America." In *The Independence of Latin America,* pp. 49–92. Edited by Leslie Bethell. Cambridge: Cambridge University Press, 1987. Anna details the widespread problems facing this region in the post-independence period.

Brading, D. A. "Bourbon Spain and Its American Empire." In *Colonial Spanish America,* pp. 112–62. Edited by Leslie Bethell. Cambridge: Cambridge University Press, 1984. Brading presents the conditions operating in the colonial empire as the Bourbon reforms were introduced and shows how the response to these reforms influenced the development of the independence movement.

Bushnell, David, and Neill Macaulay. *The Emergence of Latin America in the Nineteenth Century.* New York: Oxford University Press, 1988. Bushnell and Macaulay focus on the nineteenth-century attempts by Brazil and the former Spanish colonies to establish political and social systems after the Wars of Independence.

Farriss, Nancy M. *Crown and Clergy in Colonial Mexico, 1759–1821: The Crisis of Ecclesiastical Privilege.* London: Athlone Press, 1968. Farriss provides important information detailing the relationship between church and state in the late colonial period.

Gibson, Charles. *Spain in America.* New York: Harper and Row, 1967. Gibson's remains one of the better introductory works on the colonial era.

Hale, Charles A. *Mexican Liberalism in the Age of Mora, 1821–1853.* New Haven, CT: Yale University Press, 1968. Hale focuses on the development of liberalism in the post-independence period, and in doing so presents important details about Mexican conservatism.

Halperin Donghi, Tulio. *The Contemporary History of Latin America.* Translated and edited by John Charles Chasteen. Durham, NC: Duke University Press, 1993. Halperin Donghi provides a broad overview of colonial society and the struggle within Latin America to create viable, independent nation-states.

———. "Economy and Society." In *Spanish America after Independence, c. 1820–*

1870, pp. 1–47. Edited by Leslie Bethell. Cambridge: Cambridge University Press, 1987. The author details how economic factors influenced the Wars of Independence and post-independence developments.

Keen, Benjamin, and Mark Wasserman. *A History of Latin America*. 4th ed. Boston: Houghton Mifflin, 1992. Keen and Wasserman's textbook (especially chapters 4 through 9) provides a good overview of colonial problems confronting Latin America after independence.

Knight, Franklin W. *Slave Society in Cuba During the Nineteenth Century*. Madison: University of Wisconsin Press, 1970. Knight's work concentrates on the role of slavery in Cuba's economy and the attempts to retain the institution as abolition spread throughout the hemisphere.

Lockhart, James, and Stuart B. Schwartz. *Early Latin America: A History of Colonial Spanish America and Brazil*. Cambridge: Cambridge University Press, 1983. The authors compare the colonial experience of the Spanish and Portuguese in the Western Hemisphere.

Lynch, John. "The Origins of Spanish American Independence." In *The Independence of Latin America*, pp. 1–48. Edited by Leslie Bethell. Cambridge: Cambridge University Press, 1987. Lynch examines how conditions in Spanish America led to the independence movement.

———. *The Spanish-American Revolutions, 1808–1826*. New York: Norton, 1973. Lynch provides a synthesis of the revolutionary experience based on secondary sources and extensive research.

Mecham, J. Lloyd. *Church and State in Latin America*. Chapel Hill: University of North Carolina Press, 1967. Mecham's work provides a broad picture of the Church in Spanish America.

Morner, Magnus. *Race Mixture in the History of Latin America*. Boston: Little, Brown, 1967. Morner details racial practices of the Church and state, the role of the caste system, and slave practices in the colonial period; all the while comparing and contrasting regional differences.

Perkins, Dexter. *A History of the Monroe Doctrine*. Boston: Little, Brown, 1963. Perkins examines the impact of the Monroe Doctrine in the Western Hemisphere and the role it has played in diplomatic, economic, and political relationships.

Platt, D.C.M. *Latin America and British Trade, 1806–1914*. London: A. and C. Black, 1973. Platt captures both the nature of British trade and its uncertainty due to the poverty of the former Latin American colonies during the early stages of their independence.

Rippy, J. Fred. *British Investments in Latin America, 1822–1949*. Hamden, CT: Archon Books, 1959. Rippy evaluates the impact of British trade on both the independence movement and the post-independence period.

Rout, Leslie B. *The African Experience in Spanish America: 1502 to the Present Day*. Cambridge: Cambridge University Press, 1971. Rout gives the reader a broad survey of slavery throughout Spanish America.

Safford, Frank. "Politics, Ideology and Society." In *Spanish America after Independence, c. 1820–1870*, pp. 48–122. Edited by Leslie Bethell. Cambridge: Cambridge University Press, 1987. Safford presents a detailed account of the political struggles occurring in the former colonies after independence.

Stein, Stanley, and Barbara Stein. *The Colonial Heritage of Latin America: Essays on Economic Dependence in Perspective.* New York: Oxford University Press, 1970. The authors analyze Spain's economic goals and their impact on the relationship between Spain and its colonies.

Tutino, John. *From Insurrection to Revolution in Mexico: Social Bases of Agrarian Violence, 1750–1940.* Princeton, NJ: Princeton University Press, 1986. Tutino evaluates the nature of the social order in Mexico from independence to the Mexican Revolution.

Zea, Leopoldo. *The Latin American Mind.* Translated by James H. Abbott and Lowell Dunham. Norman: University of Oklahoma Press, 1963. Zea provides a general examination of political ideologies in the Americas.

3

The Congress of Vienna and the Age of Metternich, 1815–1848

INTRODUCTION

As the early nineteenth century's Napoleonic Wars wound down, the victors gathered to make peace. Although many European nations had opposed Napoleon, Great Britain, Austria, Russia, and Prussia had been primarily responsible for his defeat. Forming a Grand Alliance in 1813, these Great Powers committed themselves not only to defeat Napoleon but also to restrain France for at least the next twenty years. In April 1814 the Grand Alliance achieved its first goal when it forced Napoleon to abdicate the French throne.

With Napoleon's defeat, the victorious allies undertook two tasks. The first was to make peace with France. The second was to restore order and stability to the shattered Continent, an undertaking that involved redrawing the map of Europe, adjudicating innumerable claims, and perhaps creating machinery to keep the peace, or at least to assure that another Napoleon did not arise.

On May 30, 1814, the allies signed the Peace of Paris with France. After some hesitation, they had restored the deposed Bourbons to the French throne, and they negotiated peace with Louis XVIII, a younger brother of the executed Louis XVI. The terms of the treaty were quite mild since

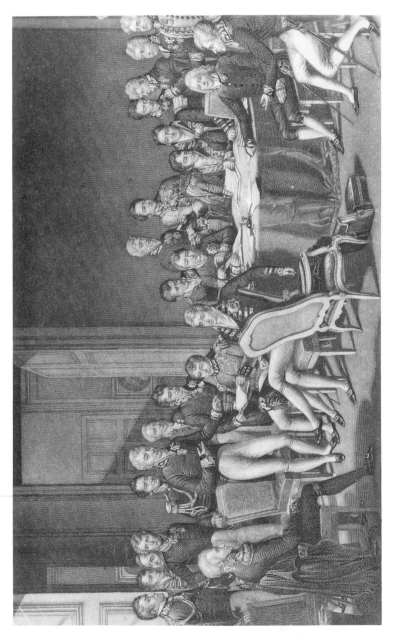

The era's most important diplomats redraw the map of Europe. Presided over by the Austrian chancellor Clemens von Metternich (standing in the left foreground), the Congress of Vienna concluded the Napoleonic Wars and set the tone for Europe for the next three decades. (Courtesy of the Bettmann Archive)

the allies feared that anything other than a magnanimous peace might undermine their aim of restoring tranquility to Europe. A humiliated France might very well seek to redress its grievances in the future, a possibility the victors wanted to avoid.

In addition to restoring the Bourbons, the First Peace of Paris allowed France to keep its January 1792 borders—its so-called natural frontiers—even though they were greater than the frontiers that had existed in 1789 when the French Revolution began. However, France surrendered its territorial gains in Germany, Italy, and the Low Countries, and it relinquished to Great Britain some of its colonies, including Tobago, Trinidad, and Santa Lucia. Louis XVIII successfully insisted that France not pay any reparations. The treaty was so lenient that France was not even required to return the art treasures that Napoleon had systematically looted while ravaging Europe. The treaty also called for a meeting to assemble shortly thereafter in Vienna "for the purpose of regulating the arrangements which are to complete the provisions of the present Treaty."

The Congress of Vienna began in September 1814, when hordes of monarchs, princes, nobles, statesmen, policy experts, influence peddlers, influence seekers, courtesans, and socialites descended on the Austrian capital. A steady round of lavish entertainments followed, severely denting the host state's finances. The social aspects were so conspicuous that one sharp-tongued observer noted that the "Congress does not progress, it dances." Of course, this was not entirely the case. The social whirl was intentional; it occupied the time and the energy of the less important attendees while allowing the representatives of the major states to concentrate on the business at hand.

During the Congress, representatives of the Great Powers made decisions behind closed doors. Originally Great Britain, Austria, Russia, and Prussia had intended to reserve decision-making power for themselves, but it soon became apparent that defeated France would have to be included as well. France was simply too important a state to exclude. Furthermore, were France not included in the inner councils, the French delegate, Prince Talleyrand, threatened to create a bloc of small countries that might have disrupted the smooth working of the Congress. Finally, at times the victors found themselves so badly split that France's presence was necessary to mediate and resolve contentious issues.

A galaxy of nineteenth-century diplomatic superstars made peace at Vienna. Prussia was ably represented by the old and nearly deaf Prince Hardenberg. Alexander I, the Russian tsar, was swelled by a sense of pride in his army's victories and buoyed by a feeling of self-righteousness and moral superiority that baffled, confused, and irritated his fellow conferees. Alexander frequently spoke in high-sounding, moralistic tones. Talleyrand, representing defeated France, had the weakest hand to play at the Congress, yet he played it with such skill that he managed not only to secure France's admission to the inner circle but on several occasions maneuvered to give France the deciding vote.

Britain's foreign secretary, Viscount Castlereagh, was a dominant figure at the Congress. Shy, reserved, and intensely disliked by many of his countrymen, Castlereagh was best able to play the role of honest broker because Great Britain had already secured its spoils of war in the First Peace of Paris. Following traditional British policy, Castlereagh sought to achieve a balance of power in order to insure peace and stability so that Britain could pursue its domestic and global interests without having to worry about continental entanglements.

The most important statesman at the Congress was its host, Prince Clemens von Metternich, the young, vain, and supremely self-assured Austrian foreign minister. Although Metternich did not neglect Austria's interests, he counseled compromise and mutual concession in order to build an enduring European peace. Metternich was so successful that not only was he regarded as the moving force behind the Vienna settlement, but he also came to dominate European affairs for the next three decades.

Once its initial ceremonies had been completed, the Congress of Vienna, or more properly the Great Powers, got down to business. Disposition of Polish lands proved to be the most contentious issue. The ancient Polish state had disappeared in 1795 when Austria, Russia, and Prussia finally partitioned it. However, Napoleon had revived it in truncated form as the Duchy of Warsaw. At Vienna, Tsar Alexander proposed to revive Poland once again, this time as a constitutional monarchy with himself as hereditary monarch. Russia's ally Prussia agreed to surrender its Polish lands to Alexander in return for territorial compensation in Saxony.

Alexander's scheme alarmed Great Britain and Austria, both of whom felt that Russia had already received adequate reward for its contribution to the allied war effort when it annexed Finland and Bessarabia. More important, both objected to such a strong Russian presence in the heart of Europe. Having just expended considerable resources to defeat an expansionistic France, neither Austria nor Great Britain was willing to aggrandize Russia to the extent it desired. Furthermore, Austria disliked sacrificing Saxony to Prussia since this would greatly enhance Prussia's standing in the German-speaking world, a sphere that Austria intended to dominate. Great Britain did not object to awarding territory to Prussia, but it wanted that territory to be in the Rhineland so that Prussia could stand guard there against a potentially resurgent France.

By the end of 1814, the disagreement over Poland had ballooned to crisis proportions. At this juncture Talleyrand stepped in and suggested a secret alliance of Britain, Austria, and France against Russia and Prussia. On January 3, 1815, his proposal was accepted, and when rumors of the alliance were intentionally leaked, Russia and Prussia soberly reassessed their position and a compromise was quickly reached. Russia received the greater part of the Duchy of Warsaw, from which it made its Polish kingdom, the so-called Congress Kingdom of Poland. Prussia and Austria both retained some of their Polish territory, and Cracow, an important hub, was made a free city. Prussia received almost half of Saxony along with Swedish Pomerania and considerable territory in the Rhineland, but the king of Saxony retained his throne and his two most important cities, Dresden and Leipzig.

The Congress of Vienna made other significant territorial changes. Austria surrendered the Austrian Netherlands (Belgium) to the newly independent Kingdom of Holland, thereby creating another barrier to potential French aggression. This was done against the wishes of the Belgians, but no one consulted them. Austria was compensated for relinquishing the distant and hard to defend Austrian Netherlands with the prosperous nearby Italian provinces of Lombardy and Venetia. Austria also gained territory on the eastern coast of the Adriatic Sea (Illyria) and the mountainous Tyrol. It is estimated that the settlement left Austria with 4 to 5 million more people than it had in 1792.

Austria also did well in the rest of the Italian peninsula as the northern Italian duchies of Parma, Modena, Lucca, and Tuscany now came under indirect Austrian control. In other changes affecting Italy, the pope and the king of Piedmont regained and even expanded their holdings, and the Bourbons recovered the Kingdom of the Two Sicilies.

As always, Great Britain moved to increase its colonial empire, and in fact did so even before the Congress got under way. Among other territories, Britain added Helgoland, Malta, the Cape Colony, Ceylon, Santa Lucia, Trinidad, and Tobago.

The final settlement also left Germany fragmented, with thirty-nine sovereign states including Austria and Prussia lumped into the German Confederation, a loose body that Austria dominated. The Congress of

Vienna also reestablished and guaranteed Switzerland's independence, restored the Bourbons to the Spanish throne, and denounced the slave trade.

In the midst of the Congress, word reached Vienna that Napoleon had escaped from his exile on the Mediterranean island of Elba, regained power in France, and was once more on the move. Napoleon's last hurrah, known as the Hundred Days, came to an end with his defeat at the Battle of Waterloo on June 18, 1815. Nevertheless, the Hundred Days had important ramifications, especially for France. The original Peace of Paris was jettisoned and replaced with a new accord, known as the Second Peace of Paris, which imposed much stiffer conditions on France. According to the terms of the new peace, signed on November 20, 1815, France surrendered territory in its north and east, thereby retreating to its borders of 1789 and losing about 500,000 people in the process. Moreover, it was ordered to pay 700 million francs in reparations and was required to support an army of occupation for at least three years. Much of Talleyrand's work had been undone.

Before it closed in June 1815, the Congress of Vienna considered Tsar Alexander's proposal for a Holy Alliance. Alexander wanted all states to base their actions on Christian principles, and the Holy Alliance was an attempt to give concrete form to this desire. Castlereagh dismissed the whole enterprise as "a piece of sublime mysticism and nonsense," and Great Britain declined to participate. However, with the additional exceptions of the Moslem Ottoman Empire and the pope, all the other states signed the Holy Alliance in September 1815. Meanwhile, Metternich edited the original proposal to include language that seemed to give the signatories the right to stifle dissent within their own countries and hinted that they also had the right to go beyond their borders to crush opposition if necessary.

A few months later, on November 20, 1815, the four victorious Great Powers also signed the Quadruple Alliance, which proved to be much more important than Alexander's Holy Alliance. The Quadruple Alliance—soon made into a Quintuple Alliance with the addition of France—committed its signatories to meet periodically to discuss the state of affairs in Europe. It also obliged them to resolve any problems that might arise and through their efforts to maintain European peace. European diplomacy appeared to have entered upon a new age of cooperation.

INTERPRETIVE ESSAY
Robert D. Billinger, Jr.

The Final Act of the Congress of Vienna was signed on June 9, 1815. Viscount Castlereagh, the British foreign minister, predicted that it would maintain European peace for at least seventy years. In fact, there would be no general European war for a century. In short, the Congress of Vienna established Europe's political geography and moral climate for most of the nineteenth century. It introduced an era of peace that lasted until mid-century and thereafter was marred only by brief, localized conflicts until World War I.

The period between the Congress of Vienna and the Revolutions of 1848 is often called the Age of Metternich because Clemens von Metternich, the Austrian foreign minister, traditionally has been seen as responsible for the Vienna settlement and its subsequent impact on Europe. It was Metternich, the self-proclaimed "Coachman of Europe," who used the Congress to create an ongoing negotiating structure that maintained the political equilibrium associated with that settlement until Metternich himself was swept from office in 1848. It was a structure that aimed at preserving both the international peace of Europe and the domestic peace of the individual European countries. Why and to what degree Metternich and the Vienna settlement succeeded, and at what cost, have been historical questions of perennial interest.

The reasons for studying the Congress of Vienna and the Age of Metternich have varied over the years. Contemporaries were concerned about preserving the past or breaking pathways to the future; later evaluators have searched for object lessons for their own times. For example, in the late nineteenth century liberals and nationalists studied the Congress in order to condemn it and its creators for delaying what they considered to be the historic development of liberalism and nationalism. By the end of World War I, historians, envious of the long peace that followed the Congress, studied it for insights about creating a stable world. During the Cold War, "realists," who saw the world through the lens of power politics, studied the Congress as an exercise in balance of power politics. They perceived a world similar to their own, one in which central Europe teetered between East and West.

In a post–Cold War world, historians still return to the Congress of Vienna and the Age of Metternich. To them what seems remarkable about the Congress is not its creators' mistakes or their ability to devise a new European balance of power, but that the Congress introduced a whole new vision of world politics characterized by a generally accepted moral code of conduct that became the basis for assessing situations in terms of desirable outcomes for all involved. In short, recent historians have suggested that such amoral eighteenth-century concepts as "reason of state" and "balance of power" were replaced with new ones. "Political equilibrium," a system of mutual stability and benefit, superseded older notions of "every state for itself and God for us all."

To understand what is remarkable about the Congress of Vienna and the Age of Metternich, it is necessary to see the period's continuity and change in its broadest sense. Customarily, historians stress the novelty of the French Revolution and the Napoleonic period. Courses and textbooks often commence with the events that unfolded in France in 1789. In that sense the Congress of Vienna and the Age of Metternich would be mere episodes in the development of the modern world; setbacks, even, to the principles of liberty, equality, and fraternity proclaimed by the Revolution and asserted by Napoleon. However, increasingly historians are beginning to reassess such a periodization of history. While it is no doubt going much too far to see the French Revolution as a retrograde detour in the history of human progress toward liberty and individualism, there is certainly much evidence to suggest that Napoleon was far from a modern man.

When Napoleon followed his star and disrupted both French and European tranquility, he based his actions on "reason of state," if not actually on princely egoism. Such thinking was characteristic of the late seventeenth and eighteenth centuries' age of dynastic wars. These wars—like the Napoleonic Wars—were all fought for the expansion of dynastic power. Moreover, they were fought within a state system that responded to such threats through traditional balance of power politics. That is, ruling dynasties and their states changed sides during or certainly at the end of each war so as to prevent any of their neighbors from becoming too powerful. It was an age of cabinet diplomacy when the interests of a dynasty, or the "state," were of prime concern and the interests of Europe and its people were of no concern whatsoever. Notwithstanding Napoleon's wartime propaganda and self-serving memoirs to the contrary, the Napoleonic Wars occurred within the context of this established eighteenth-century system.

Seen from this perspective, the Congress of Vienna and the Age of Metternich represent a major turning point in international relations. The long centuries of dynastic wars, and the more recent events of the Napoleonic period, slowly brought a new mind-set to European statesmen. This new mind-set and the determination to construct an apparatus for its international application are the pivotal changes that make the Congress of Vienna and the Age of Metternich the beginning of modern world history rather than the beginning of a retrograde "Restoration."

The last years of Napoleon's reign saw the dawning of this new mindset. While Napoleon himself never embraced this new perspective, his erstwhile ally and soon to be adversary Clemens von Metternich did. In the summer of 1813 the Austrian foreign minister attempted a grand mediation between Napoleon and Britain, Prussia, and Russia. Metternich urged the French dictator to seek a peace based on the independence and neutralization of Napoleon's Confederation of the Rhine. Such a settlement, Metternich suggested, could leave France with much of its expanded prestige, power, and territory intact, while reestablishing the European political equilibrium. Napoleon distrusted the seeming selflessness of the Austrian offer. Some historians have considered the whole mediation attempt a sham to give the Habsburgs an excuse to abandon a peace-defying Napoleon. Others have more justifiably seen Metternich as a balance of power practitioner seeking to keep Napoleon in place, while thwarting the ambitions of either Prussia or Russia by guaranteeing the neutrality and independence of the German princes who had formerly been part of Napoleon's Confederation of the Rhine. But neutrality as balance of power was a new idea, and planning for peace and stability was too.

What Metternich had in mind was neither the destruction of Napoleon's power nor the restoration of pre-revolutionary Europe. Rather, he called for the construction of a just and peaceful Europe. Metternich, the continental statesman, realized that turmoil in Europe meant trouble for the Habsburgs, and he hoped to integrate Napoleon into a peaceable and stable Europe. Then and now, both reactionaries and revolutionaries decried Metternich's commitment to the preservation of existing governmental and social relations; but in 1813 it was Napoleon, the so-called child of the Revolution, who was trapped in an earlier reason of state mind-set and did not understand Metternich's intentions. Consequently, Metternich reluctantly joined Britain, Russia, and Prussia in the March 9, 1814, Treaty of Chaumont, which guided the coalition toward a generally agreed upon peace and ended any hope Napoleon may have had of splitting the allies. Chaumont also extended the alliance for twenty years and guaranteed the signatories against French aggression. Because of Napoleon's obstinacy, he called down upon France the first Great Power alliance in European history to dedicate itself not only to the defeat of an enemy, but also to the future restraint of that former enemy in the interest of European peace and stability. Like the modern United Nations, a wartime military alliance was envisioned even at its founding as a continuing vehicle for the preservation of international security.

Napoleon's abdication on April 11, 1814, forced Metternich to join Austria's allies in insisting upon the Bourbons' return. But this should not be seen as support for counterrevolution or even real "restoration" in France. The First Treaty of Paris, signed on May 30, 1814, was generous to France because the allies' main goal was political equilibrium rather than vengeance, compensation, or even restoration. Though the period in French history between Louis XVIII's assumption of the French throne in 1814 and the 1830 July Revolution is usually called the Restoration, very little of France's pre-revolutionary constitution or its European relationships was "restored." In the interest of European stability, the allies not only imposed a moderate constitution, but they also allowed France to keep its January 1792 borders. France's constitutional habits, boundaries, and neighbors had changed since 1789, and neither Metternich nor the other allied statesmen wished to resurrect the dangerously unstable past.

The preservation of a peaceful equilibrium rather than revenge, restitution, or restoration was the theme at the Congress of Vienna when it opened in September 1814. This is not to say that Metternich or the other statesmen at Vienna were selfless models of a new world view in which the peace of Europe replaced the interests of dynasties. It does mean, however, that during the negotiations, these statesmen began to realize the benefits of a concert of European powers based on mutual respect, cooperation, and the pursuit of peace. Napoleon's reappearance in France after his flight from Elba in late February 1815 even more fully convinced them of the need for a new understanding that would place reason of state on the back burner and move European stability to the fore.

To understand the uniqueness of the Vienna settlement it is necessary to see the political realities of the post-Napoleonic period. Many options were still open, but some, such as the restoration of the pre-revolutionary status quo, would soon be closed forever. The Congress brought little "restoration" since none of the European rulers who had survived and even profited from alliances with Napoleon were interested in a return to the status quo ante bellum.

Great Britain was intent on becoming the mistress of the seas, which also meant acquiring additional colonies. Tsar Alexander wished to be recognized as the protector of Europe, which included ruling a constitutional Poland, possibly supporting constitutional principles in the surviving German and Italian principalities, and leading a community of Europe's "Christian rulers." Prussia's delegate, Prince Hardenberg, wanted to move beyond the Austro-Prussian dualism that had characterized eighteenth-century Germany to establish Prussia's supremacy at least in north Germany. Finally, Metternich, representing Austria, the multinational state most threatened by any further change in the status quo, desired a new European equilibrium, one that would restrain not only a potentially revenge-seeking France, but also a zealous Russian tsar and an expansionistic Prussia.

What was unique about the Congress was not that the small powers were ignored or that the Great Powers pursued their own interests. Nor was it surprising that France, thanks to the diplomatic skills of its delegate, Prince Charles Talleyrand, and the conflicts among the major powers, was able to become a major player in the settlement. Rather, the Congress of Vienna was unique in that traditional power politics, reason of state, and balance of power had less to do with the actual settlement than the good intentions of all the participants to achieve an equitable European equilibrium. The desire to fulfill these good intentions helps to explain not only the success of the Congress itself but also the stability of the Age of Metternich that followed.

This new moral influence can be seen in the settlement of the Polish Question, an issue that threatened to disrupt the Congress and leave the Great Powers divided. Tsar Alexander intended to revive the defunct Polish monarchy, with himself as hereditary constitutional monarch. The problem was that when Poland had disappeared in 1795, it had been divided between Russia, Prussia, and Austria. Prussia was willing to turn over its Polish lands to Alexander in return for Saxon territories. The king of Saxony, having remained too long an ally of Napoleon, seemed a fit victim. Thus a classic international problem of the eighteenth century was raised and a classic balance of power response suggested. Yet, times had changed. Indeed, on January 3, 1815, Britain, Austria, and France formed a "secret" alliance against Prussia and Russia. But it was hardly this alliance that frustrated the Northern Powers. A naval-based Britain, a recently conquered France, and a financially exhausted Austria were no match for Russia and Prussia. Dynastic desires motivated Russia and Prussia, and balance of power tactics were arrayed against them. But the tsar's willingness to compromise had more to do with his desire to uphold the European equilibrium than with his fear of military conflict. Alexander, the self-proclaimed liberator of Europe, was anxious to appear as a responsible "Christian" sovereign. He placed considerations of international morality above reason of state. A new era was dawning.

Meanwhile, what of the principles of compensation, balance of power, and "legitimacy" that are usually associated with the Congress? Should all of these concepts, remnants of the eighteenth century, be dismissed from historians' vocabularies when describing the Congress of Vienna? Were "political equilibrium" and "Christian morality" really triumphant? Yes, rather more than should have been expected, though there was enough continuity from the past to confirm several generations of historians in their belief that traditional politics dominated the Congress.

Territory did change hands, but it did so more for Europe's overall good than for reasons of dynastic expansion. For example, Metternich continued his German policy of 1813. Rather than reviving the Habsburg-led Holy Roman Empire, Metternich created a German Confederation of thirty-nine states. These states were bound in a defensive alliance in the interest of European stability, but decentralized to such an extent that each state's sovereignty was vested in the dynastic survivors of the Napoleonic era. Essentially, the German Confederation was a neutralized Confederation of the Rhine, but with Austrian and Prussian membership. The de facto Austro-Prussian dualism that emerged within the German Confederation between 1815 and 1848, and which characterized German history during the Age of Metternich, is one of the best examples of the new principle of political equilibrium that guided the thinking of Metternich and the other representatives at Vienna.

Nor did Austria demand the return of the Austrian Netherlands, conquered by France early in the revolutionary wars. Instead, Austria gave them up to be joined with the former United Provinces, also a victim of Napoleon's aggression. Together these two areas formed the Kingdom of the Netherlands. There was no matter of compensation here, nor was anything "legitimate" about the new kingdom or its equally new monarch, the Prince of Orange. As for balance of power, the Kingdom of the Netherlands was a tripwire, not a barrier, for a potentially expansionist France. The Kingdom of the Netherlands, like the later Republic of Belgium, which devolved from it with Europe's blessing in 1830, symbolized a new Great Power mind-set that featured pursuit of a peaceful equilibrium.

Only in Italy could Metternich be accurately accused of pursuing compensation and balance of power politics. The acquisition of Lombardy-Venetia certainly came through the "right of conquest." But the Austrian hegemony in Italy thus conferred by this expansion meant new European responsibilities for the Habsburgs. Later Austrian interventions in Italian politics, in the name of European stability, characterized the Age of Metternich. Such interventions were, of course, condemned by nineteenth-century liberals and Italian nationalists who preferred Italian self-government to cosmopolitan Austria's just and efficient rule.

Napoleon's escape from Elba in late February 1815 and the so-called Hundred Days did not substantially alter the European settlement. Nor did the Second Treaty of Paris, signed on November 20, 1815, change the new tone of European cooperation and moral justice. Simultaneous with the signing of the Second Treaty of Paris, Great Britain, Russia, Austria, and Prussia signed a Quadruple Alliance that for twenty years bound them to resist any French threat to Europe's tranquility. The Quadruple Alliance also called for periodic meetings to promote European peace and prosperity. At their first such meeting in 1818, a less threatening France was recognized as a full member of the concert. This concert and its moral quest for a European equilibrium united the Great Powers in a new spirit of cooperation that lasted until the coming of the Crimean War nearly forty years later.

It was the Quadruple Alliance, not the Holy Alliance, that provided the true basis for Great Power cooperation and for European stability in the Metternich era. Because of Tsar Alexander's later turn to reactionary politics, his Holy Alliance has often been misunderstood as the basis of cooperation between Austria, Prussia, and Russia for the repression of domestic reforms. It is the confusion of the Quadruple Alliance, which owes much to Castlereagh, the British foreign minister, with Alexander's Holy Alliance in the minds of nineteenth-century liberals and nationalists that led them unjustly to condemn the Concert of Europe.

More needs to be said of Castlereagh, who, as much as Metternich, was the real hero of the Congress of Vienna and the early Metternich era. While Metternich, the continental statesman, had a pragmatic as well as an ideological interest in a stable Continent, Castlereagh, the island statesman, had a more difficult time persuading the British to remain interested in continental affairs. His remarkable ability both to engage

Britain in continental stability and to act with Metternich as a "disinterested" party in search of European equilibrium cannot be overrated. But Castlereagh's achievement became obvious only after his suicide in 1822. Successors like George Canning and Viscount Palmerston, because of their distaste for Metternich's conservativism and their love of balance of power politics that allowed English bullion to promote British prestige and power, frayed the cords that bound the Concert of Europe. Consequently, for most of the period between 1822 and 1848 Metternich was virtually on his own as the Coachman of Europe, holding the potential runaway horses of competing state interests.

Because of this, the Age of Metternich is rightly named. During most of this era, Metternich worked to convince the Great Powers to support the concert system. However, his personal vanity led both contemporaries and later historians to question Metternich's advocacy of the European equilibrium. Critics have seen Metternich's statements as mere fig leaves to cover policies benefiting Austria. Contemporaries often believed that what Metternich wanted from the Quadruple Alliance was not peace and stability for Europe but protection for the fragile Habsburg Empire. Statesmen, particularly in constitutional monarchies like Britain and France, and later in reform-minded Prussia, accused Metternich of organizing Europe against the specters of war and revolution not for the good of Europe but for the survival of the Habsburg dynasty. Liberal European and American historians continue to make that accusation. What they miss, however, is the degree to which Metternich was a reform-minded conservative. What they fail to see is both the widespread support for Metternich's European system and the more dangerous alternatives his efforts avoided.

What concerned Metternich was revolution—not popular revolution as we think of it today, but revolution like that in France, which not only changed a society but also turned that society, acting through the state, into a dynamo for European conquest. Revolutionary movements, therefore, were a major concern of Metternich. Austria had fought against revolutionary and Napoleonic France because it upset the European equilibrium and threatened the internal, as well as the external, security of all states. After 1815, Metternich's fear of revolutionary states focused not only on France but also on Alexander's Russia between 1815 and 1825 and on Frederick William IV's Prussia after 1840. Both the difficulty of Metternich's efforts and the true nature of his successes can be understood only with the knowledge that Metternich saw states rather than peoples as the perpetrators as well as the victims of revolutions.

Metternich relied upon ongoing communications and personal contacts between heads of state or their chief ministers to maintain European stability. The Age of Metternich was also, therefore, the age of great conferences: the Congress of Vienna, the Congress of Aix-la-Chapelle (1818), the Carlsbad Conference (1819), the Vienna Conference (1820), and the Congresses of Troppau (1820), Laibach (1821), and Verona (1822). Additionally, there were conferences in London in 1830 and 1840, the first to settle the Belgian Question, the second to avoid a European war over the Eastern Question. Metternich organized and directed all but the last two meetings. In those cases Austrian diplomats vigorously represented his views.

At all of these conferences, Metternich managed to convince the Great Powers that good will, cooperation, and a concern for European stability superseded egoism and self-serving statism. He was successful more because of the age's new moral tone than because of the widespread fear of popular revolutions that alone would have persuaded the European monarchs to act against European liberals and nationalists. Because Metternich promoted fear of revolution among the monarchs of Europe, historians overlook the spirit of monarchic brotherhood that he so often called upon. It was this spirit of brotherhood and justice that appealed even to such critics as Tsar Alexander and King Frederick William IV. At the same time, Metternich's invocation of monarchic brotherhood wearied British and French statesmen: the former because their insularity permitted self-centeredness, the latter because they found it difficult to accept an ethic of abnegation and selflessness after the heady days of Napoleonic conquest.

Thus Metternich's congress system, far from being an agency designed solely for governmental repression of peoples—as has traditionally been asserted—was one that continually checked the self-serving instincts of the Great Powers themselves. At Aix-la-Chapelle, for instance, Metternich worked to control the zeal of Alexander and Frederick William III of Prussia for organized intervention against nationalists and liberals at the German universities. While Metternich was no friend of revolution, he had less fear of popular revolutionaries than of crowned "revolutionaries" like Alexander, whose boundless idealism repeatedly led him to exert undue influence far beyond his empire's boundaries.

Metternich did indeed move against popular revolutionary movements in Germany, as evidenced in the Carlsbad Decrees (1819) and the Vienna Conference (1820). However, to achieve his goal he used the German Confederation and did not call on the other Great Powers. Metternich wanted Germany to be an island of tranquility, disturbed neither by domestic revolutionaries nor by foreign intriguers, including a reactionary Russia and a liberal France or Britain. In Metternich's eyes, a stable Germany meant peace for fragile Austria and for the European state system as a whole. Metternich's constantly negative comments about both "reactionaries" and "revolutionaries" in the ministries of the other European states indicate his sincere conviction that overzealousness in either direction could return Europe to turmoil.

Metternich's desire to moderate Alexander was evident during the Spanish, Italian, and Greek revolutions of the 1820s. Through the Congresses of Troppau, Laibach, and Verona, Metternich caused the Great Powers not only to intervene in Italy and Spain but also to delay intervention in Greece. In the first two cases, Tsar Alexander again offered troops to quell revolutionary disturbances far distant from Russia. In each case, Metternich convinced Alexander that the intervention should be local—undertaken by Austria in Italy and by France in Spain. While liberals then and now regret Great Power intervention in Italy and Spain, it is important to remember that in both cases intervention restored order without leading either to prolonged occupation or to more power for the intervening states. Such interventions in previous centuries, and in our own, have not led to such demonstrations of European cooperation, trust, and selfless responsibility.

More dangerous than the situations in Spain and Italy was the perennial Eastern Question, which in the nineteenth century meant the fate of the Ottoman Empire. First in the Greek revolt, which began in 1821, and later in the Egyptian crisis of 1840, the narrow concerns of the Great Powers—first Russia and then France—threatened Metternich's work. The Greek revolt unleashed a brutal war that lasted for most of the decade. It aroused sympathy for the Greeks in England, France, and much of Germany, while it provoked Russia's ire against its traditional enemy, Turkey. The result was a near breakup of Metternich's congress system. The moral suasion that Metternich exercised over Alexander ended with the latter's death in 1825 and the assumption of the Russian throne by his brother Nicholas. Confronted with a Russian tsar interested in humiliating the Turks, a France desirous of breaking up the Concert of Europe, which confined it to limits determined by the European community, and a Palmerstonian England angered at Turkish atrocities, Metternich temporarily lost control of the concert system. When in 1828 a Russian, French, and British combination coerced the Ottoman Empire and brought about the liberation of Greece—with the accompanying glorification of both popular revolution and balance of power politics—Metternich could do little but accept the results.

However, the 1830 July Revolution in France refreshed Great Power memories of the dangers not only of revolutionary peoples but also of revolutionary states. Here again, it was Metternich, with his passion for stabilizing the status quo, who moved to recognize the "legitimacy" of King Louis Philippe, to bring him into the Concert of Europe, and to prevent France from becoming a revolutionary state. During an ensuing revolution in Belgium that threatened European peace through the breakup of the Kingdom of the Netherlands, Metternich urged cooperation and conciliation among the Great Powers. Success came in the 1830 London Conference when Metternich engineered a European-sponsored settlement that provided for an independent but permanently neutralized Belgium. This settlement was another triumph for Great Power solidarity in the name of justice and political equilibrium.

The last of the war scares that unsettled Europe before the Revolutions of 1848 occurred in 1840. The problem was again the Eastern Question. Turkey, besieged by Mehemet Ali, leader of Turkey's erstwhile vassal state, Egypt, verged on collapse. To avoid the consequences for Europe of a scramble for Turkish territory, Austria and Britain intervened on behalf of the Turks. But France was led by Premier Adolphe Thiers, who sought renewed prestige for France by invoking the glories of the Napoleonic period and by diplomatically supporting Egypt. Unable to strike at Metternich's Austria, which he considered responsible for France's limited European status, Thiers threatened the German Rhineland.

Once again Metternich's diplomatic maneuvering and a London conference defused the situation. He not only kept Austria from provoking France, he also prevented a provocation by the German Confederation when King Frederick William IV of Prussia incited a surge of German national patriotism. This romantic king was ready to arm the Confederation and crush France; but Metternich prevented him from thrusting Germany—and thus all of Europe—into a needless war with a temporarily overheated France. Metternich maneuvered the German Confederation, and thus Europe, onto the path of stability and political equilibrium.

Stability, of course, came at the expense of revisionist Frenchmen, Prussian statists, and German nationalists. It was these latter two groups, along with revolutionary liberals and democrats, who were particularly pleased by Metternich's downfall in March 1848. But the revolutions that inundated Europe in 1848 swept away more than the Coachman of Europe. They also undermined the Concert of Europe, which had been at the heart of the Congress of Vienna settlement and the Age of Metternich. The Revolutions of 1848 that removed Metternich also ended the July Monarchy in France and led to the popular election of France's first president, Louis Napoleon Bonaparte, who by the end of 1852 was ruling as Emperor Napoleon III. Between Napoleon III and Otto von Bismarck, who became chancellor of Prussia in 1862, Realpolitik, a nineteenth-century version of the old balance of power politics, replaced Metternich's quest for a European political equilibrium. Napoleon III and Bismarck, the two state revolutionaries of the second half of the nineteenth century, moved Europe back to the power politics that had characterized the Continent before the Congress of Vienna. These men were the kind of revolutionaries Metternich had feared more than popular revolutionaries. And White Revolutionaries that they were, they offered Europe not liberalism, democracy, and peace, but authoritarian government and war. Social Darwinism replaced monarchic solidarity and the norms of political equilibrium. The European concert system was doomed; the Metternich era, a remarkable period of European history, was at an end.

SELECTED BIBLIOGRAPHY

Baack, Lawrence J. *Christian Bernstorff and Prussia: Diplomacy and Reform Conservatism, 1818–1832.* New Brunswick, NJ: Rutgers University Press, 1980. Persuasively written study of the Prussian statesman whose "reform conservatism" made him both an ally and a rival of Metternich.

Bertier de Sauvigny, Guillaume de. *Metternich and His Times.* London: Humanities Press, 1962. Excellent topical discussion of Metternich's views and policies, using quotations from Metternich's correspondence to illustrate the Austrian's conservative principles.

Billinger, Robert D., Jr. *Metternich and the German Question: States' Rights and Federal Duties, 1820–1834.* Newark: University of Delaware Press, 1991. A revisionist, positive evaluation of Metternich's failed conservative German federalism, the keystone of his strategy for European stability.

Grimstead, Patricia K. *The Foreign Ministers of Alexander I: Political Attitudes and the Conduct of Russian Diplomacy, 1801–1825.* Berkeley: University of California Press, 1969. A useful examination of the roles played by the tsar's advisors and the emergence of the convoluted Russian foreign policy during the Vienna Congress period.

Gruner, Wolf D. "Was There a Reformed Balance of Power System or Cooperative Great Power Hegemony?" *American Historical Review* 97 (1992): 725–35. This "AHR Forum" piece responds to Paul Schroeder's "transformation of European politics" concept, which suggests a complexity to European, and particularly German, affairs that Schroeder misses.

Hartley, Janet M. *Alexander I.* London and New York: Longman, 1994. Readable survey with impressively annotated bibliography; suggests Alexander's self-proclaimed goal of Great Power cooperation for the maintenance of peace checked his religious enthusiasm to lead Europe.

Jervis, Robert. "A Political Science Perspective on the Balance of Power and the Concert." *American Historical Review* 97 (1992): 716–24. This "AHR Forum" piece supports Paul Schroeder's "transformation of European politics" concept and its depiction of movement away from balance of power politics after the Congress of Vienna.

Johnson, Paul. *The Birth of the Modern: World Society, 1815–1830.* New York: Harper Collins, 1991. Marvelous popular social history of the political, economic, cultural, and demographic transformations that dramatically changed the world in this period.

Kissinger, Henry A. *Diplomacy.* New York: Simon and Schuster, 1994. The former secretary of state, who favors pragmatism rather than ideology in the conduct of foreign affairs, argues that very pragmatic statesmen devoted to the balance of power system created the Concert of Europe.

———. *A World Restored: Metternich, Castlereagh and the Problems of Peace, 1820–1822.* Boston: Houghton Mifflin, 1957. A readable study that focuses on the political pragmatism of the "continental statesman," Metternich, and the "island statesman"—the real hero of the story—Castlereagh.

Kraeh, Enno E. "A Bipolar Balance of Power." *American Historical Review* 97 (1992): 707–15. This traditional realist's "AHR Forum" piece critiques Paul Schroeder's rejection of balance of power conceptions as applied to the Congress of Vienna.

———. *The Metternich Controversy.* New York: Holt, Rinehart and Winston, 1971. Part of the European Problem Studies series, this volume presents representative excerpts from the evolving literature on Metternich.

———. *Metternich's German Policy.* 2 vols. Princeton, NJ: Princeton University Press, 1963–1983. These volumes covering the period from 1809 to 1818 are micro-historical balance of power narratives by the dean of America's Metternich scholars.

Nichols, Irby C., Jr. *The European Pentarchy and the Congress of Verona.* The Hague: Martinus Nijhoff, 1971. A study based on British and French documents which argues that France's decision to intervene in Spain against the wishes of Britain, Austria, and Prussia ended the congress system.

Reinerman, Alan J. *Austria and the Papacy in the Age of Metternich.* 2 vols. Washington, DC: Catholic University Press, 1979–1989. These revisionistic volumes covering the period from 1809 to 1838 present a moderate Metternich whose suggested reforms for Italy were undermined by reactionaries associated with the papacy.

Schroeder, Paul W. "Did the Vienna Settlement Rest on a Balance of Power?" *American Historical Review* 97 (1992): 683–706. This "AHR Forum" article persuasively argues that a transformation of European politics took place during the Congress of Vienna; that political equilibrium and moral suasion, not balance of power, are the more useful concepts for understanding the post-Vienna European international system.

——. *Metternich's Policy at Its Zenith, 1820–1823.* Austin: University of Texas Press, 1962. Schroeder's early book on the post-Vienna settlement emphasizes Metternich's de facto pragmatism despite his proclaimed conservative idealism.

——. *The Transformation of European Politics, 1763–1848.* Oxford: Oxford University Press, 1994. Schroeder's trend-setting interpretation, a part of the Oxford History of Modern Europe series, has the most complete and up-to-date bibliography.

Sked, Alan, ed. *Europe's Balance of Power, 1815–1848.* New York: Barnes and Noble, 1979. Eight provocative essays, with usefully annotated bibliographies, by six distinguished British historians.

Webster, Charles K. *The Foreign Policy of Castlereagh, 1815–1822.* London: G. Bell and Sons, 1925. A sympathetic study of the man Webster considered the real founder of a European alliance system designed "to restrain the Great Powers rather than oppress the small."

Viereck, Peter. *Conservativism Revisited.* New York: Scribner's, 1949. Writing in the wake of World War II, Viereck portrays Metternich as a defender of Europe against nationalistic fanatics.

4

The Reform Bill of 1832

INTRODUCTION

Ever since the Glorious Revolution of 1688–1689, which deposed King James II, England's Parliament had increasingly guided that country's affairs. Parliament was aristocratic in nature, but it proved flexible and capable of passing reform measures. However, the French Revolution and the Napoleonic Wars badly frightened many members of both the House of Commons and the House of Lords. Fearing the spread of revolution to the British Isles, they turned a jaundiced eye toward any proposal to alter the status quo. Resistance to change was particularly evident during the half decade or so after Napoleon's defeat, since an especially reactionary faction of the Tory, or conservative, political party controlled Parliament. However, this was also a time of significant dislocation throughout Great Britain, caused by recession, rapid industrialization, and a rocky transition from a wartime to a peacetime economy that included the dumping of hundreds of thousands of soldiers into an already saturated labor market.

Faced with growing discontent that sometimes took a violent form, the reactionary Parliament suspended habeus corpus, stifled the press, and restricted public meetings. In August 1819, soldiers broke up a large

O'Connell and the Prime Minister at the bar. The election to Parliament in 1828 of Daniel O'Connell, an Irish Catholic radical, helped to split the Conservative Party of the Prime Minister, the Duke of Wellington, and to usher in an era of reform. (Reproduced from the Collections of the Library of Congress)

but peaceful protest meeting at Manchester, killing 11 protesters and wounding about 400. This "Peterloo Massacre" not only inflamed public opinion, but also confirmed the reactionaries in their fear of revolution and prompted them to push through Parliament the Six Acts, a set of statutes that expanded the government's right to conduct searches and seizures. Parliament also imposed an indirect form of censorship and banned public gatherings. A year later, revolutionaries conspired to murder the entire cabinet and proclaim a republic, but they were caught and executed.

Despite the best efforts of conservative Tories, including such well-known figures as the Duke of Wellington, Napoleon's conqueror, and Lord Castlereagh, the foreign secretary, support for reform continued to grow. The English middle class, or bourgeoisie, who prospered thanks to the Industrial Revolution, demanded political power equal to its growing economic wealth. English workers, who were being exploited in the new factories, and English farmers, who were being driven from the land, also cried out for reform.

The reform movement even affected the Tories, and there emerged a reformist wing led by George Canning, William Huskisson, and Robert Peel. The liberal Tories supported moderate reform as a way to get the country moving again and to dampen revolutionary sentiments. In 1822 Lord Liverpool, the politically adroit Tory leader and prime minister since 1812, eased the conservative Tories from office and replaced them with reforming Tories. Not surprisingly, moderate reform followed.

Huskisson, president of the Board of Trade, guided legislation through Parliament that significantly liberalized trade by reducing tariffs and modernizing the antiquated Navigation Laws, which had impeded the movement of goods. Peel, the home secretary, turned his attention to "law and order" matters. He persuaded Parliament to reform the barbaric penal code, which imposed the death sentence for more than 600 crimes, and he began to clean up the scandalous prison system, which was both inhumane and a training ground for future criminals. Peel is best known for creating a professional police force for London, the famous "Bobbies," who were so successful in maintaining order and combating crime that other cities soon copied Peel's idea.

Canning, the foreign secretary, distanced Great Britain from the extremely conservative views that dominated the European continent. In his role as leader of the House of Commons, Canning successfully moved Huskisson's and Peel's reform measures. In 1827 he replaced the ill and aged Liverpool as prime minister; but he died several months later, and the prime minister's post eventually went to Wellington, one of the most conservative Tories. This was an ironic development since it fell to the conservative duke to bring in the last and most controversial Tory reform measure, Catholic emancipation.

Since the turbulent seventeenth century, laws had been on the books discriminating against Catholics and Dissenters or Nonconformists, that is, Protestants who were not members of the Church of England. Over the years, the force of these laws had eroded, but Irish Roman Catholics in particular continued to suffer disabilities. They could not sit in Parliament, serve in the officer corps, or hold civilian office. In 1828 Daniel O'Connell, an Irish Catholic lawyer and orator of note, forced the issue of Catholic emancipation. In defiance of the law, he ran for a seat in Parliament and was elected overwhelmingly. With O'Connell's victory, it became obvious that Irish Catholics intended to run for (and undoubtedly win) Irish seats in Parliament. Wellington and the Tories now faced a dilemma. They could refuse to seat O'Connell, and perhaps spark civil war in Ireland, or they could lift the restrictions against Catholics. Reluctantly, Wellington chose the latter course, and in March 1829 the Catholic Emancipation Act became law. Catholics could now hold office, but the Tories, who were split to begin with between moderate reformers and staunch conservatives, found themselves even more fractured.

With the Tories in disarray and their opponents, the Whigs, in scarcely better condition, attention shifted once again to the question of reforming Parliament. For a number of years, many thoughtful Britons had viewed parliamentary reform as a necessity if not something of a panacea. The basic problem with Parliament was that it failed to reflect the nature of nineteenth-century Great Britain. With the Industrial Revolution, both population and wealth had shifted from the south of England to the Midlands. However, there had been no corresponding shift in parliamentary representation. In fact, no new borough had been created since 1688. Consequently, large and growing centers of wealth and population such as Birmingham, Manchester, Leeds, and Sheffield were not represented in Parliament. This galled the wealthy manufacturers who populated the new industrial cities.

The suffrage, where it did exist, was restricted and unequal. Of the approximately 660 members of Parliament, 465 came from boroughs; but there were no uniform rules to determine who possessed the right to vote. While some boroughs were quite democratic, the majority had a limited suffrage that allowed the local gentry to control the electoral process. The worst examples of this abuse were the rotten boroughs and the pocket boroughs, so called because the few voters who did exist were perceived to be "in the pocket" of the wealthy landholder. Old Sarum, the best example of a rotten borough, had no inhabitants at all. Whoever owned the land comprising Old Sarum had the right to send whomever he wished to Parliament. Another rotten borough, Dunwich, was virtually uninhabited since it was being swallowed by the North Sea. Boroughs were commonly bought and sold.

There were 190 representatives from the counties, elected by "forty-shilling freeholders," or men possessing land which produced an annual income of at least forty shillings. However, the number of Britons who met this requirement was shrinking due to agricultural consolidation. Furthermore, many of those who met the requirement were tenants and thus susceptible to the landlord's pressures. The end result was that a small group of powerful landowners tended to dominate county elections.

Studies indicate that in 1820 fewer than 500 men selected a majority of the House of Commons. Furthermore, most of these men sat in the House of Lords, a body that exercised considerable power at that time. It is estimated that in 1827, the landed gentry controlled 276 seats in the House of Commons, and that the most powerful eight landholders commanded 51 seats.

Despite growing pressure for parliamentary reform, Wellington and the conservative Tories resisted; but they overplayed their hand. The badly divided Tories had only a slight majority in the House of Commons, and when Wellington intemperately praised the existing electoral system and announced that he (and the Tories) would consider no changes, the Tory government collapsed.

With the Tories discredited, the Whigs under Earl Grey formed a government and introduced a bill calling for sweeping parliamentary reforms. In March 1831 the Commons narrowly defeated this first attempt at reform, thereby prompting a general election. The May 1831 election brought Grey and the Whigs a majority in Parliament for the first time in the nineteenth century. The Whigs reintroduced the Reform Bill, and it passed the House of Commons in September 1831, only to have the House of Lords kill it the following month.

Undaunted, the House of Commons passed yet another Reform Bill in March 1832. But the aristocratic and reactionary House of Lords could not be converted to the cause of reform, and when it appeared that Lords would reject the Reform Bill again Grey resigned. Wellington now attempted to form a government, but popular opinion was firmly against him. Workingmen went on strike, public protests occurred, and the supporters of reform, reacting to the slogan "Go for Gold," engineered a run on the Bank of England that threatened to plunge the nation into fiscal chaos.

With Wellington unable to form a government, the king, William IV, turned to Grey. Grey took up the challenge, but only after the reluctant king promised to create enough new, reform-minded members of the House of Lords to insure the Reform Bill's passage. Once Grey's strategy and the king's acceptance of it became clear, the House of Lords capitulated. Rather than see its ranks diluted by an influx of newcomers, the House of Lords acquiesced to reform on June 4, 1832.

Following in the wake of the Reform Bill of 1832, Parliament passed several other reform measures. In 1833, slavery throughout the British Empire was abolished. In the same year, the first Factory Act was passed, outlawing child labor for children under the age of nine and limiting working hours for children between the ages of nine and thirteen to nine hours per day and forty-eight hours per week. Children between the ages of thirteen and eighteen were limited to twelve hours of work per day. In 1835 Parliament passed the Municipal Corporation Act, which reformed the way local urban government was chosen. Henceforth, almost every adult male who paid taxes over a three-year period gained the right to vote in municipal elections. Less successful, perhaps, was the Poor Law of 1834, which ushered in the odious workhouses that Charles Dickens described so evocatively.

INTERPRETIVE ESSAY
Daniel W. Hollis III

Beginning with the eighteenth-century Enlightenment, European reformers cited England as a historical model for a variety of changes they sought in government, society, economics, and religion. Indeed, philosophers such as Voltaire tended to romanticize English institutions and individual freedoms in order to call attention to inequities in their own states. Yet, the issues for English reformers were different than for those on the Continent because English institutions had advanced beyond the authoritarian system prevalent in most of Europe. Thus, although England was not the idyllic society depicted by some philosophers, its flexible constitution allowed the peaceful reformation of institutions and the further extension of individual opportunities. Such a system inevitably inspired reformers in Europe and ultimately the entire world to believe in the possibility of ordered change.

The fact that England's constitution included a significant role for the representative legislature, Parliament, could be matched by only a few other European states. Yet, Parliament's primary constitutional role was to counterbalance the executive power of the monarchy. The franchise (right to vote) was available only to those with wealth, although the definition of wealth included social status as well as economic prosperity. That the unreformed Parliament—in both the House of Lords and the House of Commons—was aristocratic should not obscure the fact that it usually responded to the concerns of most Englishmen on major issues. Still, contested parliamentary elections before the Reform Bill concentrated on local issues and leadership rather than national matters.

During a long period of one-party Whig rule when King George I (r.1714–1727) and King George II (r.1727–1760) delegated considerable policy-making authority to the cabinet, a marked increase in corrupt election practices began to injure the integrity of the parliamentary system. Further, the truly revolutionary implications of economic expansion and advances in agriculture, commerce, and especially industry in the eighteenth century not only weakened the traditional social structure but also disrupted the function and purpose of political institutions. The population shifts—mainly from southern England to the Midlands—caused by increased commercial-industrial expansion and urbanization led to growing inequities in the representative nature of the boroughs, which possessed by far the largest number of seats in the House of Commons.

When George III (r.1760–1820) attempted to resume an active role for the king as a hands-on chief executive in the 1760s, the professional Whig politicians resisted his efforts to control the appointment of cabinet ministers and dictate policy to Parliament. The opposition to the purported growth of royal authority coincided with a unique parliamentary reform campaign revolving around the unlikely figure of John Wilkes. In a periodical called the *North Briton*, Wilkes boldly attacked the person of the king as well as the office. The crown had Wilkes arrested, but because the government used unconstitutional "general warrants" to seize Wilkes and his publication, a court released him. After being condemned by Parliament as an outlaw, Wilkes left England for a few years. When he returned in 1768 to face a prison term, London voters overwhelmingly elected him to Parliament. The House of Commons refused to allow

Wilkes to take his seat and scheduled new elections, only to have Wilkes elected again and denied his seat once more.

The Wilkes affair in the 1760s, especially the image of a government attempting to thwart the wishes of the voters, served to create the first parliamentary reform organization, the Society of Supporters of the Bill of Rights, which called for an end to corrupt elections, a redistribution of borough seats reflecting population shifts, and uniform property qualifications for voting, which would have increased the number of voters in many boroughs. However, by 1770 Tory opposition and a fractured Whig Party derailed the reform movement.

The government's concern with defeating the revolution in America from 1775 to 1783 further frustrated reform efforts. After the American Revolution, the Whig Party leadership continued to promote parliamentary reform, but once more internal divisions between its leaders, Edmund Burke and Charles James Fox, undercut the movement. The rivalry affected reform most seriously during the French Revolution (1789–1799) because bloodshed in France soon gave reform a bad name. Meanwhile, the government, led by William Pitt the Younger (previously an advocate of reform), associated reform efforts with subversion because England was at war with France. Its repressive policies silenced the various reform organizations and their leaders, and curtailed traditional English constitutional rights such as freedoms of speech and press. The long war with France, continuing through the Napoleonic era, further damaged and delayed the reform cause. Nonetheless, the issue of parliamentary reform was resurrected gradually in the years following the Napoleonic Wars in large part because social and economic issues pricked the national conscience.

The structure of Parliament from the eighteenth century to the passage of the Great Reform Bill of 1832 must be understood to appreciate the purpose of reform. Since membership in the House of Lords automatically included all bishops and peers (i.e., titled nobles), there were no elections to the upper body. Prior to the Union of England and Scotland in 1707, the House of Commons contained 489 seats from England, including 82 county seats, 403 borough seats, and 4 university seats (2 each for Cambridge and Oxford). Wales elected twenty-four members, half from the twelve counties and half from the boroughs. Scholars have estimated that there may have been 250,000 eligible voters for House of Commons seats in 1700.

County voters were determined uniformly by the ancient forty shilling freehold, but in the English boroughs property qualifications varied greatly. In the thirty-eight scot-and-lot boroughs, the franchise was held by all who paid the poor tax. The fourteen potwalloper boroughs allowed the franchise to residents of at least six months who were not on the poor roll and had a family and a boiling pot. The burgage franchise in thirty-five boroughs was held by those who owned an ancient parcel of real estate. Perhaps the narrowest of all the franchises was the corporation borough (twenty-nine total), where only members of the town corporation could vote, generally a few dozen at most. The eighty-six freeman and freeholder boroughs contained the most voters, yet there was no residency requirement.

The Act of Union with Scotland in 1707 allowed the Scots to elect sixteen peers to the English House of Lords and forty-five members to the House of Commons, including thirty county and fifteen borough seats. However, the number of voters in Scotland (about 4,500) was proportionally much smaller than in England. The 558 members of the House of Commons in 1707 remained the same until the union of Ireland with Great Britain in 1800. In 1801, the Irish obtained 100 seats in the Commons: sixty-four from the thirty-two counties, thirty-five borough seats, and one university seat for Trinity College.

Another aspect of Parliament's political evolution during the eighteenth century was the decline in contested elections. Although the number of voters roughly doubled from the early eighteenth century to the early nineteenth century due to increased prosperity, there was not a corresponding increase in the number of electoral challenges. Probably half of the enfranchised boroughs had fewer than 300 voters in 1815, and most often a local elite controlled them. Thus, in 1815 a political patron commanded at least half of the borough seats in the Commons compared to about one-fifth at the beginning of the eighteenth century. Of course, those powerful few who determined the representatives for most seats in Parliament had a vested interest in keeping the unreformed system intact. Throughout the reform era, they argued against any tampering with the constitution.

The traditionally conservative Tory Party, nominally headed by Robert Banks Jenkinson, Earl of Liverpool, managed the government after 1812. Because the administration's previous concerns had been overwhelmingly foreign, the real power in the cabinet was Foreign Secretary Robert Stewart, Viscount Castlereagh, who also served as leader in the Commons. Unfortunately, despite his foreign affairs competence, Castlereagh was ill-equipped to deal with mounting domestic problems after 1815. The early grievances were economic, related to wartime inflation, a recession during 1816–1817, and the demand of factory workers for increased wages. Spurred by radical orators like Henry Hunt, several clashes occurred between frustrated workers and British troops, which only worsened the situation. The Spa Fields riot in 1816 at a textile mill outside London resulted in the government suspending the right of habeas corpus so that suspects might be arrested without being brought to trial. The larger "Peterloo Massacre" caused eleven deaths; yet Parliament's only response was to pass the restrictive Six Acts.

The opposition Whig Party had been disillusioned by events and frequently divided since the 1760s. Although virtually all Whigs embraced some type of reform in theory, they seemed unwilling to act without a groundswell of popular support from both the middle and lower classes. Among the working classes, the tide of reform sentiment rose and fell according to the boom and bust cycles of the economy, so that the agitation between 1815 and 1820 promoted by hard times was followed by apathy during the more prosperous 1820s. The middle class—whether merchants, manufacturers, or small shopkeepers—embraced self-interested change. It resented aristocratic power and privilege evident in Parliament's decisions, yet it feared laboring-class democratic radicalism.

By the 1820s, some Whigs had revived the liberal positions of Charles James Fox to attack parliamentary corruption and the power of the privileged few. Radical journalists founded the Manchester *Guardian* in 1821 and the *Westminster Review* in 1824 to express their philosophy, which separated them from most Whigs and Tories. The moderate Utilitarian philosopher James Mill wrote a widely quoted essay for the *Encyclopaedia Britannica* in 1820 that favored the enfranchisement of the new industrial middle class. Central to the radical attack on the political system was the electoral process. However, just as Whigs debated the type and extent of reform needed, the Tories experienced their own internal tensions. Castlereagh's failure to resolve the domestic dilemmas ended with his suicide in 1822, and Liverpool selected as Castlereagh's successor a progressive Tory, George Canning, who pledged to end repression and enact modest reforms.

Although Canning officially opposed parliamentary reform, he pursued limited social and economic reforms designed to defuse popular dissent. William Huskisson, president of the Board of Trade, began the first serious assault upon the old mercantilism system by gradually lowering tariffs, a policy long advocated by the liberal economic followers of Adam Smith. The stimulation of trade indeed fostered job growth and even allowed minor wage adjustments for workers. Home Secretary Robert Peel abolished the government's domestic spy system, revised the penal code to eliminate many capital crimes, and established a model London police force to replace the military in law enforcement. Peel also persuaded Parliament to repeal the Combination Acts (1799–1800), thereby allowing workers to organize trade unions. These measures abated somewhat working-class hostility to law enforcement officials and the government, thereby muting calls for parliamentary reform.

While many reactionary Tories recoiled at even the tame social and economic changes wrought by Canning, it was the issue of franchise reform associated with the Catholic emancipation in Ireland that split the party. In order to remove a long-standing electoral anachronism, in 1828 the Tory Parliament repealed the seventeenth-century Test and Corporation Acts. These measures originally disfranchised Catholics and Protestant dissenters, though the latter had been allowed to vote for several decades despite the ancient laws. The repeal of the Test and Corporation Acts set the stage for action on Catholic emancipation. Originally promised in connection with the union of Ireland and Great Britain in 1800, Catholic emancipation would allow Irish Catholics to vote and to hold office. The issue was brought to a head when Daniel O'Connell, a Catholic, was defiantly elected to Parliament in 1826. Although Canning died before enacting emancipation legislation in 1827, his more conservative successor, the Duke of Wellington, caved in to fears of an Irish uprising and pressure from O'Connell's Catholic Association. The Catholic Emancipation Act of 1829 enfranchised Catholics while at the same time raising the property qualification to eliminate perhaps 200,000 voters, thereby regulating the type of Irish Catholic who could vote.

Catholic emancipation prepared the way for parliamentary reform in several ways. It demonstrated how easily the constitution could be altered, split the Tory Party into three factions, and, because of its unpopularity with Protestants, tended to shift voter attention from local to national affairs as never before. Religion proved an even more potent voter motivator than socioeconomic status. O'Connell's Catholic Association also illustrated to English reformers the value of popular political lobbying. Radical leaders Thomas Atwood and Joseph Parkes founded the Birmingham Political Union in 1829, which called for an alliance of the middle and working classes to promote parliamentary reform. Atwood secured the backing of Daniel O'Connell and Francis Place for the reform program. Radical journalist William Cobbett began a speaking tour in late 1829 advocating reform. The unity of middle- and working-class radicals persuaded many aristocrats that reform was needed to prevent more serious upheavals.

In February 1830, Lord John Russell introduced a Whig bill to create Commons seats for the industrial cities of Birmingham, Manchester, and Leeds. Wellington's Tory government opposed the measure, and it was defeated 188 to 140. Another Russell proposal to give seats to several manufacturing towns was beaten back in May. Irish leader Daniel O'Connell brazenly proposed manhood suffrage in the Commons in May, but the measure was easily defeated. Nonetheless, mounting pressure for reform generated considerable discomfort for the Wellington administration, whose future prospects appeared dim.

Upon the death of King George IV in June 1830, Parliament was dissolved and new elections scheduled. The 1830 election gave little indication of the events that were to follow. Only 83 electoral contests materialized (compared to 156 in 1722 and 89 in 1826), and a typical number of new members were elected (175 compared with 171 new members in 1826). Still, the Tory government lost most of the contested elections, and Whig reformers such as Henry Brougham of Yorkshire won many seats previously held by Tories. After the election, Wellington opted to seek allies among the anti-reform Tories instead of the moderate Whigs led by Earl Grey. This decision sealed the Tory fate. The government was defeated on a procedural vote in November, and the cabinet resigned.

Grey proceeded to form a Whig government, and almost immediately named a four-man committee to draft a parliamentary reform bill that would satisfy the public clamor for change, but not include manhood suffrage or equal electoral districts. The draft bill that finally emerged in 1831 would practically end representation for the infamous depopulated "rotten boroughs." Furthermore, forty-seven boroughs with populations of between 2,000 and 4,000 would lose one of their two seats. The bill would create ninety-seven new seats for towns that had experienced population increases, such as those Midland manufacturing cities. Twenty-six counties would also receive additional seats. A uniform property franchise, set at £10, was established for borough voters. The forty shilling freehold franchise in the counties would be preserved, but copyholders with property valued at £10 per annum and leaseholders whose rent was at least £50 per year would also be enfranchised. The maximum length a Parliament could meet was five years. Certain election traditions that permitted corruption were altered, such as reducing the polling period from fifteen days to two, adding a residency requirement for all borough candidates, and preventing urban freeholders from voting in county elections also. Grey persuaded King William IV to support the bill.

Meanwhile, a nearly bloodless revolution in France in July 1830 had led to a dynastic change. This was followed by a Belgian revolt for independence from the Netherlands. Undoubtedly, France's July Revolution (and, to a lesser degree, events in Belgium) influenced the 3,000 petitions that various well-organized reform groups around the nation presented to Parliament over the next several months. Additionally, an economic recession led to sporadic outbreaks of violence among agricultural laborers in southern England. Whig historian and M.P. Thomas Babington Macaulay argued in the Commons that passage of the Reform Bill would provide the best defense against revolution.

After the Commons defeated the Reform Bill in April 1831, the king agreed to dissolve Parliament and call new elections. In contrast to the 1830 election, the 1831 election resulted in major Tory losses for those opposed to the Reform Bill. When the new Parliament convened, the Reform Bill was put forward once again, this time passing the Commons, 346-235. It was then sent to the House of Lords, where Grey and Brougham defended it during five days of debate; but the Lords rejected the measure by forty-one votes. Serious riots, in which aristocratic property was destroyed, erupted in Nottingham, Derby, Bristol, and London, and the radical political clubs vented their anger. Francis Place, backed by Sir Francis Burdett, founded the National Political Union in London to further coordinate middle- and working-class agitation for reform. Neither middle-class organizations like the Birmingham Political Union nor working-class groups such as the National Union of Working Classes dissuaded their members from arming themselves.

After several changes designed to accommodate the Lords, the Commons approved the revised bill, 324 to 162. The focus then turned to persuading the king to create sufficient new peerages for a favorable majority in the Lords. Despite mounting pressure upon the Lords to enact the bill, in May the government lost a procedural vote in the upper house on a motion to postpone the borough disfranchisements 151 to 116, causing the cabinet to resign in protest.

The king directed Wellington to try to form a Tory government committed to a much more modest reform, but Wellington lacked support from key progressives such as Peel in his own party. Threatening rhetoric and petitions pushed by middle-class radicals such as Francis Place, which spoke about armed resistance against a new Wellington government, frightened many Tories, though not Wellington himself. A week later, when Wellington ended efforts to organize a government, King William prevailed upon Grey to reestablish a Whig administration. The anti-reform Tory peers quietly withdrew and in June allowed the Reform Bill to pass the House of Lords, 106 to 22. The king gave his royal assent to make the Reform Act of 1832 law. Parliament was dissolved to allow new elections under the reform structure. Separate reform bills were enacted for Scottish and Irish representation in July and August. The more significant franchise reform in Scotland increased the number of eligible voters from 4,500 to 65,000.

As an instrument of political change, the Reform Act was neither as great as its most ardent backers supposed nor as fearful as its major detractors predicted. The Reform Bill was indeed a compromise, but one which showed why the unique British Parliament had existed for hundreds of years. The Whig leadership hoped that none of the new boroughs would have less than 300 voters. Although that goal was not achieved, only thirty-one reformed boroughs had less than 300 voters, and twenty-nine had over 2,000 voters. Because the number of voters in England and Wales increased by perhaps 80 percent (from about 366,000 in 1831 to 653,000 in 1832), participation in government greatly expanded. Yet only about 18 percent of the adult males could vote after the Reform Bill passed, compared to about 11 percent before. Thus, unquestionably the Reform Bill did not create a democracy, though it became a necessary first step toward that end. Manhood suffrage would be completed in two installments in the Second Reform Bill (1867) and the Third Reform Bill (1884). By that time, other nations including France and Germany had enacted full manhood suffrage. Nonetheless, it is fair to conclude that England's Reform Bill of 1832 again demonstrated to the rest of Europe how organized citizen participation in government could accomplish change without revolution through a constitutional framework.

The question of both the Whig leaders' motives and the impact of the new franchise and representative provisions contained in the Reform Bill has been debated continuously without agreement since 1832. The older view that the Reform Bill was a concession by frightened property interests to avert a revolution has been modified. Some of the aristocratic Whig leaders such as Grey indeed feared the possibility of revolution. Yet Grey also believed that participation in government should be broadened to a limited degree and that the aristocracy must balance its interests with those of the larger community. Indeed, Grey later argued that reform in fact had preserved aristocratic interests, although Henry Brougham thought that their power had been broken by the middle class. Tory leaders such as Wellington believed that the bill dangerously advanced the interests of the working classes, while progressive Tories like Peel argued that the beneficiaries were the middle classes. While some political leaders portrayed the Reform Act as solidifying the existing social and political order, radicals viewed the measure as a tool for future social and political innovation.

That the Reform Act of 1832 ushered in additional reform measures cannot be denied. The abolition of slavery in the British Empire, a factory act that regulated child labor, reform of municipal governments along the lines of the Reform Act, and a revamping of the Elizabethan poor law were a direct result of the Reform Act. By the mid-1830s, the reform zeal of the Whigs waned, and continued efforts to bring change originated outside of Parliament. By appealing more directly to the working classes, the Chartists—the logical heirs of the radical political unions which promoted the reform of Parliament—sought to exploit class consciousness more than the political unions. Their Great Charter was a petition to Parliament calling for the abolition of property qualifications for voting (i.e., manhood suffrage), regular reapportionment of the House of Commons according to population, electoral districts with equal populations, a secret ballot, and salaries for members of Parliament. Each time it was presented to Parliament, in 1839, 1842, and 1848, the Great Charter was rejected. Yet, the Chartist proposals were adopted later in the century. Led by John Bright and Richard Cobden, merchants and manufacturers advocating laissez faire economic policies formed the Anti–Corn Law League in the 1830s, which called for repeal of the last vestige of mercantilism, the tax on imported foodstuffs. It was not until a disastrous potato famine in Ireland in 1846 that the Corn Laws were finally repealed. These extra-parliamentary movements, clearly fruits of the Reform Act, continued to engage the popular middle- and working-class cultures in constitutional political action.

If anything can be said categorically about the Reform Act, it is that it enhanced the role of Parliament, which in turn increased the importance of partisan politics, which thereby enlarged the function of parties. Although earlier periods of English history had assured Parliament's significance in the governance of England, the Reform Act of 1832 elevated its importance. The character of the constitution changed from a "mixed government" of "Kings, Lords, and Commons" to a representative government in which Commons was preeminent. Parliament eventually assumed the diverse responsibilities of executive, administrator of the bureaucracy, protector of consumer and citizen rights, and director of foreign policy, all of which broadened its traditional legislative function.

Because Parliament had become the most important government institution, the political parties also became more critical to the success of the political system. At the least, the newly enfranchised voters forced both parties to compete for their votes. Since issues after 1832 tended to focus more on national than local matters, after the Reform Act voters tended to act in a more partisan manner, so that there was much less fluidity between parties than in the past. Historians usually emphasize the ideological differences between Whigs and Tories (or later Liberals and Conservatives) as the reason for expressive partisanship. Yet their political principles were remarkably similar, especially when compared with continental political parties. Both parties endorsed the constitution and accepted their responsibility to respond to public concerns so as to govern in the best interests of the nation. Also, because there was little correlation between socioeconomic status and voting behavior, the Reform Act did not guarantee permanent political dominance for the Whigs. What did change for both parties because of the Reform Act was the shift of attention away from local politics, traditionally of much greater concern to communities, to national affairs.

SELECTED BIBLIOGRAPHY

Brock, Michael. *The Great Reform Act*. London: Hutchinson University Library, 1973. The standard monograph, emphasizing the historical process leading to reform and the Reform Bill's conservative aims yet significant results.

Butler, James R.M. *The Passing of the Great Reform Bill*. London: Longmans, Green, 1914. Traditional interpretation focusing on the immediate events surrounding the Reform Bill's passage.

Cannon, John. *Parliamentary Reform, 1640–1832*. London: Cambridge University Press, 1972. Detailed historical background concluding that the Reform Bill had far-reaching effects.

Davis, Richard W. "Toryism to Tamworth: The Triumph of Reform, 1827–1835." *Albion* 12 (1980): 132-46. Argues that reformers intended to broaden participation in government.

Dinwiddy, John R. *From Luddism to the First Reform Bill: Reform in England, 1810–1832*. Oxford: Basil Blackwell, 1986. A concise review revealing the complexity of reform politics; especially strong on the radicals.

Evans, Eric J. *The Great Reform Act of 1832*. London: Methuen, 1983. Another brief survey, primarily focused on reform politics within Parliament.

Flick, Carlos. *The Birmingham Political Union and the Movements for Reform in Brit-*

ain, 1830–1839. Folkestone, Kent: Dawson, 1978. Detailed analysis of the most important middle-class extra-parliamentary organization backing reform.

Gash, Norman. "English Reform and French Revolution in the General Elections of 1830." In *Essays Presented to Sir Lewis Namier,* pp. 258-88. Edited by Richard Pares and A.J.P. Taylor. London: Macmillan, 1956. Shows that the 1830 French Revolution played only a marginal role in Reform Bill politics.

————. *Politics in the Age of Peel: A Study in the Technique of Parliamentary Representation, 1830–1850.* London: Longmans, Green, 1953. View that the Reform Bill was only one aspect of a gradual and complex political change.

Hamburger, Joseph. *James Mill and the Art of Revolution.* New Haven, CT: Yale University Press, 1963. Suggests that Mill and other radicals coerced Whig leaders into support for reform by threatening revolution.

Hill, Brian W. *British Parliamentary Parties, 1742–1832.* London: George Allen and Unwin, 1985. Argues that Reform Bill politics unified both parties by healing serious splits.

Maccoby, Simon. *English Radicalism, 1786–1832.* London: George Allen and Unwin, 1955. A detailed treatment by a leading authority on the radical tradition, viewing the Reform Bill as a watershed in English history.

Milton-Smith, John. "Earl Grey's Cabinet and the Objects of Parliamentary Reform." *Historical Journal* 15 (1972): 55–74. Defends Grey's motives as genuinely pro-reform and the Whigs as responsive to public opinion.

Mitchell, Austin. *The Whigs in Opposition, 1815–1830.* London: Oxford University Press, 1967. Argues that Whig acquisition of power in 1830 was due to popular backing rather than the weakness of the Tories.

Mitchell, L. G. "Foxite Politics and the Great Reform Bill." *English Historical Review* 108 (1993): 338–64. Sees similarities between reform-era Whigs and earlier Foxite Whigs, and argues that the redistribution of seats to Whig advantage was more important than the number of new voters.

Moore, David Cresap. *The Politics of Deference: A Study of the Mid-Nineteenth Century English Political System.* Hassocks, Sussex: Harvester Press, 1976. A leading revisionist, Moore argues that the Reform Bill was deliberately limited by aristocrats to protect their interests and preserve deferential politics.

O'Gorman, Frank. *Voters, Patrons, and Parties: The Unreformed Electoral System of Hanoverian England, 1734–1832.* Oxford: Clarendon Press, 1989. Argues that the unreformed electoral system was less corrupt and had more popular support than supposed.

Phillips, John A. *The Great Reform Bill in the Boroughs: English Electoral Behavior, 1818–1841.* Oxford: Clarendon Press, 1992. Argues that the Reform Bill redefined yet solidified party behavior along partisan lines.

————. "The Many Faces of Reform: The Reform Bill and the Electorate." *Parliamentary History* 1 (1985): 115–35. Suggests that parliamentary reform increased an already large participation in government.

Porritt, Edward. *The Unreformed House of Commons.* 2 vols. Cambridge: Cambridge University Press, 1903. Detailed account of Commons before reform as well as enactment of the Reform Bill itself; condemns the unreformed system as corrupt.

Rowe, D. J. "Class and Political Radicalism in London, 1831–32." *Historical Journal* 13 (1970): 31–47. Suggests that the absence of class consciousness during the reform era permitted cooperation between middle- and working-class groups.

Smith, E. A. *Lord Grey, 1764–1845.* Oxford: Clarendon Press, 1990. Views Grey as a pragmatic reformer who aimed to preserve existing institutions, especially the influence of the aristocracy.

Thompson, Edward P. *The Making of the English Working Class.* New York: Random House, 1963. This classic account of the radical cause concludes that the Reform Bill betrayed working-class interests to protect aristocratic positions.

Tuberville, Arthur S. *The House of Lords in the Age of Reform, 1784–1837.* London: Faber and Faber, 1958. Shows the House of Lords to have been both realistic and flexible toward reform, hence able to retain a viable role in Parliament for decades following.

Wasson, Ellis Archer. "The Great Whigs and Parliamentary Reform." *Journal of British Studies* 24 (1985): 434–64. Argues that the aristocratic Whigs genuinely favored reform and were the key to its success.

Woodbridge, George. *The Reform Bill of 1832.* New York: Thomas Y. Crowell, 1970. Concise but excellent account that examines the Reform Bill's limited but significant changes.

5

The Revolutions of 1848

INTRODUCTION

The Revolutions of 1848 swept over Europe from Paris to Budapest and from Copenhagen to Sicily. Among Europe's important nations, only Great Britain and Russia were spared. Rising tensions dating back decades, if not centuries, caused the revolutions. One source of tension was the growth of liberal ideas derived from the eighteenth century's Enlightenment and from that century's American and French Revolutions. Mid-nineteenth-century liberals, although never in complete agreement with each other, usually called for constitutions and the rule of law, legislative assemblies elected by at least some of the citizenry, religious toleration, equality under the law for some, and laissez faire economics that would remove the state from the marketplace. Europe's conservative leadership, consisting chiefly of the monarchical courts, the nobility, established religious bodies (especially the Roman Catholic Church), and the officer corps, bitterly opposed liberalism and clung to the status quo.

The growth of national sentiment proved another source of tension. Inspired by figures such as the apostle of nationalism Guiseppe Mazzini, demands for either national unification or national independence in-

The crowned heads of Europe contemplate their fate. The Revolutions of 1848 challenged monarchical rule in many countries; however, by the end of 1849 most monarchs had regained their power. (Reproduced from the Collections of the Library of Congress)

creased dramatically. Germans and Italians were interested in the former; Poles, Hungarians, and the Irish sought the latter.

Technology also fostered tension. The Industrial Revolution was in the process of either destroying or marginalizing age-old economic relationships. Artisans, who could not compete against machines, desperately sought relief. The new working force, the proletariat, tended the machines for long hours in uncomfortable and unsafe factories at low wages and with no job security. After work, they returned to crowded, unsanitary, and dangerous slums. Even the bourgeoisie, the owners of the machines, repudiated the status quo. Growing rich thanks to the Industrial Revolution, they wanted political power and social prestige equal to their wealth. When the established authorities barred them from their inner circle, the bourgeoisie grew restless.

Finally, in much of central Europe the peasantry was unhappy. Although basically conservative, the peasantry resented the continuing vestiges of medieval feudalism that interfered with their lives at every turn, and they began to demand emancipation. However, the conservative rulers were not inclined to grant their wishes.

During the 1840s, two additional factors heightened tension and helped to produce a revolutionary atmosphere. In one instance, an industrial boom based on the construction of railroads collapsed, giving way to an industrial depression. Many workmen now found themselves unemployed, and there was no social welfare "safety net" to protect them. As the numbers of unemployed grew, so too did the level of discontent. In the other instance, Europe experienced agricultural problems culminating in a devastating series of crop failures that brought skyrocketing food prices in the towns and malnutrition and even starvation in the countryside. Desperation set in among Europe's peasants; but the governments could not or would not do anything to alleviate the suffering.

Although a revolution had broken out in Sicily in January, the real starting point for the Revolutions of 1848 was France. Discontent with King Louis Philippe's stagnant and corrupt reign had been growing, and when his ministers flatly refused to consider reform, crisis ensued. Barricades went up in the working-class districts of Paris, and on February 23 demonstrators and army units clashed, resulting in dozens of casualties. On the following day, Louis Philippe abdicated and a republic was proclaimed. Louis Philippe's unexpected overthrow electrified Europe. However, the revolution in France was far from complete. It had been something of a spontaneous event, and now those who had seized power faced the awesome task of ruling.

Fundamental differences among the revolutionaries surfaced almost immediately. One faction, consisting chiefly of the bourgeoisie and led by the poet Alphonse Lamartine, wished to implement liberal ideals and, at the same time, validate the bourgeoisie in their control of the French state. Another faction, led by the socialist Louis Blanc, aimed for a radical social revolution. The vast majority of Frenchmen—peasants living beyond the superheated atmosphere of Paris—held basically conservative views.

Peasant conservatism carried the day in April elections for a National Constituent Assembly. While the Constituent Assembly cautiously embraced political reform, it rejected social experimentation. In particular, it objected to Blanc's socialist proposals and the National Workshop scheme that had been implemented in a hasty and incomplete manner in order to mollify Blanc. The National Workshops gave work to the unemployed in public works projects. Very quickly, the number of men enrolled in the National Workshops far exceeded the amount of work available to them. Consequently, many were being paid for doing little or nothing.

Antagonism between the socially conservative Constituent Assembly and the supporters of the National Workshops, including the Parisian working class and others who had been drawn to Paris by the prospect of work—or at least a daily handout—steadily mounted, and in late June it erupted into violence. Civil war, or perhaps more accurately class warfare, engulfed Paris. The forces of the Constituent Assembly triumphed, but the June Days, as the conflict was called, left more than 10,000 killed or wounded.

In the wake of the June Days, the Constituent Assembly drew up a new constitution which envisioned a strong president. In December 1848, elections took place; the surprise landslide winner was Louis Napoleon Bonaparte, a nephew of the great Napoleon. Despite his public commitment to the new republic, Louis Napoleon wanted absolute power. Three years later he engineered a coup d'état that destroyed the republic and replaced it with an empire headed by himself.

The news of revolution in Paris stunned the Habsburg Empire, an antiquated dynastic state that sprawled across central Europe. The Habsburg Empire included sizeable numbers of Germans, Hungarians, Czechs, Slovaks, Poles, Ruthenians, Romanians, Slovenes, Serbs, Croats, and Italians. The Habsburgs also dominated much of Germany and the

Italian peninsula. The empire's chancellor, the elderly Clemens von Metternich, who opposed both liberal ideas and nationalism, guided Habsburg fortunes.

News of Louis Philippe's fall galvanized the Hungarian, or Magyar, aristocracy, many of whom feared and resented German encroachment into the Hungarian lands. On March 15, 1848, the Magyar diet (parliament), under the influence of radical journalist Louis Kossuth, issued a new Hungarian constitution that guaranteed Hungary's autonomy at Vienna's expense. Several weeks later, the Czech lands (Bohemia) followed suit.

Meanwhile, the old regime in Vienna was collapsing. On March 13, students and workers rose in revolt. Metternich, the living embodiment of the post-Napoleonic era, fled to exile in Great Britain. Rioting spread throughout the empire, and disturbances broke out in both Germany and Italy. These March Days, as they were known, forced the Habsburgs to grant several reforms; but with one exception it was a case of too little too late as revolution swept the empire.

Nevertheless, by early summer the revolutionary tide had crested and the revolution began to ebb. The Habsburg decision to emancipate the peasantry speeded this process. Abolition of serfdom defused peasant anger and destroyed any enthusiasm the conservative peasants may have had for the revolution.

In the Czech lands, ethnic suspicions undermined the revolution. When the Czechs and Germans fell out, the way was open for troops loyal to the emperor under General Alfred Windischgratz to reassert imperial authority. In mid-June Windischgratz bombarded Prague, thereby bringing an end to the Czech phase of the revolution.

In March the Habsburgs' Italian holdings, the provinces of Lombardy (Milan) and Venetia (Venice), had broken free. Charles Albert, the ruler of the independent Italian kingdom of Sardinia, or Piedmont, supported the breakaway provinces and declared war on Austria. Parma, Modena, Tuscany, and Sicily, states closely aligned with Austria, also experienced revolution. However, the Austrians were not beaten, and in July the Austrian army defeated Charles Albert at the Battle of Custozza and reestablished Habsburg rule in Lombardy. In the following year, the Habsburgs defeated Charles Albert once again and reabsorbed Venetia into their empire.

Next came the turn of the Hungarians. During the summer of 1848, the Magyars had acted in an extremely chauvinistic manner, thereby antagonizing other nationalities living within Hungary. In particular, the

Croats resisted the Hungarians. In September, Joseph Jellachich, the governor of Croatia appointed by Vienna, led the Croatians in open revolt against the Magyars. Shortly thereafter, the Habsburgs also made war on the rebellious Magyars. Early in 1849, the Hungarians won a series of victories over the Austrians and their allies, and declared their independence. The new Austrian emperor, Francis Joseph, called on Russia for help. The Russian tsar, Nicholas I, the most reactionary ruler in Europe, quickly accepted this opportunity to crush revolution. He sent 140,000 troops into Hungary, where they routed the Magyars by August 1849.

Meanwhile, the revolution in Vienna itself had failed. From the start, radical socioeconomic demands and unrestrained street violence had frightened the Viennese bourgeoisie, who favored political reform but abhorred social revolution and disorder. The empire's apparent disintegration also prompted second thoughts about the revolution. As rioting continued and the demands of the students and workers became more radical, the middle-class supporters of revolution began to drift away. For many, a return to the pre-revolutionary status quo had growing appeal. When fresh rioting occurred in October, the property owning classes had had enough. They abandoned the revolution at the very time that Windischgratz mounted a military counterstrike. By the end of October, the Habsburgs once again controlled Vienna.

The Revolutions of 1848 also engulfed the German-speaking lands. In Prussia, the news from Paris and Vienna, as well as a severe economic recession and the unwillingness of the Prussian king, Frederick William IV, to heed calls for reform, provoked rioting. The king hastily granted concessions, but troops fired into a crowd of demonstrators, killing several dozen. Chaos ensued and barricades went up. Although the Prussian army held the upper hand, the shocked king ordered it to leave Berlin, but in doing so he became the unwitting prisoner of the crowd. Under popular pressure, Frederick William appointed a cabinet of moderate liberals and consented to the election of a national assembly charged with writing a constitution.

The national assembly was elected in May, but real power rested with the army. Frederick William gradually regained his nerve, and he now refused to surrender any of his autocratic powers. As the national assembly moved at a snail's pace, in June Berlin's lower classes once again took to the streets. Many moderates who had wished for mild political reform now washed their hands of the revolution and looked to the king and the army to restore law and order. In November Frederick William moved decisively against what remained of the revolution. He suspended the national assembly and recalled the army to Berlin. Minor opposition was quickly overcome, and the revolution in Prussia was dead.

At this time Germany was not a unified country. At the Congress of Vienna, thirty-nine independent German states—including Prussia and Austria—formed the German Confederation, a loose body dominated by Austria. In spring 1848, revolution shook virtually all these states; traditional authority disappeared and a huge vacuum opened. German revolutionaries seized this opportunity to create a liberal, unified Germany. For that purpose, they elected delegates from throughout Germany. The resultant Frankfurt Assembly opened in May 1848.

The assembly consisted almost exclusively of moderate, middle-class professionals. It never seriously considered the socioeconomic questions of the day; rather, it focused on the issue of German unification. The assembly split badly over the question of what to do with Austria, a multinational empire. The *Grossdeutsch*, or large German, solution would include the Austrian lands, except Hungary, in any unified German state. The *Kleindeutsch*, or little German, solution would exclude Austria—both its German and non-German subjects—from any unified state.

While the delegates at Frankfurt endlessly debated this intractable issue, events took their own course. Upon regaining control of their empire, the Habsburgs rejected overtures from Frankfurt, indicating that they were as opposed to German nationalism as they were to any other kind of nationalism. Consequently, the *Kleindeutsch* forces won by default. However, the *Kleindeutsch* choice for German monarch, the king of Prussia, was not interested either. In fact, Frederick William brusquely refused what he contemptuously called a "crown from the gutter" offered by "butchers and bakers." With his refusal, the Frankfurt Assembly broke up. As elsewhere in Europe, the revolution in Germany was over.

INTERPRETIVE ESSAY
Paul D. Lensink

The year 1848 was unique in European history. Never before had the revolutionary current been so strong. In all, some fifty separate revolts and uprisings took place, and many of these were amazingly successful.

Within the space of a few weeks, revolutionary forces had succeeded in toppling several governments. Remarkably, these revolutions took place in an area marked by great geographic, social, political, and economic diversity. Some regions in western Europe were more economically and socially advanced, while large areas in southern and eastern Europe remained backward. Political systems under attack ranged from a constitutional monarchy in France to the absolutist multinational empire of the Habsburgs. The revolutionaries themselves had different motives and often pursued contradictory aims. Nationalism galvanized some of the revolutions, while economic hardship and political alienation sustained others. The bourgeoisie wanted to ensure property and voting rights, while urban workers demanded job security and food. Peasants, who formed the vast majority of Europe's population, demanded an end to serfdom, the legal system which made them virtual slaves to the landlords.

Because of the diverse nature of the Revolutions of 1848, assessing their significance is a complex task. No general interpretation can explain each case, or even the whole revolutionary episode. Each of the revolutions took place under particular national and local circumstances. Nonetheless, the revolutions did share more than the time frame in which they occurred. The impact of the revolutions spread well beyond the particulars of each situation. Some common conditions and attitudes had to prevail for the revolutionary current to spread so quickly across national boundaries. While it is important to remember that none of the revolutions was exactly alike, the best way to determine their overall historical significance is to identify some of their fundamental characteristics and consequences.

One of the most obvious features of the revolutions was that they all eventually shared the same fate: failure. By the summer of 1848, most of the revolts had lost momentum as the revolutionaries began to experience serious differences over methods and aims. This allowed the antirevolutionary forces time to regroup and to gain strength. By 1849 only the Hungarians and Venetians held out against the conservative reaction sweeping across Europe. Then in August, the Habsburg army, with some outside help from the Russians, defeated these revolutions as well. Although the Revolutions of 1848 started with great promise, no revolutionary regime was able to maintain power. Most of the European aristocracy preserved its entrenched position at the top of society, and, with the exception of France, the pre-1848 governments regained power and reestablished authoritarian rule. Even many moderate liberals sided with the conservative elements of society because of the threat of social revolution posed by the lower classes. The conservatives seemed to become even more unified and powerful in the wake of the defeated revolutions.

In France, after the socialist revolutionaries were crushed during the June Days, the Constituent Assembly passed a constitution that called for a strong presidency. In December, Louis Napoleon, the nephew of Napoleon Bonaparte, won the election for president by an overwhelming majority, thereby inaugurating the so-called French Second Republic. Louis Napoleon was to have a four-year term. However, the new president, dissatisfied with this limit on his rule, illegally dismissed the assembly in 1851 and took power in a coup d'état. He then called an election which extended his presidency to a ten-year term. There was some resistance to this move, but protests were crushed by the army. The following year Louis Napoleon held another plebiscite which named him hereditary emperor. Louis Napoleon, now Napoleon III, replaced the Second Republic with his own personal dictatorship. Although his rule was ratified by popular vote, the government was basically authoritarian and composed mainly of men of the old order. This appeared to be a resounding defeat for the ideals of the 1848 revolution in France.

In the German states, the liberals in the Frankfurt Assembly had failed to create a unified Germany. Although the assembly elected Frederick William emperor of the new German state, the Prussian king refused the throne, not wishing to accept a crown offered by an elected parliament. This proved to be a major defeat for liberalism in Germany. In 1849 Frederick William disbanded Prussia's Constituent Assembly. He granted a basically conservative constitution that allowed conservatives to maintain control over a weak parliament. Prussia, like other German states, lapsed into a period of reaction during the 1850s.

In a similar pattern, the Habsburg Empire became even more centralized and reactionary than it had been prior to the revolutions. The government in Vienna returned to the system created by the archconservative Metternich and strengthened it even further. In 1851, the government repealed the constitution passed in 1848 and canceled the list of rights granted in 1849. New laws abolished elected councils at virtually all levels, even those that had existed prior to 1848, and created a new, highly centralized administration. The laws also introduced Austrian law into the Hungarian lands of the empire and assured a superior position to German-speaking subjects. There were virtually no institutions left to check the power of the central authorities. For several years Vienna ruled the empire as a kind of conquered territory.

The conservative reaction was also strong in various Italian states. The regime in Modena jailed liberals and closed universities. Pope Pius IX became an opponent of both liberalism and nationalism, and denounced the war against Catholic Austria. In Naples, the government worked with organized crime in order to strengthen its authority. Only in the kingdom of Piedmont did the government maintain the liberal constitution passed in 1848.

In the short term, the 1848 revolutions, or rather their defeat, led to strengthened authoritarianism. Government authorities and police censored potentially revolutionary publications, arrested political opponents, and, in general, created a climate of repression. The power of the military also expanded in most of the countries that had experienced revolution. The French revolutionary Pierre-Joseph Proudhon lamented, "We have been beaten and humiliated. We have been scattered, imprisoned, disarmed, and gagged. The fate of European democracy has slipped from our hands—from the hands of the people—into those of the Praetorian Guard."

Because of the defeat of the revolutions, many of the problems that had caused the upheaval in the first place were not immediately addressed. The urban poor still endured the misery of filthy living conditions, and workers did not gain greater access to education or shorter hours. Artisans still faced the prospect of losing their livelihood because of industrialization. The middle classes did not establish a lasting government enshrining liberal values, though in many cases they did gain expanded voting rights. On the surface, it appeared that many average Europeans became politically apathetic, having lost hope for meaningful change.

Many observers have considered the Revolutions of 1848 an episode that might have advanced ideas such as liberalism and democracy. History seemed to be progressing in that direction. The political philosophy of liberalism had spread with the success of the French Revolution and the conquests of Napoleon. The revolutions in the first half of the nineteenth century suggested that it was only a matter of time until governments based on liberal values replaced the conservative monarchies. At first, it seemed that the revolutions in 1848 might accomplish just that. This made their ultimate failure all the more disappointing. The conservative reaction that ensued made the defeat of the revolutions appear even more complete. The famous British historian G. M. Trevelyan even asserted, "1848 was the turning point at which modern history failed to turn." The revolutions should have been the point at which the old regime was finally and completely overthrown, but this was far from the case. Some historians have argued that the revolutions were not really revolutions at all, for they did not succeed in advancing a new political system or structure. Considering this interpretation, one might be prompted to ask, does a discussion of the 1848 revolutions even belong in a volume on "events that changed the world in the nineteenth century"?

To answer this question it is necessary to look beyond the immediate political aftermath of the revolutions. Even though conservatives managed to regain and even to consolidate power, they had to operate under a new set of realities. Revolution had proved capable of spreading quickly, and although the revolutionaries were defeated in 1848, the ideas brought to the forefront during the unrest could not easily be swept away. Concepts like nationalism and universal suffrage were now an undeniable part of political life. The conservatives could not simply turn back to pre-1848 policies; they had to develop new and more effective ways to meet the challenge of revolutionary ideas. Ironically, the same authoritarian leaders who crushed the revolutions eventually came to institute many of the ideas first brought to the forefront during the upheaval of 1848. Though defeated in the short run, the revolutions unleashed ideas that became a natural part of political and social life in the ensuing decades. In this way the revolutions helped transform Europe.

Although conservatives returned to power after the 1848 revolutions, people no longer simply accepted monarchy as the natural order of politics and society. The traditional system of the old regime had lost its authority. Very few leaders could hope to survive as champions only of absolutism and reactionary politics. As the post-1848 leaders came to terms with this fact, they began to see that they would have to pursue new policies to reinforce their power. They had to learn the politics of the people. Even conservative leaders began to talk about influencing public opinion, and they adopted strategies to integrate discontented social groups into the existing political systems. Because they were still fearful of revolution, conservatives recognized the need to provide some outlet for political and social dissent. Thus, in many cases, the post-1848 regimes granted limited political rights and created some form of democratic institutions. However, conservatives generally maintained control of the political process through skillful manipulation of the voters and the political institutions. Ultimately, the authoritarian governments that emerged in the aftermath of 1848 proved quite different than their predecessors.

Examples of the new authoritarian tactics can be found in several of the major states that experienced revolution in 1848. In France, Napoleon III became a masterful manipulator of popular politics. He was sensitive to public opinion and tried to foster popular support for his policies. He reintroduced universal male suffrage and repeatedly tested his right to rule by calling elections. Parliament also remained intact, though it had little say in important government matters. The French emperor helped build economic prosperity by promoting public works projects and creating new investment banks. Napoleon III was one of the first modern leaders to rule not simply by force or claim to divine right, but by propaganda and populist appeal that could be managed well by a capable authoritarian.

Prussia also made steps toward a modern political structure, even though conservatives retained control over the governing process. The parliament, though weak, proved to be an important feature of politics since it provided an outlet for dissenting viewpoints. The Prussian government also made decisions to appeal to large segments of the population. The peasantry benefited from the abolition of serfdom and the limited redistribution of land. At the same time, these reforms did not greatly threaten the interests of the landowning class. The middle classes also made important gains as the Prussian government started to promote industrial development and economic growth, and reformed the bureaucracy and judicial system. These policies helped Prussia out of the stagnation that had contributed to the revolution in 1848. Certainly not all problems were solved, but there was enough progress so that most segments of society no longer favored revolution as a solution.

In the Habsburg lands, the Revolutions of 1848 demonstrated that nationalism had the potential to rip the multinational empire apart. If the Habsburg monarchy was to survive, its leaders had to do more than simply revert to traditional policies. Consequently, the Habsburg government began to modernize and reform the empire's antiquated administrative structure. Emperor Francis Joseph issued laws intended to make government more efficient and effective. They reformed the civil service, standardized the tax system and commercial laws, and encouraged economic development. Francis Joseph also maintained one important change made during the revolutions, the abolition of serfdom. This met the most basic demand of the peasantry. Even under the most authoritarian systems, leaders had to come to terms with a political environment altered by the revolutions.

The events of 1848 enabled many Europeans who had previously had little political experience to participate in the political problems of the day. Those who usually had little say in politics and society, such as women, workers, and artisans, provided the muscle for revolutionary demonstrations. People came to believe that politics had relevance for their daily lives and that they could gain better living conditions. "All change!" was a common slogan of the revolutions. Ideas that had once been discussed only by liberal-minded intellectuals became open to many more people. The concepts of nationalism, democracy, and equality supplied powerful motivation for large segments of the population. Although the defeat of the revolutions caused some people to withdraw from political involvement, the experience gained during 1848 generated a loyalty to certain political ideas. Such ideological commitments survived to resurface in better times.

The revolutions also revealed the social division and new class structure that was emerging in Europe. One of the primary reasons the revolutions failed was the lack of unity among the revolutionary elements of society. In most cases the revolutions actually began as mass protest movements of the urban poor. Workers and artisans fought most of the street battles and manned the barricades. At first the real revolutions had no leaders. Rather, the lower classes actually pushed politically aware intellectuals who also favored change to participate in the revolution. Although intellectuals, workers, peasants, and others found a common cause in making revolution, this did not provide a basis for lasting political cooperation. When the time came to form new governments and make reforms, the different groups promoting revolution split apart. Advocates of liberalism, many of whom came from the bourgeoisie, hoped to consolidate their own positions by assuring property rights and limited political democracy. The lower classes, especially poorer urban workers, wanted real equal rights, social justice, and secure employment. For these people liberalism did not go far enough; they wanted social revolution. The attitude of the lower classes and the prospect of more violent agitation worried liberals. While they wanted some reforms, they could not go along with social and political change that would threaten stability and social order.

In the end, liberals proved more willing to acquiesce in a return to conservative control than to accept social revolution. They were unwilling to battle openly against the established order. Hence, liberals withdrew from the revolutions and made it possible for dedicated conservatives to reassert authority. The revolutions failed not because the conservatives defeated progressive forces, but because those classes of society with some power and wealth, including most liberals, favored order over true social revolution.

As a result of this split, the revolutions served to promote a new kind of class antagonism. The lower classes found that they could not count on liberal intellectuals and the bourgeoisie for support. The lack of revolutionary solidarity demonstrated that simply overthrowing the old order was not enough to achieve real change. The resulting disillusion convinced many workers that socialism and class solidarity were the only answer. This created a basis for the radical socialism advocated by Karl Marx and Friedrich Engels, two German political theorists. The men first outlined their socialist ideas in the *Communist Manifesto* (1848), which asserted that class conflict was inevitable and that workers, if they wanted real power, would have to overthrow the bourgeoisie in a violent revolution. The conflicting goals and aspirations of different classes revealed in 1848 remained an important feature of politics in the second half of the nineteenth century. Nineteenth-century liberals and socialists continued to disagree greatly in their views on the role of government and the classes of society.

The power of nationalism also proved to be one of the most important legacies of the 1848 revolutions. Prior to 1848, nationalism was largely the purview of intellectuals, who were primarily interested in cultural aspects of nationalism such as literature, history, and language. However, the 1848 revolutions demonstrated that nationalism could have broad political appeal and provide a rationale for changing government. Many liberal revolutionaries argued that sovereignty should rest with the people of the nation, not with a monarchy. In the German- and Italian-speaking lands, these revolutionaries advocated national unification as a way to make political change. Both Germans and Italians had long been separated into different states and principalities, and many revolutionaries hoped that a constitutional government could be created for a unified state.

Although neither Italy nor Germany was unified in 1848, nationalism and national unification did become more acceptable notions. Just as with some other political ideas, the authoritarian leaders realized that nationalism was a force they could manipulate for their own purposes. It provided ready justification for strengthening central control and military power. It could also help to reconcile class conflicts within the state.

Italian unification was ultimately achieved in 1860, under the leadership of Count Camillo di Cavour, the prime minister of the northern Italian Kingdom of Piedmont. Cavour was sympathetic to liberalism and the ideas of 1848, but realized that diplomacy and warfare rather than persuasion and democracy were necessary to unify Italy. The goal of German unification, first put forward in 1848 by the Frankfurt Assembly, was finally realized in 1871. However, the real power in the newly unified German Empire rested with the Prussian government and army rather than with a democratically elected parliament. Prussia had defeated both Austria and France on the battlefield to make unification possible. Otto von Bismarck, the Prussian chancellor who engineered this feat, noted that "it is not by speeches and majority decisions that great questions of the day are decided—that was the mistake of 1848—but by blood and iron." Both Italy and Germany opted for strong central control. Although the unifications of Italy and Germany were not managed in the way that the 1848 revolutionaries advocated, these achievements were clearly influenced by the revolutions. The goal of national unification set forward in 1848 had revealed the power of nationalism and had set the agenda for leaders like Cavour and Bismarck.

In the multinational Habsburg Empire, nationalism played a divisive rather than a unifying role. During the 1848 revolutions, self-determination first became a concrete goal for many of the nationalities in the Habsburg lands. The revolutions also awakened national feeling among the empire's Slavic population, including Czechs, Slovaks, Croats, Slovenes, and Serbs. Slavic intellectuals held a congress in Prague in 1848. The participants in the Slav Congress advocated ethnic and linguistic unity as a way to defend against German nationalism, and some even called for an independent Slavic state in Europe. Nationalism was also the primary cause for the Hungarian revolution, which was successful in large part because the disparate classes in Hungary joined forces against the imperial authorities. Unfortunately, nationalism frequently was transformed into chauvinism when people became prejudiced against other nationalities. Hungarians, for example, wanted national independence for themselves, but they were not willing to grant the same rights to national minorities living in Hungarian-controlled lands.

Although the Habsburg government managed to quash national aspirations for a time, it could not do so indefinitely. The government passed reforms to improve the bureaucracy, but this did little to solve the empire's nationality conflicts. To the contrary, some of the new pol-

icies actually made the nationality problem worse. For example, the reformed civil service was overwhelmingly German, and this antagonized
much of the empire's non-German population. The Hungarians, who had
the most success fighting for independence in 1848–1849, finally gained
autonomy through an agreement called the Compromise of 1867, which
gave the Hungarians control over their domestic affairs, but preserved
a unified imperial army and ministry of foreign affairs. This satisfied the
Hungarians for a time, but the other nationalities in the Hungarian lands,
such as Slovaks and Croats, chafed under Hungarian control and continued to aspire to autonomy for their own nations.

The realization of nationalist goals in the decades after 1848 prompted
a significant shift in the European balance of power. As a unified nation,
Germany became stronger and exerted much more influence in European
politics. Unified Italy also entered the ranks of the Great Powers. Napoleon III, the new emperor of France, deliberately cultivated French
nationalism as he sought to restore France to the position of grandeur
and power that it had lost in 1815. Meanwhile, the Habsburg Empire
became weaker as nationalism continued to threaten its stability and
integrity. The 1848 revolutions, by legitimating and encouraging national
aspirations, helped to change the international power structure of Europe.

The economic consequences of the revolutions are more difficult to
determine. There was unprecedented economic growth in Europe in the
two decades after 1848, but it would be inaccurate to portray this wholly
as a result of the revolutions. It can be said, however, that the revolutions
did promote some changes that certainly facilitated economic growth.
The breakdown of old customs and the spread of new ideas encouraged
people to move from their traditional activities and environment. The
abolition of feudal restrictions made it possible for peasants to migrate
to cities and to work in factories. The fear of revolution also led many
post-1848 regimes to modernize their administration. Governments promoted economic growth by establishing uniform laws and lowering
trade barriers. In general, the middle class made the most significant
economic gains after 1848. It benefited greatly from economic expansion,
and greater wealth ultimately led to more influence in politics.

Despite its failure to establish new political structures, the mid-century
upheaval represents a pivotal point in the history of nineteenth-century
Europe. For nearly sixty years, since the French Revolution in 1789, Europe had experienced recurrent revolts and revolutions. However, this
"age of revolutions" came to an end with the Revolutions of 1848. After

them, there were no significant revolutions in Europe except under the stress of war. Yet many of the goals of the revolutionaries were met in more gradual ways. People no longer accepted traditional notions of politics such as aristocratic privilege and divinely appointed dynasties. Authoritarian governments learned to offset potential unrest by granting limited concessions to certain groups in society. Hence, the very leaders who defeated the revolutions later helped to advance many revolutionary ideas.

The year 1848 also marks the opening of an era. The issues and goals raised by the revolutions, although not met at the time, later spread and became a common part of the political and social order. Socialism, political democracy, liberalism, and nationalism all promoted the development of a modern political consciousness. Change could be achieved more gradually because the state became more organized, prosperity expanded, and the middle classes renounced revolution. Peasants also were less likely to support revolution since governments granted their primary demand, an end to serfdom. The lower classes developed a political sense which in time gave them a stronger voice to demand reforms. Workers began to form unions, and universal suffrage became more common and accepted. The year 1848 became known as the "springtime of peoples," and many nationalities looked to 1848 as the moment of national awakening. The changes did not occur immediately, but the revolutions did pave the way for the transition from a feudal society to an industrial society with a modern state structure. In this sense, the 1848 revolutions did change the world, though not as quickly as the revolutionaries would have liked.

SELECTED BIBLIOGRAPHY

Agulhon, Maurice. *The Republican Experiment, 1848–1852.* Cambridge: Cambridge University Press, 1983. Offers a synthesis of the historiography on the revolution in France.

Deak, Istvan. *The Lawful Revolution: Louis Kossuth and the Hungarians, 1848–1849.* New York: Columbia University Press, 1977. A biography of Louis Kossuth, leader of the Hungarian revolution of 1848, which also analyzes the political scene in the Hungarian lands.

Fejtö, François, ed. *The Opening of an Era, 1848: An Historical Symposium.* New York: Howard Fertig, 1966. Contains a wide variety of essays on the 1848 revolutions including separate entries on many of the nations involved.

Hobsbawm, Eric J. *The Age of Capital, 1848–1875.* New York: Charles Scribner's Sons, 1975. Emphasizes social and economic developments in Europe during the post-1848 period.

Jones, Peter. *The 1848 Revolutions*. 2nd ed. New York: Longman, 1991. A short, up-to-date introduction to the 1848 revolutions; contains some primary source material.

Langer, William L. *Political and Social Upheaval, 1832–1852*. New York: Harper and Row, 1969. Emphasizes social change in the period leading up to and during the revolutions.

Lovett, Clara. *The Democratic Movement in Italy, 1830–1876*. Cambridge, MA: Harvard University Press, 1982. An examination of the democratic movement in Italy with good chapters on the 1848 revolutions and the unification of Italy.

Namier, Lewis. *1848: The Revolution of the Intellectuals*. Garden City, NY: Doubleday, 1946. Offers a very critical view of the accomplishments of the revolutions.

Pech, Stanley. *The Czech Revolution of 1848*. Chapel Hill: University of North Carolina Press, 1969. Examines the revolutionary events in the Czech lands of the Habsburg monarchy.

Price, Roger. *The Revolutions of 1848*. Atlantic Highlands, NJ: Humanities Press International, 1988. A brief interpretive account that places the revolutions in the context of the larger revolutionary period.

———, ed. *Revolutions and Reaction: 1848 and the Second French Republic*. New York: Barnes and Noble, 1975. This collection of essays covers the topic from various perspectives.

Rath, R. J. *The Vienna Revolution of 1848*. New York: Greenwood Press, 1969. Older but still valuable study of the revolution in the Habsburg capital.

Roberston, Priscilla. *Revolutions of 1848: A Social History*. Princeton, NJ: Princeton University Press, 1952. An interesting and readable survey of the events and personalities of the revolutions.

Sked, Alan. *The Decline and Fall of the Habsburg Empire, 1815–1918*. New York: Longman, 1989. A synthesis of the historiography on the decline of the Habsburg Empire containing several good chapters on the 1848 revolutions.

———. *The Survival of the Habsburg Empire*. New York: Longman, 1979. Although its title is misleading, this work is a valuable study of the Habsburg effort to regain control of the Italian provinces of Lombardy and Venetia.

Sperber, Jonathan. *The European Revolutions, 1848–1851*. Cambridge: Cambridge University Press, 1994. An introductory survey incorporating the latest scholarship on the period.

———. *Rhineland Radicals: The Democratic Movement and the Revolution of 1848–1849*. Princeton, NJ: Princeton University Press, 1991. Examines the revolutions in Germany and includes analysis of the broader impact of the revolutions.

Stadelmann, Rudolf. *Social and Political History of the German 1848 Revolution*. Translated by James G. Chastain. Athens: Ohio University Press, 1975. Stadelmann gives a comprehensive view of the revolution in the German-speaking lands.

Stearns, Peter N. *1848: The Revolutionary Tide in Europe*. New York: W. W. Norton, 1974. Emphasizes how the revolutions opened the way for the modernization of Europe.

6

The Emancipation of the Russian Serfs, 1861

INTRODUCTION

By the middle of the nineteenth century, the Russian Empire found itself in dire straits. For more than five decades, Russia's leaders had neglected its domestic problems, and stagnation now characterized the state. Any attempt to revitalize Russia would have to begin with serfdom, a form of human bondage that had distinguished Russia for centuries. The Russian nobility owned not only the land, but also the peasants, or serfs, who worked the land. The royal family, the Russian Orthodox Church, and the state itself also owned millions of serfs. Although there were laws on the books to mitigate the evils of serfdom, in practice Russian serfs differed little from American slaves save for the color of their skin. Estimates indicate that of a population totaling approximately 74 million in 1858, there were 23 million privately owned serfs, 25 million state peasants, or serfs owned by the state or its appendages such as the church, and perhaps 2 million appanage serfs, or serfs owned by the tsar.

An immense mass of ignorant, illiterate, isolated, superstitious humanity, the Russian serfs lived in grinding poverty. They had no civil liberties or human rights and found themselves at the mercy of their

Recently freed Russian serfs pose for the camera. The emancipation of the Russian serfs freed tens of millions of peasants from bondage. (Reproduced from the Collections of the Library of Congress)

owners. Often sullen and noncooperative, the serfs resented their status but lacked the means to change it.

Most serf holders preferred to perpetuate the status quo; however, by mid-century a growing number of Russians had concluded that serfdom needed to be reformed drastically if not eliminated entirely. Several factors led to this conclusion. For some, Russia's gradual transformation from a feudal economy to a capitalist one demanded the end of serfdom. Free labor, one of the foundations of a capitalist economy, was more efficient and more cost effective than serf labor. Other Russians, especially those who had visited western Europe, supported emancipation for humanitarian reasons. For them, enserfment was not only barbaric and uncivilized, but also undermined Russia's claim to be part of the European mainstream.

Additionally, there were important reasons of state that required serfdom's elimination. Serf disturbances or rebellions were a seemingly permanent but nonetheless threatening feature of the Russian landscape. Although the vast majority of these disturbances were minor and easily put down, and none even vaguely approached the size and ferocity of the eighteenth century's massive Pugachev Revolt, fear of a large serf uprising persisted.

Russia's miserable showing in the Crimean War also stimulated the reform movement. The army's recruits, drawn from the serfs, performed poorly, and the entire wartime experience painfully demonstrated Russia's backward, inefficient, and ultimately dangerous condition.

The task of reforming Russia fell to an unlikely hero, Tsar Alexander II, who ascended the throne in 1855 at the age of thirty-seven. Alexander was a shy, unassuming man who inclined toward conservatism rather than reform. However, he was acutely aware that change must come lest the empire be swept away, and he was stubborn on this score. In the March 1856 imperial manifesto announcing the end of the Crimean War, Alexander intimated that change was on the horizon. A few weeks later, in an address to the nobility of the Moscow region, he observed, "It is better to begin to abolish bondage from above than to wait for the time when it will begin to abolish itself spontaneously from below." With this speech, the question of emancipation became a public one and moved to the head of the government's agenda.

In late 1856 Alexander appointed a secret committee of high officials —most of whom were also large landowners—to examine the serf question. Not surprisingly, this committee, later renamed the Main Committee of Peasant Affairs, concluded that serfdom was indeed an evil; but the committee decided that any attempt to eliminate it should proceed at a glacial pace. Alexander was undaunted, and in 1857 he began to create committees of the nobility in the various Russian provinces and ordered them to prepare proposals for emancipation. Dominated by noblemen who opposed the end of serfdom, the provincial committees reluctantly followed the tsar's instructions. However, they determined to emancipate the serfs according to provisions designed to gain the greatest advantage, or compensation, for themselves.

By the end of 1858, the provincial committees had finished their work and submitted their recommendations to the Main Committee. The actual task of preparing draft legislation was turned over to an Editing Commission first headed by General J. I. Rostovtsev and, after his death, dominated by Nicholas Miliutin, the energetic deputy minister of the interior and a supporter of emancipation. The Editing Commission completed its work in December 1860, and after some minor revisions the laws emancipating the private serfs were signed on March 3, 1861. Similar laws applying to appanage serfs and to state peasants were announced in 1863 and 1866, respectively.

The emancipation statute proved to be a mixed bag. At last serfs were regarded as something other than chattels. No longer could they be bought or sold. They no longer worked at their master's whim and could no longer be sent off to Siberia for insubordination or dispatched to the army to meet a conscription quota. Serfs could now own property and marry without securing their master's permission. Nevertheless, the former serfs still had to pay a head tax, and they were subject to customary instead of statutory law.

Reflecting Alexander's belief that his throne rested upon the nobility, the emancipation was designed with the interests of the nobility in mind. Nowhere was this more evident than in the provisions pertaining to land distribution. While it is true that the serfs acquired about 50 percent of the arable land, the nobility did quite well. A series of convoluted regulations requiring the peasants to pay for the land they received compensated the gentry for the loss of their serf labor. The regulations varied from province to province and region to region in order to fit the gentry's particular needs. According to the government's scheme, the nobility immediately received interest-bearing notes from the government equal to approximately 75 percent of the value of the land given to the peasants. The peasants were obligated to pay the remaining 25 percent directly to the nobility. Furthermore, the peasants were also obligated to give the government annual payments extending over forty-nine years for the land they received.

In dividing up the land, the interests of the nobility predominated. Usually they received the more fertile 50 percent of the land. They also tended to maintain their pasture, water, and forest rights at the expense of the newly emancipated serfs.

The state also worried that emancipation might create a landless proletariat, and it feared the end of the gentry's traditional administrative and judicial powers over the serfs. To deal with these problems, the state reinforced the village or commune. Title to the land given to the serfs was vested not in the individual, but in the commune; and the land division took place between the noble landlord and representatives of the commune. The commune elders assigned landholdings to the former serfs and decided for everyone in the commune such basic questions as what to sow and when to plant and harvest. The government made the commune responsible for the annual payments due the government, and in turn the commune assessed its individual members. The commune also exercised administrative and judicial powers previously held by the nobility. For example, the commune applied traditional peasant law, issued internal passports, and supplied recruits for the army.

The emancipation of the serfs necessitated several other major reforms that, taken collectively with the emancipation, became known as the Great Reforms. With the end of gentry authority in the countryside, the government not only strengthened the commune, but also created a new administrative body called the *zemstvo*. The 1864 Statute on Zemstvos provided for district and provincial representative assemblies elected according to a suffrage weighted in favor of the well-to-do. The *zemstvos* handled many local duties including roads, education, health care, poor relief, and agricultural services. However, the *zemstvos* were handicapped because they had only a very limited right of taxation and were all too often subject to the authority of bureaucrats sent out from St. Petersburg.

In 1870, the emperor promulgated a Municipal Reform that helped to rationalize city government. Seen as a companion piece to the Statute on Zemstvos, the Municipal Reform extended much greater self-government to Russia's cities. The statute gave the right to vote to all urban males who paid taxes; but, as was the case with the *zemstvos*, the suffrage was weighted in favor of the wealthy. Among other things, municipal governments gained authority over education, public safety, and social welfare programs; however, like their rural counterparts they had only a very limited right to levy taxes, and they frequently found themselves subject to the commands of imperially appointed bureaucrats.

Prior to emancipation, Russia's judicial system was the worst in the Western world. It was characterized by exceptional incompetency, corruption, and stupidity. All that changed in 1864 when an extensive judicial reform placed Russian jurisprudence on a firm footing. Most important, the judicial reform liberated Russian courts from administrative control; they now operated independently. The reform introduced public trials and the jury system to Russia. It also extended to the accused the right to counsel, and it provided for an independent judiciary appointed for life. For minor cases, a system of justices of the peace was established. Nevertheless, problems with the Russian legal system persisted. The principle of equality under the law remained elusive as the former serfs continued to be treated as a class apart. Furthermore, some of the pre-reform courts—with all their shortcomings—continued. This was especially true of ecclesiastical courts and military courts.

The last Great Reform dealt with the Russian military. Between 1861 and 1881, the Russian military underwent a thorough reorganization under the leadership of Dmitri Miliutin, the minister of war and brother of Nicholas Miliutin, who had played such an important role in pushing forward serf emancipation. Prior to its reorganization, the Russian army drew its foot soldiers exclusively from the serf population, drafting young men for a twenty-five-year term of service. The inductees were treated with incredible cruelty and subjected to brutal discipline and barbaric punishments. Their lot was an altogether unenviable one.

Miliutin, with the steadfast support of the tsar, attacked these shortcomings. The cornerstone of the military reform was the 1874 law that made military service universal. Henceforth, upon reaching the age of twenty, every able-bodied Russian male was subject to military service. Other changes included lowering the term of service to six years with further reductions contingent upon the recruit's level of education, the elimination of corporal punishment, the establishment of a military reserve organization, the creation of specialized military schools, and the introduction of elementary education for all recruits.

The entire reform process, which proceeded in fits and starts during Alexander's reign, ended with the tsar's assassination in 1881.

INTERPRETIVE ESSAY
Bruce F. Adams

Slavery in the United States and serfdom in Russia were abolished contemporaneously in the 1860s. In both countries emancipation was divisive, dangerous, and momentous. Both countries were much changed as a consequence.

In the United States, the abolition movement had complicated and embittered politics for decades before the 1860s. The failure to resolve the problem of slavery by political means led the country into a civil war, which became the bloodiest war in America's history. On the eve of the war, American slaves numbered approximately 4 million, or just over 12 percent of the total population. The 3.2 million slaves living in what became the Confederate States of America comprised somewhat more than 35 percent of its population. When President Abraham Lincoln eventually freed the slaves, it was in the midst of the Civil War, and he temporarily exempted the 830,000 slaves living outside the Confederacy. Although the newly freed Americans often continued to live and work where they had been enslaved, they received no land to help support them in freedom.

In Russia unfree peasants—serfs who belonged to gentry landlords, state peasants who lived on land belonging to the government, and appanage peasants owned by the imperial family—numbered, between 45 and 50 million, accounting for more than three-quarters of European Russia's population. (There were practically no serfs in Siberia.) When abolition began to be discussed seriously, Russian serf owners, like American slave owners, were frightened and angered by the prospect of losing their human property and much of their real estate. Many would in fact be economically ruined as a consequence. Russian statesmen too were frightened by the immensity of the change they contemplated. Ten times before the 1850s, officially appointed committees had discussed the problems of serfdom and had generally agreed that reform was needed. Along the way they enacted some small and mostly ineffectual reforms, but each time they had failed to carry through. At several stages of the final process in the 1850s they almost turned back. In the end, however, in separate major acts from 1858 to 1866 (and many subsequent smaller laws), Russia managed to free all its serfs, providing most of them with land and avoiding significant bloodshed.

The reasons for freeing the peasants were many and powerful. All of them had been advanced more than half a century before the emancipation. But it took a full fifty years to overcome the inertia, fear, and greed that sustained serfdom and to convince leaders of the Russian government that, as daunting as it was, emancipation was necessary.

The humanitarian argument was the easiest to make, and it was easier to make in Russia than in the United States; Russia's peasants were Caucasian and Orthodox Christian, just like their masters. Although many gentry viewed the serfs as shiftless and expressed fears that they could not support themselves in freedom, they did not consider them less than human. It was not enough to condemn serfdom as unjust and dehumanizing to bring it to an end, however. Economic and statist reasons had to become more compelling before the institution could be destroyed. The humanitarian argument helped undermine serfdom and then supported the more "modern" arguments.

Economic arguments grew more powerful in the nineteenth century. Serfdom had died a more or less natural death in western Europe long before Russia seriously contemplated emancipation. As the Commercial Revolution created a money economy, landlords came to recognize that they could make more money from free laborers and/or vacant land than they could from serfs, and they sold or granted serfs their freedom. It was a gradual process in most places, spread out over several centuries. Where it was quickly done, it was often cruelly done. The enclosure movement in England, for example, forced peasants off the land on which they had traditionally lived and worked, leaving them in dire poverty and driving many into crime. But by the nineteenth century, Europe's capitalist economy was much more productive and prosperous than Russia's, which was still based on serfdom.

As Russia's gentry became better educated and more widely traveled, more of them came to accept the superiority of the European model. Well before 1860, many of them were familiar with and convinced by the arguments of what we today call classical liberalism. It was in applying that general lesson to their particular property, human and real, that they balked. And for good reason. The money economy that had driven enlightened landlords to free their serfs in Europe was still very underdeveloped in Russia. As a matter of fact, when the emancipation occurred, it was in this regard artificial. Emancipation was carried out more to create a capitalist economy than because capitalism had made serfdom obsolete.

However, changes had occurred in the nature of Russian serfdom over the several centuries of its existence. Especially in the nineteenth century, as a money economy slowly developed in Russia, landlords in the northern and central regions had transformed their serfs' obligations from labor or payment in kind to a money rent. In these regions the soil was poor and the growing season short, making agriculture less profitable than in the steppe, with its rich soil. But crafts production, industry, and trade were more developed, and the peasants dealt more in cash. In the agriculturally rich black soil areas, landlords continued to demand feudal obligations in labor or in kind. In neither area, however, did landlords feel an urgency to free their serfs in order to increase the income from their land.

The largest serf owners, few in number, were immensely wealthy and had no need to change their relations with the serfs. Their social standing and their income were more than adequate. The great majority of serf owners, however, possessed very few serfs and often very little good agricultural land. Many of them led lives little different from the serfs', and few dreamed of transforming their holdings into capitalist farms. Most did not have the knowledge or the capital to do so. Like American slave owners, they preferred the devil they knew. Owners had been legally able to free their serfs with land since 1803, but fewer than 1 percent had chosen to do so.

That is where the statist component of the economic argument comes in. It was not the landlords but the bureaucrats who perceived the necessity of emancipation and enacted it. Many of these men came from the same gentry background as the serf owners, but most had had weak ties to the land for several generations. The majority of them owned few or no serfs and little land. They had followed their fathers into government service because they could not be supported by serfdom and agriculture, making their careers in service to the state. Sons of clergymen and other men, whose origins were not always clear, made similar careers. By the 1850s, although the ministers of the tsar's government were still for the most part wealthy serf owners, these career civil servants occupied most of the middle and some of the upper ranks of the bureaucracy.

From their perspective, the interests of the state were paramount. And increasingly toward the middle of the century, they saw serfdom as a brake on both Russia's agricultural and industrial development. Measured by crop yield per land area, Russian agriculture was only about one-seventh as productive as western European and American agriculture of the same period. And largely because the peasants were tied to the land, they had not drifted off to cities to become an urban working class, and the Russian industrial revolution had barely begun. As a consequence, the Russian government was poor and the state was becoming weaker relative to its more industrialized neighbors. This was seen most clearly in the effort to man, pay for, and utilize Russia's very large military.

Before the beginning of the nineteenth century, Russia had expanded rapidly to become the largest nation on Earth. Its borders were lengthy, and its neighbors—China, the Ottoman Empire, Austria, and Prussia, among others—had all been enemies at one time or another. The Russian army was thus necessarily large. Russia's technological backwardness compounded this problem. To compensate for inferior organization and equipment, Russia always put more men in the field. Since the Napoleonic Wars, Russia's army had been the largest in the world, and that of course was very expensive.

The event that brought all these problems into focus was the Crimean War (1853–1856). From the time Russia drove Napoleon back to Paris in 1813 and helped forge the peace at Vienna in 1815, everyone assumed that Russia was the greatest land power of Europe. To mid-century, little had seemingly happened to change that impression. It was in those years that the British humor magazine *Punch* had invented the image of Russia as a great, shaggy bear, menacing all Europe. But when Russia fought England and France on Russian soil from 1854 to 1856 and lost, the reason for its defeat was painfully clear. The industrialized West had forged so far ahead of "feudal" Russia that Russia's great size and manpower resources could no longer compensate. The need for military reform and for industrialization now made it urgent that serfdom be swept away.

The "enlightened" bureaucrats knew what had to be done, but in Russia's strictly autocratic government they could do nothing without the emperor's support. Nicholas I, emperor from 1825 until 1855, understood that there was a serious problem. He appointed committees to investigate serfdom, but none came close to recommending emancipation. This may have been because Nicholas himself was extremely conservative. He was overly fond of bayonets, close-order drill, and everything old-fashioned about the army and the country in general. More likely it was because in Nicholas's time Russia continued to expand into Central Asia, where its foes were even less advanced, and until the Crimean War, Russia experienced no military reverses in Europe. The gravity of Russia's problems was not yet evident. We will never know what Nicholas might have done in the wake of the Crimean defeat; he died shortly before the war ended. His son, the new emperor Alexander II, immediately made it clear that he was more than willing to contemplate change; he would insist on it. In his first year he loosened the very strict laws regulating censorship, higher education, and foreign travel. And at the end of that year, traditionally and officially a year of mourning for his father, Alexander began the process of emancipation.

In a speech to the gentry, gathered for his coronation, Alexander told them that it was time to consider how to free their serfs. In the most quoted sentence of that speech, he told them that it was time to free the serfs from above before they began to free themselves from below. Soviet historians repeatedly cited this specter of serf revolt as the emancipation's primary cause. There is very little evidence, however, either in the words of the serf owners or the bureaucrats, or in the numbers of mostly petty rebellions, to support this contention; the last major peasant rebellion had occurred almost a hundred years earlier. Alexander may have hoped to frighten the gentry, to soften them up for the assault that the government was soon to mount on their property.

Writing the emancipation laws proved to be very complex. It required the concentrated work of many talented men over several years and involved reports and testimony from serf owners all over Russia. The work began in earnest when Alexander II appointed a secret committee, later renamed the Main Committee of Peasant Affairs. By December 1858, it had decided on the basic principles of the emancipation: the peasants would be freed, but they would have to remain in the collective structure of their villages or communes. The communes would become the lowest level of government authority in the countryside, carrying out for the central government many of the functions of the former landlords. The peasants would receive an allotment of land so that they could continue to live and work in their villages, support themselves, and pay taxes and other obligations, but this land would be owned by the village collectively, not by individual peasants, and the peasants would have to compensate the gentry (or the state or the imperial family) for that land. At the same time, the government required the gentry to form committees in every province which were to discuss the emancipation of their serfs and send their recommendations to Moscow. The last of these reports also arrived in December 1858. Not surprisingly, they strongly advocated the interests of the gentry.

In March 1859 Alexander appointed an Editing Commission to draft the emancipation statue. It fell to this commission to study the gentry's reports and to hear testimony from the provincial committees, and somehow to reconcile these sentiments with the Main Committee's general principles. Of course that was not possible. The Editing Commission produced its draft of the emancipation law largely by ignoring the gentry's more conservative demands. The commission's chairman also integrated many separate points from the commission's minority reports to produce the final report.

For another year and a half the Main Committee, and then the State Council, reworked the document. Despite the death of the committee's chairman and signs that the government's will might waver, they made only minor revisions to the law before Alexander signed it on March 3, 1861.

Historians have interpreted the process variously. Some have seen it as a cynical attempt by the bureaucrats to pretend to listen to the serf owners while doing precisely what the government wanted to do. However, the use of so many minority reports makes it difficult to say who, beyond Alexander II, comprised that government. On the other hand, because the emancipation can be seen as unfair to the peasants and because it did not solve all the problems created by serfdom, other historians have seen it as a cynical collusion between the gentry-dominated government and the serf owners. The committee's disregard for the provincial reports and the gentry's reaction at the time make this interpretation hard to support. A third group emphasizes the complexity of the problem, acknowledges that other more complete solutions might not have been possible at the time, and claims that the outcome was not as bad as has usually been claimed. They find the emancipation an imperfect but impressive compromise in a most difficult situation.

Having labored for four years to end what many saw as an ancient shame, the government might have been expected to trumpet the peasants' new freedom as soon as possible. But the serfs' emancipation was not announced for another month. Meanwhile, a brief manifesto was prepared summarizing the 360-page law, and troops were dispatched to areas where disturbances were anticipated. The government did not expect the peasants to welcome the emancipation. On the first Sunday in Lent, when the government hoped that the peasants would be sober and preparing themselves for Easter confession, priests across the country read the emancipation manifesto in their churches.

As the government expected, the peasants were disappointed, in some cases bitterly and angrily disappointed. News that freedom was coming had, of course, leaked out, but this was neither what they expected nor what they believed they deserved. The terms of the emancipation were extremely complex. It is fair to say, judging from the difficulty historians have had in explaining the terms clearly, that they must have been beyond the comprehension of many peasants. But it is also easy to understand that even had they understood the terms perfectly the peasants would have been unhappy. Under the terms of the new law the peasants were declared to be "free," but this meant little more than that they could not be sold as property any longer and could not be made to pay or perform any new obligations. For the next two years at least, however, they were required to continue to pay their former owners all they had in recent years and also remained under their judicial control. When "land charters," registering the peasants' land holdings and traditional obligations, were drawn up and signed by the landlords and the peasants, the latter would then become judicially free of their lords. But the peasants then still remained "temporarily obligated" to the lords for another indeterminate number of years until it was decided what land the peasants would purchase from the lords at what price. Eventually the peasants would be required to accept land allotments and to begin to pay for that land. For some, it turned out, "temporarily" lasted until 1883.

In most places the peasants unhappily but peacefully accepted their new status. In more than a few villages, however, the peasants rejected the terms of the emancipation, usually showing their recalcitrance at first by refusing to perform their "feudal" obligations and later by refusing to sign the land charters. If the gentry and priests could not persuade these peasants to obey, the government sent in provincial officials to harangue and threaten. When persuasion failed, the government used troops to command obedience. The threat of force generally brought the peasants around, but in a few places there were skirmishes between peasants and troops. Altogether a few hundred peasants were killed. Several thousand more were subjected to corporal punishment and/or exiled to Siberia. By 1863 the countryside was sufficiently calm that the government felt secure enough to abolish most applications of corporal punishment.

To help the gentry and the peasants work out the land charters and to help the peasants organize their institutions of self-administration, the government created a new class of officials called the peace mediators. Although some Soviet historians charge these officials, who were nominated by and for the most part drawn from local gentry, with being agents of the landlords, other Soviet historians and most Western historians agree that they acted effectively and for the most part impartially. By the end of 1863, peasant institutions were in place throughout the country, peasant unrest had largely ended, and almost all the land charters had been approved.

It took much longer for the peasants and lords to agree on what portion of the land the peasants would receive and what they would pay for it. The four local statutes within the emancipation law applied very different criteria to various parts of Russia, taking into consideration, among other things, regional differences in soil type, land usage, traditional serf obligations, and the ethnicity of the landlords. Each local statute specified minimum and maximum norms for land holdings and set norms for payments in either cash or labor. Except in the western Ukraine, where most of the landlords were Polish, the landlords were given the upper hand in determining what land the peasants would have to accept. Within these parameters the parties bargained, often for many years.

In the end the ex-serfs received less land than they had been using under serfdom, losing about 10 percent across the country, but with wide regional variations. In general, the better the soil in a given area, the more land the gentry managed to keep for themselves. Significantly, the peasants lost the use of much of the meadowland on which they had grazed their animals and from which they had collected manure for their fields. They also lost access to many sources of water and to all forest land, which the statutes did not consider productive land. As a consequence, their economic dependence on the landlords actually increased in many areas. Historians generally agree that the peasants also paid more for the land they purchased than it was actually worth. Although the general charter specifically forbade it, it is clear that the peasants' redemption payments were based not only on the value of the land they received but also on the cash payments formerly made to landlords by serfs engaged in handicrafts and other industrial labor.

The gentry did not prosper as a consequence, however. Many were deeply in debt before the emancipation. One of the reasons that there had not been more gentry opposition to emancipation was that the gentry had mortgaged a large percentage of their serfs as collateral on government loans. They hoped that the government, in freeing the serfs, would forgive their debts. Instead, at the beginning of the redemption the government retained all the money owed it by the gentry, somewhat more than a quarter of all the money due them. Most of the rest of the payments to the landlords were made in 5 percent bonds, which quickly depreciated in value as cash-short gentry sold them long before maturity. Without money most gentry, who had little or no experience in this area anyway, were unable to convert to modern, capitalistic farming methods. Living among undeveloped markets, and separated from cities by distance and poor roads, the gentry were as dependent on their ex-serfs for labor as the peasants were dependent on the gentry for land. Most wound up renting to the peasants the land they had previously worked as serfs. Few adapted to modern methods, and gentry landholding fell steadily in the next decades.

Appanage serfs were much easier to deal with. They numbered only about 2 million, and all belonged to a single, collective landlord, the imperial family. There was much greater uniformity among them as they had all been administered by a single government office, and they had long enjoyed better conditions and much greater independence (village self-administration) than the proprietary serfs. The statutes of 1858 and 1859 granted them personal freedom. The land they received in 1863 was slightly larger on average than the proprietary serfs' plots, and when redemption began in 1865, they paid only half as much for it.

State peasants were almost as numerous as the proprietary serfs, but they too had had a single landlord, the state, and had long been administered by a governmental ministry. In the 1830s and 1840s, the Ministry of State Domains had carried out significant reforms that had considerably improved their welfare. Before the emancipation, they held more land and paid much less for it than the serfs. When they were freed in 1866, they kept almost all of this land, thereby receiving significantly more land than either the appanage or proprietary serfs. Although their redemption price was much higher than their former obligations, on average they paid considerably less for their land than the serfs did.

Historians disagree profoundly over the emancipation's long-term consequences both for the peasants and for the nation. One school believes that the peasants' economic condition deteriorated as a result of the emancipation. They see the heavy burden of redemption payments, combined with increasing taxation in the late nineteenth century, as equivalent to a new enserfment, and believe that these conditions sped the coming of revolution in 1905 and 1917. Many other historians believe that the emancipation was a necessary step in Russia's modernization, particularly of its economy; but they see it as only partially successful because it preserved the peasant commune. They believe the commune's collective structure and the traditional agriculture it helped preserve held back the development of modern farming and modern attitudes among the peasants. Reaching the same conclusion, several Russian statesmen in the inter-revolutionary period, 1905–1917, attempted to free the peasants from collective ownership of their land and collective responsibility for their obligations.

Other historians, who seem to be the majority in recent decades, emphasize the emancipation's successes. Although they acknowledge the incompleteness of the peasants' freedom, they see the emancipation as a major step in the creation of a capitalist economy. Some gentry and more enterprising peasants did begin to practice modern farming on a larger scale and with new crops, and many more peasants found it easier to leave the communes to work in the rapidly industrializing cities. In recent years a few Western historians have strengthened this interpretation through population studies. They have found that the Russian peasants in the late nineteenth century comprised one of the fastest growing populations in the world. Since medical services did not significantly improve in the countryside during those years, they attribute the growth to improved nutrition, which in turn can be traced to improved agricultural productivity resulting from changed agrarian conditions. There is no question that agricultural output increased significantly in those decades. Although average productivity remained well below western European and American standards, Russia's growing cities were well fed, and for most of the years from 1880 to 1914 Russia was the world's largest food exporting nation.

The emancipations were but the first major steps in a series of reforms carried out mostly in the 1860s. Other parts of what came to be called the Great Reforms included an extensive revision of Russia's university statutes in 1863, which gave much greater freedom and power to faculty. That same year most remaining corporal punishments were abolished and the severity of the few that remained was reduced. In 1864 the government carried out an extensive overhaul of the judiciary, introducing many features of Western judicial systems. Also in 1864, organs of local administration, the *zemstvos*, were established. Urban administration was reformed in 1870, devolving much power from the St. Petersburg ministries to the cities. And military service was considerably redefined in

1875 in an effort to create a professional officer corps and a large reserve of trained soldiers.

From the perspective of the reformers and many of their contemporaries, the Great Reforms were enormously exciting proof that Russia was becoming a modern western European nation. That Russia did not is another story, as interesting as the reforms. The reforms restructured and redefined Russia, but like all major social and political transformations, they aroused unrealized hopes, fears, and resentments. They would not be carried much further before Russia experienced backlash and several revolutions. The courts and *zemstvos* became seedbeds of a liberal movement which sought to defend and expand the democratization of Russia. The emancipation's perceived failure spawned a populist movement which quickly became radical and then revolutionary. Conservatives, who had been routed in the early 1860s, had regrouped by the time a radical student tried to assassinate Alexander II in 1866. The tsar listened attentively to them for the rest of his reign, and after revolutionaries did kill him in 1881, conservatives dominated the reign of his son, Alexander III (1881–1894), who imposed a series of counter-reforms.

SELECTED BIBLIOGRAPHY

Blum, Jerome. *Lord and Peasant in Russia from the Ninth to the Nineteenth Century.* Princeton, NJ: Princeton University Press, 1961. A long account of the history of lord-peasant relations, including enserfment and the abolition movement before the emancipation. Published in 1961, this has been superseded in many areas by more recent research.

Eklof, Ben, and Stephen P. Frank, eds. *The World of the Russian Peasant: Post-Emancipation Culture and Society.* Boston: Unwin Hyman, 1990. A good collection of articles on various aspects of peasant life, culture, and economy after the emancipation.

Eklof, Ben, and Larissa Zakharova, eds. *Russia's Great Reforms, 1855–1881.* Bloomington: Indiana University Press, 1994. An excellent collection of articles about many aspects of the Great Reforms by scholars from the United States, Russia, England, and Australia.

Emmons, Terrance. *The Russian Landed Gentry and the Peasant Emancipation of 1861.* Cambridge: Cambridge University Press, 1968. The story of the gentry's interaction with the bureaucracy during the development of the emancipation legislation and of the emancipation's impact on the gentry.

———, ed. *The Emancipation of the Russian Serfs.* New York: Holt, Rinehart and

Winston, 1970. Part of the European Problem Studies series, this offers excerpts of major articles and books on the whys and hows of the emancipation.

Emmons, Terrance, and Wayne S. Vucinich, eds. *The Zemstvo in Russia: An Experiment in Local Self-Government*. New York: Cambridge University Press, 1982. A series of outstanding essays examining the newly created organ of local self-government.

Field, Daniel. *The End of Serfdom: Nobility and Bureaucracy in Russia, 1855–1861*. Cambridge, MA: Harvard University Press, 1976. Another look at the ground covered by Emmons.

Kolchin, Peter. *Unfree Labor: American Slavery and Russian Serfdom*. Cambridge, MA: Harvard University Press, 1987. A superb side-by-side description of the culture of American slavery and Russian serfdom.

Lincoln, W. Bruce. *The Great Reforms: Autocracy, Bureaucracy, and the Politics of Change in Imperial Russia*. DeKalb: Northern Illinois University Press, 1990. The best full account in English of the whole Great Reform era.

———. *Nikolai Miliutin, an Enlightened Bureaucrat*. Newtonville, MA: Oriental Research Partners, 1977. A splendid biography of perhaps the most important bureaucrat involved in the emancipation process.

McCauley, Martin, and Peter Waldron. *The Emergence of the Modern Russian State, 1855–81*. Totowa, NJ: Barnes and Noble Books, 1988. A quirky summary, written almost in outline form, of the major acts, movements, and changes of Alexander II's reign.

Pereira, N.G.O. *Tsar Liberator: Alexander II of Russia, 1818–1881*. Newtonville, MA: Oriental Research Partners, 1983. A brief biography of the tsar, offering a limited view of the Great Reforms.

Rieber, Alfred J., ed. *The Politics of Autocracy: Letters of Alexander II to Prince A. I. Bariatinskii, 1857–1864*. Paris: Mouton, 1966. The tsar's correspondence with his friend suggests reasons for the emancipation and indicates Alexander's commitment to it.

Robinson, Geroid Tanquary. *Rural Russia under the Old Regime: A History of the Landlord-Peasant World and a Prologue to the Peasant Revolution of 1917*. Berkeley: University of California Press, 1967. An old but still interesting account of lord-peasant relations before and after the emancipation.

Starr, S. Frederick. *Decentralization and Self-Government in Russia, 1830–1870*. Princeton, NJ: Princeton University Press, 1972. This extensive, if not exhaustive, survey considers the slow development of local government in nineteenth-century Russia.

Vucinich, Wayne S., ed. *The Peasant in Nineteenth-Century Russia*. Stanford, CA: Stanford University Press, 1968. Still useful thematic articles on the peasants and the emancipation, religion, the army, the factory, etc.

Wcislo, Francis William. *Reforming Rural Russia: State, Local Society, and National Politics, 1855–1914*. Princeton, NJ: Princeton University Press, 1990. A long view of the agrarian-political problem in Russia, beginning with a chapter on the emancipation.

Zaionchkovskii, Peter. *The Abolition of Serfdom in Russia.* Edited and translated by Susan Wobst. Gulf Breeze, FL: Academic International Press, 1978. A thorough account of the emancipation process by one of the finest Soviet scholars.

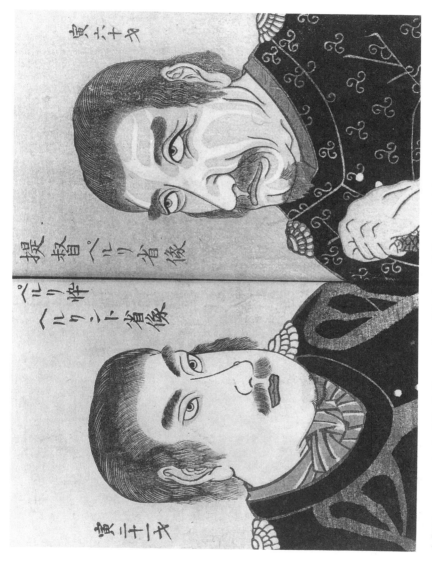

A Japanese woodcut of U. S. Commodore Matthew C. Perry (right) and his son, Lieutenant Oliver Hazard Perry (left). The arrival of the Perrys at the head of a fleet of U. S. "black ships" in 1853 and 1854 signaled the end of Japan's isolation. (Reproduced from the Collections of the Library of Congress)

7

The Meiji Restoration, 1868

INTRODUCTION

At the beginning of the nineteenth century, Japan had been isolated from the rest of the world for 200 years. This was by choice, not chance. Soon after the start of the seventeenth century, Japan's rulers had made the conscious decision to sever all but the most minimal contact with the outside. In part this drastic decision was prompted by a growing European presence. European encroachment, especially the growth of Christianity, alarmed the Japanese. After 1640, Japan permitted limited and closely supervised contact with only the Chinese, Koreans, and Dutch. Japanese wishing to go abroad were punished with death.

However, during the first decades of the nineteenth century the outside world began to intrude upon Japan with greater frequency. The Russians, having crossed Siberia, pressed down from the north; the British sought to expand their East Asian trade; and the Americans increasingly turned their eyes toward the Pacific. The Japanese viewed these foreigners with alarm, seeing in them a threat to their values and traditions. In turn, this apprehension sparked debate and intensified a rising feeling of uneasiness about domestic affairs.

Japan was ruled by the Tokugawa shogunate that had loosely dominated the country since the early seventeenth century. The Tokugawa had brought order to chaotic Japan, but in the process they had pushed aside the emperor. Already considered a demigod, the emperor—whom all Japanese revered—served as a figurehead for the ruling Tokugawa, who made sure that he was detached from politics and that he and his court were financially dependent.

Eventually, real power in Tokugawa Japan rested with the *bakufu*, a sort of board of directors or central administration. While the *bakufu* ruled in the shogun's name, the *daimyō*, or feudal lords, retained a significant degree of autonomy; however, the *bakufu* required the *daimyō* to spend part of the year at the shogun's castle in Edo (later Tokyo) in order to keep an eye on them. Below the *daimyō* were the samurai, or men at arms. Formerly a warrior caste, many samurai became petty administrators after the Tokugawa takeover. Within the ranks of the samurai there was great differentiation. Some samurai were wealthy and powerful, but many were virtually destitute and lacked visible means of support other than a dwindling hereditary stipend paid by their lord.

During the long Tokugawa era, Japan enjoyed an extended period of peace and stability that allowed it to mature into a well-ordered, prosperous, and sophisticated society. However, by the middle of the nineteenth century, the Tokugawa consensus started to break down. The regime's finances were in bad shape, peasant uprisings became more frequent, and the *daimyō* of western Japan seemed less inclined to obey the *bakufu*. Tokugawa government had degenerated into a cumbersome, corrupt, and inefficient bureaucracy. Under these circumstances, the appearance of foreigners plunged Japan into crisis. For many the *bakufu*'s failure to ward off the perceived foreign threat signaled the end of its usefulness and the need to replace it with something more effective. However, Japan split on the question of how to deal with the foreign menace. Some would challenge the foreigners at every turn, while others, more cognizant of the foreigners' technological superiority, would learn from and copy foreign ways in order to resist the foreigners and preserve Japan's sovereignty.

Great Britain's victory over China in the Opium War (1839–1842), which "opened" five of China's ports to foreign traders, first alerted Japan to the threat posed by well-armed foreigners. The minuscule Dutch trading outpost at Deshima warned the *bakufu* that Britain's victory inevitably meant more contact with the West and suggested that Japan abandon its policy of isolation. However, the *bakufu* rejected this advice.

Throughout the 1840s, Japan experienced increased contact with the outside world, but the deciding event was the arrival of U.S. commodore Matthew Perry's naval flotillas in 1853 and 1854. Perry's "black ships," technologically superior to anything the Japanese had, greatly accelerated the opening of Japan to foreigners and deepened the domestic crisis.

As a result of Perry's second voyage (1854), Japan and the United States signed the Treaty of Kanagawa. While the treaty was not extensive—it opened the ports of Shimoda and Hakodate for the resupply of American vessels, but did not provide for trade—it helped to undermine Japan's seclusion. Within the year, Great Britain and Russia secured similar treaties. These treaties foreshadowed additional agreements in the late 1850s that opened Japan to trade with the Western powers on a basis unfavorable to Japan. These so-called unequal treaties allowed foreigners to control Japanese tariff policy; tariffs were kept low in order to facilitate the importation of foreign goods. They also imposed extraterritoriality on Japan, a legal device that exempted foreigners living in Japan from Japanese law.

The *bakufu* response to the foreigners' intrusion proved fatal to the Tokugawa shogunate. A series of reforms, including the purchase of Western-made armaments, establishment of military training facilities, and permission for the *daimyō* to increase the size of their personal armies, proved to be a case of too little too late. When a confused and fractured *bakufu* sought advice and support from the *daimyō* and the emperor's court, it only undermined its own unlimited authority. Shortly thereafter, the *bakufu*'s opponents challenged the shogunate in the name of the emperor, a step the emperor's long-repressed advisors did not condemn.

The belief that Japan might be sliding into civil war was strengthened when a wave of terrorism swept the country between 1860 and 1863. Carried out by *shishi*, or "men of high purpose," who were outraged and humiliated by Japan's failure to rebuff the foreigners, the terror campaign claimed the lives of several prominent *bakufu* figures and further undermined the shogunate's authority. Moreover, the *shishi* even attacked some of the foreign merchants and diplomats, prompting Western retaliation. In 1863 the British shelled Kagoshima and burned the city. The following year a combined Western fleet successfully opened the straits of Shimonoseki, which the local *daimyō* had closed.

In the midst of this confusion, several powerful *daimyō* from western Japan rose against the *bakufu*. In 1866 the rebels held off the *bakufu* forces. During 1867, the *bakufu* tried to regroup, but early in 1868 the Tokugawa shogunate collapsed and was replaced by a restored monarchy. This was the Meiji Restoration, the era-name Meiji being given to Mutsuhito, who succeeded to the throne in 1867 as a fourteen-year-old boy and reigned until his death in 1912.

According to the Meiji Restoration's main premise, the emperor was supposedly restored to the authoritative position that he had held prior to the Tokugawa seizure of power; but in fact the emperor was to continue as a symbol. Real power initially devolved upon a coalition of victorious *daimyō* and reforming samurai and their court allies. During the next few years, most of the *daimyō* were squeezed out and the court officials receded into the background. Control of Japan passed to an oligarchy of activist samurai.

Many of Japan's new leaders had either been *shishi* or sympathized with *shishi* aims. However, exposure to Western influences had convinced them that an unreformed Japan could not resist the technologically superior West. Consequently, they concluded that in order to save Japan from the foreigner—which was their overriding goal—drastic changes were essential. Specifically, they would copy the West in order to save Japan from the West. This radical formula proved to be highly successful.

Initially, Japan's leaders centralized the state and restructured Japanese society. They established the *Dajōkan,* a sort of grand state council, and several ministries including war, foreign affairs, finance, justice, and education. They also broke the *daimyō's* power. Over a period of several years, the Meiji leadership outlawed *daimyō* armies, persuaded the *daimyō* to return their land to the emperor (although they would stay on as "governors" of this land), and finally ended the governorships by converting the former *daimyō* lands into prefectures governed by Tokyo-appointed officials. Surprisingly perhaps, given the composition of its leadership, the Meiji state also abolished the samurai. This was done gradually, with some concern for the samurai's welfare; nevertheless, by 1876 the samurai as a special class had virtually disappeared.

The Meiji leadership also undertook a whole series of reforms designed to modernize Japan according to the Western model in order to ward off Western threats. In the decades after 1868, the entire legal system was reorganized. The principle of equality under the law was introduced, although the state continued to exercise almost complete authority over the individual. The criminal code was drastically altered, and new legal procedures based on the Napoleonic Code were introduced.

Given the reason for its existence, it is not surprising to learn that the Meiji leadership concentrated much of its energy and resources on military reform. It created a modern national army based on first French and then German ideas. Later, Japan built a formidable navy modeled after that of Great Britain.

The 1872 Education Ordinance created a modern, Westernized national school system. However, in 1890 Japan amended that statute in order to restore to the system a measure of traditional Japanese values.

In its drive to strengthen the central government, Meiji authorities assumed control of the country's financial affairs, which heretofore had been fragmented and chaotic. They created a rational system of taxation that placed the state on a sound fiscal footing. They also established a national currency and a central bank. These steps greatly aided the process of industrialization. Even before the Meiji Restoration, signs of industrialization had begun to appear. After 1868, and especially after 1885, industrialization hit its stride as Japan became a major producer of textiles, steel, machinery, ships, coal, and chemicals.

The Meiji Restoration arose from an impassioned desire to defend Japan from the perceived threat posed by the West. Consequently, once Japan embarked upon reform, it turned its attention to foreign affairs. Its major objective was to regain complete independence by securing revision of the unequal treaties. This proved difficult since the Western powers continued to regard Japan as just another "uncivilized" nation ripe for exploitation. On several occasions the Western nations, particularly Great Britain, refused to modify the existing treaties; however, by 1900 Japan achieved success. New treaties were gradually put into effect that ended extraterritoriality and returned to Japan the right to set its own tariffs.

Japan was determined to achieve equality with the West, and this led the Meiji rulers to pursue imperial goals in much the same fashion as Western nations of that era. Although Japan failed to force China to sign unequal treaties with it similar to those China was signing with the Western powers, it did open Korea in 1876 in an operation reminiscent of Japan's opening two decades earlier. Korea soon became a major bone of contention between Japan and China, and in 1894 the Korean rivalry provided the pretext for war between these two large Asian states. Japan won a decisive victory, clearly indicating its new strength. In the Treaty of Shimonoseki (1895), Japan received a large indemnity, the island of Taiwan, the Liaotung peninsula on the mainland, and treaty revisions that lifted it to the same status in China that the Western powers enjoyed. Japan, however, had overreached itself. In the same year, the European powers forced it to return the Liaotung peninsula.

Nevertheless, Japan's increased international status was confirmed in 1902 when it signed a defensive alliance with Great Britain. This time the British treated the Japanese as equals. However, the event that heralded Japan's arrival as a true equal of any Western nation occurred in 1904–1905, when increased friction between Russia and Japan over Korea and Manchuria resulted in war. During the course of the Russo-Japanese War, the Meiji state defeated the Russians on both land and sea. The Treaty of Portsmouth (1905) not only confirmed Japan's victory, but also marked the first time that a nonwhite nation had defeated a white one. Japan had come a long way from the days of Commodore Perry and the "black ships."

INTERPRETIVE ESSAY
George M. Wilson

Wherever we look in Meiji Restoration studies, the historical event seems to dissolve in a field of ambiguities. Contrary impressions highlight the restoration's two faces—one of change and progress, the other suggestive of a powerful leaning to custom and reaction. Such a dichotomy permeates the images generated by all readings of this epic event. The restoration's time frame is also divided into before and after. The two phases correspond to a preparatory period leading up to the emperor's return to formal sovereignty in 1868, and a follow-up period of reforms that issued forth from government offices in the decades after 1868. Two phases and two faces—they are always there, but no structural similarity appears to connect them. The restoration's phases fit no feature of the ideological tenor of nineteenth-century Japanese history, nor do its faces mirror the predominant patterns that come out of the chronological sequence of events. Faces and phases, phases and faces: they are dimensions of a complex and confusing episode in world history.

This essay will focus on the problem of the restoration's evident duality. While sorting out the potential for multiple explanations generated by the apparent contradictions in restoration imagery, it is important to note the related point that the history of this episode is normally written with two explanatory models in mind. The first says that foreign affairs overrode domestic issues and dictated the process of change, while the other holds that Japan's leaders, rather than the common people, were responsible for the country's rapid rise to modern nationhood. These models may be compatible, but they disregard the degree of mass commitment (or popular will) that existed in 1868, when the long-lived feudal system of early modern Japan (1600–1868) at last collapsed.

Photography came to Japan with the foreigners in the 1850s. As a result, the entire restoration era is captured in the faded and flecked black-and-white images of thousands of daguerreotypes and other surviving photographs. One photo will serve to introduce the age. A bright-eyed young male, dressed more for show than for battle, carries a long sword of the type identified with the samurai, Japan's elite corps of feudal warriors. The military estate was legally abolished in 1876, and even in this photo his sword and vestigial topknot are the only things "traditional" about him. He wears a black European-style suit much like schoolboy uniforms worn in Japan today. His leather shoes give him a trim and nimble look. Gloves adorn his hands. His slender frock coat is well cut. His shirt has a collar, but he wears no tie and his shirt is buttoned at the neck. He is the picture of a restoration activist of the 1860–1870 years.

This portrait of a youthful warrior in new garb adroitly sums up Japan's situation at the time of the Meiji Restoration. He dresses Western yet discloses a Japanese heart in sword and topknot; and he conveys the impression of high competence and utter fearlessness. Looking intent on taking care of business, this youngster joined his whole generation in a struggle to regain their country's independence, hamstrung as Japan was by unequal treaty arrangements with the Western powers. He might as well be a famous person, though he was not, for they looked much like him—doleful but determined to plunge ahead into the new in order to build a bright future for Japan.

Novelty is the Meiji Restoration's lasting emblem. Those who made it happen did not wish to rescue the old, fearing that bad habits would persist (as many did) and that Japan would be unable to deal with the onslaught of Western military and commercial power. Their purpose was to bring change to Japan by a skilled insertion of European and American ways into Japanese society. Three hundred years earlier, the entire system of islands that make up Japan had been reconstructed as a kind of feudal monarchy. After 1600 the shogun, the hereditary head of the Tokugawa house, sat astride an awkward but effective political system designed to support the relative autonomy of the great feudal barons, the *daimyō*, numbering more than 250 and spread out all over the country. Headquartered in Edo in the east of Japan, on the site of what is today Tokyo, the shogun scarcely interacted with the city's 1 million residents, who lived and worked in their own quarters while the aristocratic samurai occupied the high ground. The city meandered across hills, valleys, and waterways, revealing little and concealing most of the byplay among its huge and disparate population. Edo's police kept the wives and children of *daimyō* in town to guarantee their loyalty while traveling to and from their home territories. Not even the shogun, however, could give orders to the feudal lords, whose official status equaled his own. A complex parlor game bound shogun and *daimyō* throughout the Edo years from 1600 until the emperor's restoration in 1868.

The "story" of the restoration necessarily begins with the entry of Western military might into Japanese waters in the mid-nineteenth century. As a result, the restoration is chiefly datable from the arrival of Commodore Matthew Perry of the U.S. Navy in 1853. Nothing other than this "definitive event," as Maruyama Masao, Japan's preeminent postwar social scientist, terms it, occurred to set off such a storm. Efforts to situate the origin of the restoration at some earlier time and to align it with domestic developments take many forms and may shed some light on the process, but they ignore the obvious. To be sure, problems beset the country, such as food shortages and economic rivalries; but such issues had been there for a long time and did not worsen appreciably in the early nineteenth century. Japan's total population leveled off somewhere close to 30 million; the overall figure hardly changed between 1720 and 1850. Famine broke out here and there, as did earthquakes and fire, but in general Japan boasted a vibrant economy resulting from the massive urbanization brought about by the growth of castle towns to serve the lifestyles of the *daimyō* and their trusted warriors, the samurai. This urban growth of the seventeenth century was followed by the development of new crops and new ways to work and do business in rural Japan.

Although some thinkers began to question the extent to which the shogun and his advisors exercised governmental authority through the *bakufu* (military government, that is, the shogunate), very few people challenged the legitimacy of the feudal system based on vassalage between *daimyō* and samurai. Feudalism had successfully maintained a balance of tension in Japan ever since the Tokugawa side won the Battle of Sekigahara in 1600. Installed by the multitude of *daimyō* as a glorified peacekeeper, the shogun had only to preserve order and keep Japan safe from outside predators. The Tokugawa family was not expected to centralize governmental power and never sought such an arrangement. Over time Japan was closely governed by the feudal authorities, facing no external threat of any consequence. So it went until the arrival of Western sea power.

In 1853 Perry brought the old order to an instant state of crisis. Unlike earlier Western visitors, he proceeded straight to Edo Bay instead of putting in at Nagasaki, the customary place where foreigners might speak with representatives of the shogun's government. Two of his eight ships were the latest naval frigates, something like today's destroyers, powered by steam engines. They were terrifying with their blackened iron hulls, intimidating for their speed and firepower. The public was no less amazed by the flotilla Perry brought to Japan than were the officials who went to meet him. Like the ordinary people who saw Perry's "black ships," the officials who had to negotiate with him hoped that the Americans would tire and withdraw. In fact, Perry did leave Japan abruptly, but only after indicating that he would be back in the spring of 1854 with a larger force.

In preparing for the American's return, the shogun's advisors tried to compose a broad policy to deflect this alien intrusion into ancestral Tokugawa house rules dating back to the 1630s, when Japan had entered a state of self-imposed seclusion that discouraged trade and other routine overseas contacts. Perry was having none of that: his mission was to bring Japan into the community of "civilized nations," which joined together for "commercial intercourse" and diplomatic representation. Bearing a letter from U.S. president Millard Fillmore, Perry insisted that Japan open its closed door, at least wide enough to allow the provisioning of American vessels plying the China trade and the repatriation of shipwrecked American sailors and whalers. If the shogun (whom Perry referred to as the emperor) refused, the Americans were prepared to use force to gain their way. Perry demanded an agreement in principle. How would the shogun's government respond?

Edo's leaders understood the *bakufu*'s role as arbiter of foreign policy for all of Japan. They also knew that they could not resist Perry given the naval power he commanded. The *bakufu* tried to meet the crisis by asking the *daimyō* what they thought about Perry's demands. That was not all; Edo even asked for the views of the ancient imperial court located in Japan's old cultural capital of Kyoto. So, on the one hand, a process of consultation allowed everyone concerned to be informed and thereby alleviate the *bakufu*'s anxiety over its military inability to repel Perry. On the other hand, this very policy was without precedent. Never in the history of the *bakufu* since Edo became its seat in 1603 had the shogun found it necessary to ask for advice about foreign affairs. No one could miss the implication that the *bakufu* could not cope. Harvard's eminent historian of Japan, Edwin O. Reischauer, was moved to conclude that the Edo government had initiated the process of its own demise. Its decision to survey *daimyō* opinion may have been "an understandable effort to win national support," wrote Reischauer, but it signified "the beginning of the end of Tokugawa rule." No wonder historians call the years after Perry's arrival *bakumatsu*, referring to "the end" (*matsu*) of the shogun's government (*baku*).

Perry got his treaty and Japan ended its official isolation. Not a lot changed, however, since Edo's negotiators gave up rather little. U.S. ships could enter Japan at two ports—Shimoda on the Pacific coast west of Edo, and Hakodate on the underpopulated northern island—but this treaty did not approve trade, let alone encourage it. It did create circumstances in which a diplomatic officer known as a consul might be dispatched. In 1856 Townsend Harris appeared with his translator, a young Dutchman named Henry Heusken, to take up the American consul's duties in Shimoda. To his dismay, the Japanese declined to recognize his official status. It took Harris another two years to gain a trade treaty from the Japanese. Even that 1858 treaty contained terms that were hardly onerous for Japan by comparison with the treaties then applying to China. No opium was to be imported; missionary and diplomatic involvement was to begin gradually; and ports of trade were to phase in over an eight-year period. Yet even these limited concessions were contrary to Japan's will and opened the *bakufu* to charges of incompetence. Given the state of the world, *bakufu* officials had no choice but to agree to Harris's demands; they had worked hard to minimize ill effects.

Any concessions injured the political order, and the wider public became aware of the *bakufu*'s weakness. Critics called for reforms to meet the threat of foreign intervention. If the Westerners were strong, the devices through which their strengths were shown—guns, steamships, scientific instruments—could be learned and imitated by Japanese who would keep faith with their ancient heritage. Hence arose the first watchword of the age. *Tōyō dōtoku, seiyō gei*—"Eastern ethics, Western science"—called on Japan to maintain the values of the East while cultivating the West's "techniques" (*gei* means "arts" but here indicates science and technology). This combination, first proposed in 1854 by Sakuma Shōzan, a devotee of Western science who specialized in gunnery, appealed to critics who wanted to innovate yet also worried about holding onto traditional values.

The *bakufu's* days were numbered unless shogunal leaders could devise a way out. Overseas expeditions were undertaken; in 1860 the *Kanrin Maru*, Japan's first steam-powered vessel, carried students and learned men to America and Europe. The young Fukuzawa Yukichi made the trip, returning in time to lead Japan's intellectuals into an age of "civilization and enlightenment" early in the Meiji period. The *bakufu* did all it could to build up its defenses and strengthen its arms. Scholars in its employ cultivated an encyclopedic body of knowledge about the West. But all for naught.

The end of the Tokugawa system came at the beginning of 1868. It followed an 1867 maneuver by the last shogun, Tokugawa Yoshinobu, to cede power to a grand council of *daimyō*, thereby retaining a semblance of feudal authority. This solution was too narrow to work. First, it weakened central leadership just when a stronger hand was required to deal with the foreigners. Second, the idea of a council could pull in the lords but not the samurai, who still made up the core of feudal power. Third, it altogether ignored other elements of the population who had also put up with the confusion of recent Japanese politics. Commoners found no place in such a settlement, despite their chagrin over foreign inroads into Japan and the emergence of new religious cults as well as rowdy popular behavior on the eve of the restoration. Nor was there any involvement of the old imperial court in Kyoto.

The late entry of the imperial family into politics after a millennium of quiescence is a remarkable fact of restoration history; without it the Meiji Restoration would be a quite different phenomenon. That anyone should want to "restore" a spiritual recluse who served more as a high priest of the Shinto religion than as a secular ruler was startling in the first place. In addition, for this ancient institution of kingship to be mobilized in an imperialist world filled with technological challenges seemed anachronistic even to many Japanese. The emperor's great strength, however, lay in his symbolic role. The shogun had stood only for the 7 percent of the population who were samurai, and for the dominion exercised by their lords, the feudal *daimyō*. When the shogun could no longer keep foreigners out, his raison d'être vanished. The emperor might be a retiring figure draped in mystery, but he could be brought forward to appeal to all Japanese, those of low station as well as high, common people as well as feudal personages. A new government could project him in order to unify everyone in a common national purpose. Hence arose the second watchword of the age, *Sonnō jōi*—"Respect the emperor and repel the barbarian." This slogan captured the emerging Japanese dream of national community in which foreigners were to be kept under control. The foreigners did not have to be ousted in a literal sense, but Japan had to tame them by mastering the techniques that had made them so potent. That had been the point of the first watchword, *Tōyō dōtoku, seiyō gei*.

Foreigners resident in Japan found much to surprise them in the events of 1868. The new regime's quick putdown of resistance by forces loyal to the shogun amazed some, who thought that the entrenched power of the feudal establishment would insure its perpetuation. The decision to move the emperor to Edo and rename the city Tokyo (Eastern Capital), in emulation of Kyoto (Capital City), was scarcely unexpected inasmuch as Edo had been the key site in the growth of trade and diplomatic representation. But it did convey a surprising boldness.

Most surprising was the absence of a new shogun. To the foreigners, the Tokugawa failure signaled less a collapse of feudalism than a broken political alliance; they expected one of the feudal lords to step forward as shogun at the head of a new alliance. Instead, the obvious candidates for such a post, the great lords of Satsuma and Chōshū in southwestern Japan, swore loyalty to the emperor and gave up their ancestral lands. With all the feudal territories accounted for, the new government possessed a unique mandate for change. Under the emperor's stewardship, Japan embarked on a set of far-reaching reforms.

These reforms affected every dimension of life and gave Japan at long last the capacity to compete in the world. Their purpose was to destroy the unequal diplomatic and trade treaties with the Western powers. This required a new legal system and the creation of a modern army and navy. It also called for a new educational system to train skilled workers for an industrial future. The emperor's first message to his people, the Charter Oath of April 1868, pointed the way. In five terse articles it promised to take Japan down a new road leading to stability and prosperity:

1. Political assemblies shall be organized across the land and all matters decided by public opinion.

2. All persons high and low shall join energetically to manage the state and promote the economy.

3. Civil and military officials, and the common people as well,

shall be permitted to pursue their ambitions so that discontent does not arise.

4. Evil customs of olden days shall be broken off and everything [shall be] based on universal justice.

5. Knowledge shall be sought all over the world to exalt the foundations of imperial rule.

The first article of the Charter Oath took the longest time to attain because the Imperial Diet, or parliament, did not open until 1890. The constitution, setting forth the formal rules of the political system, preceded the Diet by only a year. By the time these two major political events occurred, the emperor had also issued a letter on education, affirming a full-blown Confucian paternalism vis-à-vis the people of Japan, whom he proposed to treat as his "family." Articles 2 through 4 were achieved more expeditiously. Moreover, this was done largely as stated in the oath, although the democratic flourishes were missing. Distinctions between samurai and commoners were legally abolished, and the government paid off the samurai with bonds while terminating the annual stipends they had formerly received from their *daimyō*. Japan's economic welfare was addressed through a vast program of government initiation of industry that lasted all the way through the 1870s. Faced with an inflationary crisis at the turn of the 1880s, the government reversed course and sold off the new industries at bargain prices, but they were bought by former samurai and merchants who took care to shepherd them into the future. In general this process established the modern Japanese *zaibatsu*, the famous financial conglomerates such as Mitsui and Mitsubishi.

As the oath promised, the reforms ended the separation of status between civil and military. Old ways were abandoned at every turn. New "ministries" in Tokyo coordinated the government's domestic and foreign policies. Education was required for every child in Japan. The new army and navy were thrown open to recruits from all walks of life. These reforms marked a sustained attempt to foster a policy of state capitalism in an effort to redress an unfavorable balance of power with the nations of the West. Such a strategy was costly and daring, but for the most part it succeeded. By the time Japan defeated China in the Sino-Japanese War of 1894–1895, observers everywhere had been impressed with Japan's success in constructing a modern nation out of an aggregation of feudal territories.

The fifth and final article in the Charter Oath was the one most faithfully observed. Japan literally searched the world for models to follow in building a new society. The fact that the advanced capitalist countries provided the lion's share of prototypes surprised no one. Educational methods and practices from France and America were grafted onto a Japanese base, as were military models drawn from Germany and Britain. French bureaucracy and American agriculture (especially on the northern island of Hokkaido) became exemplars. A system of universities was introduced to cap a public educational system that required universal schooling through the fourth grade (later changed to the sixth grade).

The whole edifice of the modern Japanese state sometimes looked like a foreign construct. Meiji reforms had an exotic quality stemming from the foreign derivation of so much of the reform program. It was an age of such novelty that the Japanese had trouble identifying a valid past to claim as a basis for reform, notwithstanding Japan's experience a millennium earlier of borrowing from Chinese civilization. Usually history is mobilized to showcase the triumphs of a country and its people when precedents are needed to support new endeavors. In Meiji Japan, however, the restoration appeared to be a unique project for which no Japanese precedent could adequately account. A German physician, hired to treat high government officials and to organize a medical school, inquired of a Japanese friend about the country's history, only to be told: "We have no history. Our history begins today." Responding to the same question, another friend informed the doctor, "That was in the days of barbarism."

In the absence of history, science acquired the ability to authorize change, and its prescription was to adopt Western ways of doing things. Beer and beefsteak became popular. Ministers of state wore morning coats and escorted their wives to parties featuring ballroom dancing. Fancy dress balls took place at the Deer Cry Pavilion (*Rokumeikan*), an imposing two-story brick building located in the Hibiya district of downtown Tokyo. The Meiji emperor did without his white Shinto robes, appearing instead in a Prussian-style field marshal's uniform and sporting a mustache. The prime minister staged a masquerade ball where the guests all dressed in costume. A young ex-samurai, who served as Japan's first envoy to the United States and later became minister of education, entered into a contractual marriage with his wife in 1875 and then divorced her in 1886 (divorce was another importation from the West). His name was Mori Arinori, and he also proposed adopting English as the national language on the assumption that it could equip people better than Japanese for the tests of a competitive world. This sort of agenda probably arose as a result of the worldwide spread of Social Darwinism, but it did represent bold (not to say wild) thinking by the Japanese themselves in the face of a cultural identity crisis.

Another watchword circulated everywhere in Meiji Japan. It was not enshrined in the legal codes or the formal apparatus of government, but it was universally known nonetheless. *Fukoku kyōhei*—"Rich country, strong army"—epitomized the goals of the Meiji reformers. Fukuzawa Yukichi, the brightest and most influential of Japan's many intellectuals who called for "civilization and enlightenment" through adaptation from European and American culture, argued that only an informed citizenry operating a system of organized institutions could bring forth wealth and power on a scale required to compete in the world. Wealth leading to power thus carried the day, fusing the intent of the two *bakumatsu* watchwords that had promoted Japan's original decision to adopt Western science and technology under a political system headed by the emperor. Western techniques grafted onto Eastern morality, governed by an Eastern monarch, could "repel" the West itself through a process by means of which Japan would match the West's industrial prosperity and military might.

At the close of the Meiji period, when the emperor himself died in 1912, the world could appreciate what Japan had accomplished during his long reign of forty-five years. By that time the unequal treaties of old were no more, and the Japanese had gained a respected place in that Darwinian age of imperialism. When Japan emerged from World War I as a great power in its own right, it seemed as if a miracle had been wrought in short order. Trouble was brewing, however, and it would lead Japan into the morass of war in China, expanding in 1941 into a war against the West. How did such a reversal happen so abruptly?

In looking at the development of Japan after 1868, it is clear that frictions and stresses were bound to arise in an era marked by so much change. Seeking to match the Western nations by building its own national wealth and power, Meiji Japan shortchanged most of its own people. Farmers, for instance, making up the largest segment of the populace, bore the huge tax burden that fueled industrial growth. However they might be educated, all Japanese were expected to do the emperor's bidding in all matters, especially that of going to war. While the Japanese Empire was being created, again in emulation of Western powers such as Britain, Japan rode roughshod over its Asian neighbors, who came to seem little more than impediments to progress despite their proud heritage as sources of Eastern civilization. The Japanese preoccupation with success through wealth and power consumed virtually every national resource. Japan's wealth was not to be enjoyed by a responsible citizenry anyway; rather, it was to be endlessly augmented by the emperor's loyal subjects.

The legacy of the Meiji era seems even more contradictory than its beginnings, for the Meiji Restoration was ultimately a cultural revolution, and such an event inevitably destroys as much as it creates. Western science and technology may appear to be neutral instruments for bringing a country into the fold of civilized nations, but nothing is spared in such a process, and "traditional" ethics could not protect people from loss of identity, of prestige, of welfare. Those who advocated an absolute code of emperor worship in order to produce wealth that might buy strength and gain an empire for Japan led the nation into sacrifices that became ritual events to be renewed in every crisis. The whole Meiji experience was unidirectional—from the top down, not the bottom up. Energy flowed from rulers and bureaucrats to the masses, from the rich to the poor; the energy of those below was blocked in its upward thrust, absorbed, and turned to the purposes of the powerholders.

In a sense, the country had managed to run a hard course from feudal disunity to centralized monarchic nation-state without changing all that much except on the surface. Still the captive of its own small size and poverty of resources, Japan mobilized its talented people to produce for production's sake and to carry the burden of imperialism to the rest of Asia. As early as 1885, the persuasive "enlightener" Fukuzawa Yukichi warned his fellow countrymen to avoid associating with bad neighbors by choosing to "break with Asia":

> On principle we must break with Asia. [Japan's] spirit has already taken leave of Asia's backwardness and shifted over to Western civilization. Unfortunately, two countries in our vicinity—one China and the other Korea—[do] not know the way to progress.... We cannot put off the rise of Asia while we wait for them to see the light. Instead we must renounce them and move forward along with the civilized nations of the West.... Those who fraternize with bad friends cannot avoid sharing their bad name. In our hearts we must turn away from bad friends in the eastern part of Asia.

Fukuzawa's celebrated generosity of spirit failed him here, and his cautionary words amount to an indictment (if also an unintended by-product) of Japan's rush to "civilization." His warning probably results as much from the characteristic nineteenth-century penchant for Social Darwinism as it does from typical Japanese conceptions of the international order. Yet such an ideological leaning might have been anticipated in light of Japan's long feudal past. In their haste to become like the West, the Japanese turned their backs on their Asian heritage, only to reinvent it as a vehicle for tutoring their "backward" Asian brethren. So they violated the first of the watchwords that had started them on their way—"Eastern ethics"—in favor of its corollary—"Western science." No amount of patriotism, no love of country and emperor, could justify such a stance. It turned the very resources that Japan cultivated for its own independence into a weapon against the rest of Asia, leaving a dark legacy for future generations.

Much the same conclusion applies to the years since World War II, and especially to Japan's miraculous postwar economic boom. Recovering from wartime ruin through self-sacrifice and hard work, the Japanese people fashioned the world's second largest economy by 1985. In the process they impressed others as "economic animals" and reconfirmed their distance from their Asian neighbors. In this sense, the triumph of the restoration's second and third watchwords has left Japan a paragon of "nationalism," even today. It is a country of great talent and great wealth, but one that has essentially forsaken Eastern ethics to pursue the Promethean muse of industrial hyper-development.

The two faces of the Meiji Restoration remain ever before us. Yes, it was a radical event, ushering in a cultural revolution. The Other (the West) became the ideal even as the Subject (Japan) launched a vast program of industrial and imperial aggrandizement. It was a grandiose exercise in what has come to be called nation-building, yet even the radicalism of this project came from on high in the name of an emperor and a leadership elite bent on pursuing wealth and power as ends in themselves.

A question persists about what the general public stands to gain from the state-sponsored acquisition of great wealth and power of this kind. *Who benefits from such aggrandizement?* The unresolved tension from this question runs through Japan's modern history and continues to puzzle observers today, almost a full century after the restoration era drew to a close.

SELECTED BIBLIOGRAPHY

Akamatsu, Paul. *Meiji 1868: Revolution and Counter-Revolution in Japan.* New York: Harper and Row, 1972. An old-style narrative long on detail about the plots and machinations of the *bakumatsu* years.

Akita, George. *Foundations of Constitutional Government in Meiji Japan.* Cambridge, MA: Harvard University Press, 1967. Positive assessment of the cooperation of Meiji leaders with the political opposition to create the Meiji constitutional order.

Beasley, William G. *The Meiji Restoration.* Stanford, CA: Stanford University Press, 1972. Broad synthesis based on the nationalist thesis of Meiji Restoration history.

Bellah, Robert N. *Tokugawa Religion: The Cultural Roots of Modern Japan.* New York: Free Press, 1985. Brilliant restatement of Max Weber's Protestant-ethic thesis in relation to premodern Japanese civic values, including those associated with *bushidō*, the samurai code.

Bernstein, Gail Lee, ed. *Recreating Japanese Women, 1600–1945.* Berkeley: University of California Press, 1991. Wide-ranging essays look at women's roles in early modern and modern Japan.

Bowen, Roger W. *Rebellion and Democracy in Meiji Japan: A Study of Commoners in the Popular Rights Movement.* Berkeley: University of California Press, 1980. Portrays common people in the rural rebellions of the 1880s, arguing that their resistance movements were crucial for the course of Meiji history.

Craig, Albert M., and Donald H. Shively, eds. *Personality in Japanese History.* Berkeley: University of California Press, 1970. Multi-author volume of essays about the psychology and behavior of individual Japanese, including studies grounded in Tokugawa and *bakumatsu* history.

Gluck, Carol N. *Japan's Modern Myths: Ideology in the Late Meiji Period.* Princeton, NJ: Princeton University Press, 1985. Convincing summary of the social and cultural production of an emperor-system ideology for Japan.

Hall, John W., and Marius B. Jansen, eds. *Studies in the Institutional History of Early Modern Japan.* Princeton, NJ: Princeton University Press, 1968. Collection of incisive essays on organizational and behavioral aspects of life in Japan during the long Tokugawa period (1600–1868).

Harootunian, Harry D. *Toward Restoration: The Growth of Political Consciousness in Tokugawa Japan.* Berkeley: University of California Press, 1970. Imaginative psychological reinterpretation of *bakumatsu* politics as a revolutionary youth movement.

Huber, Thomas M. *The Revolutionary Origins of Modern Japan.* Stanford, CA: Stanford University Press, 1981. Argues that the restoration arose from the attitudes and behavior of an ambitious and frustrated class of "service intelligentsia."

Irokawa, Daikichi. *The Culture of Meiji Japan.* Translated by Marius B. Jansen. Princeton, NJ: Princeton University Press, 1984. A leading Japanese popular historian depicts Meiji culture as an original and independent variable.

Jansen, Marius B., ed. *The Cambridge History of Japan. Volume 5: The Nineteenth Century.* Cambridge: Cambridge University Press, 1989. Encyclopedic coverage by both Western and Japanese authors summarizing and analyzing the political, social, and cultural history of late Tokugawa and Meiji Japan.

Jansen, Marius B., and Gilbert Rozman, eds. *Japan in Transition: From Tokugawa to Meiji.* Princeton, NJ: Princeton University Press, 1986. Multi-author volume of essays exploring economic and political changes that suggest the ease of Japan's transition through the restoration years.

Koschmann, J. Victor. *The Mito Ideology: Discourse, Reform, and Insurrection in Late Tokugawa Japan, 1790–1864.* Berkeley: University of California Press, 1987. Argues that radical ideas in traditional places failed to remake Japan during the Meiji Restoration.

Najita, Tetsuo, and J. Victor Koschmann, eds. *Conflict in Modern Japanese History: The Neglected Tradition.* Princeton, NJ: Princeton University Press, 1982. Argues that conflict rather than consensus drove Japan's modern transformation.

Norman, E. Herbert. *Japan's Emergence as a Modern State.* New York: Institute of Pacific Relations, 1940. Makes a case for the class-driven economic basis of change during and after the Meiji Restoration.

Pyle, Kenneth B. *The New Generation in Meiji Japan: Problems of Cultural Identity, 1885–1895.* Stanford, CA: Stanford University Press, 1969. Argues that generational change conditioned the growth of new kinds of political thought midway through the Meiji period.

Sansom, George B. *The Western World and Japan: A Study in the Interaction of European and Asiatic Cultures.* New York: Alfred A. Knopf, 1950. Inclusive look at Western involvement in Japanese history from 1500 to 1900.

Smith, Thomas C. *The Agrarian Origins of Modern Japan.* Stanford, CA: Stanford University Press, 1959. Shows how rural concerns and changes in the organization of rural life produced skilled workers and institutional resources for modern Japan.

———. *Native Sources of Japanese Industrialization, 1750–1920.* Berkeley: University of California Press, 1988. Argues that economic and social capacities generated during the Tokugawa era prepared the ground for Japan's industrial revolution.

Totman, Conrad D. *The Collapse of the Tokugawa Bakufu, 1862–1868.* Honolulu: University Press of Hawaii, 1980. Hardy political history of the Tokugawa shogunate's tortuous decline and fall.

———. *Early Modern Japan.* Berkeley: University of California Press, 1993. Magisterial institutional history of Tokugawa Japan up to 1850.

Wiley, Peter Booth. *Yankees in the Land of the Gods: Commodore Perry and the Opening of Japan.* New York: Viking, 1990. Japan's entry into the world seen via the saga of Perry and other Americans.

Wilson, George M. *Patriots and Redeemers in Japan: Motives in the Meiji Restoration.* Chicago: University of Chicago Press, 1992. Argues that unsung commoner efforts to redeem society complemented the well-known patriotism of the samurai elite to bring about the Meiji Restoration.

Otto von Bismarck (1815–1898), chancellor of Germany from 1871 to 1890. Bismarck, as chief minister of Prussia, engineered the unification of Germany under Prussian leadership in 1871. (Reproduced from the Collections of the Library of Congress)

8

The Unification of Germany, 1871

INTRODUCTION

For centuries, political fragmentation had characterized the German-speaking lands of north central Europe. Hundreds of small principalities, duchies, free cities, ecclesiastical states, and kingdoms dotted the political landscape. The Holy Roman Empire, which the eighteenth-century thinker Voltaire described as being neither holy, nor Roman, nor an empire, provided a semblance of unity; but that was a mere facade. In practice, the Holy Roman Empire failed to unite the Germans.

In 1806 Napoleon dissolved the Holy Roman Empire. However, when the French emperor was defeated in 1815 no attempt was made to revive the Empire. Instead, the statesmen at the Congress of Vienna created the German Confederation, a union of thirty-nine German states that quickly fell under the domination of the Austrian chancellor, Clemens von Metternich. Metternich was no friend of German unification, and he used his power over the German Confederation to stifle German national sentiment.

The Revolutions of 1848 drove Metternich from power, and German nationalism appeared triumphant. However, the Frankfurt Assembly failed to create a unified German state as the wishes of the *Kleindeutsch* (those who would exclude Austria from a unified Germany) clashed with the wishes of the *Grossdeutsch* (those who would include the German-speaking parts of the Austrian Empire within the new German state).

When the Revolutions of 1848 failed, the movement for German unification stalled. A resurgent Austria adamantly opposed a unified German state. The German Confederation was revived, and Austria set about destroying German national sentiment.

However, over the previous half century that sentiment had put down deep roots among Germany's growing middle class and its intelligentsia. In the face of Austria's steadfast opposition to German unification, German nationalists increasingly turned to Prussia. Prussia appeared to be a strange choice to lead the fight for German unification. Although a Great Power, it was weaker than the other Great Powers, including Austria. Furthermore, Prussia had never shown any inclination to support German unification. Rather, it was a conservative, authoritarian state that rested upon the twin pillars of its army and its nobility, the Junkers, who had vast holdings east of the Elbe River. Both the military and the Junkers thought almost exclusively in terms of Prussia; for most, German unification remained a remote and somewhat disquieting thought. Consequently, it is one of history's curiosities that Prussia united Germany and that the unification's chief architect was Otto von Bismarck, the living embodiment of Junkerdom.

In 1862 Prussia found itself in the midst of a domestic crisis over the reform of its army. William I, the king of Prussia, in a move generally regarded as one of desperation, appointed Otto von Bismarck chancellor. The forty-seven-year-old Bismarck had toned down his youthful exuberance, which had earned him the nickname "Wild Bismarck," but he was still a man of strong passions. Above all he was a Junker, revering the Prussian nobility and their arrogant, autocratic traditions. Physically imposing, Bismarck had spent his career in the Prussian foreign service. He was an arch-conservative and completely devoted to Prussia. He also believed in the use of force to achieve his objectives. In his most famous speech, he announced to the Prussian parliament that the great questions of the day would be decided by "iron and blood."

With this background, it seemed unlikely that Bismarck would become the father of German unification. However, it appears that Bismarck saw in German nationalism a suitable vehicle to advance Prussian interests. By placing Prussia at the head of the movement for German unification, Bismarck could create a large, powerful, wealthy German state that, in fact, would be little more than a greatly enlarged Prussia. This is not to say that Bismarck came to power with a preconceived master plan for German unification; rather, he proved exceptionally pragmatic, skillfully taking advantage of opportunities that he found. Nevertheless, he always strove to enhance Prussia's power and prestige.

Initially Bismarck defused the domestic crisis that had brought him to the chancellorship. He directly confronted the weak and insecure Prussian parliament, or diet, asserting the monarch's right to do as he pleased. Threatening the diet, Bismarck succeeded in preserving for the monarchy a virtually unfettered hand, but in doing so he earned the enmity of many deputies.

Bismarck then turned to foreign affairs, where he achieved a series of stunning successes that converted even his most bitter political enemies into enthusiastic admirers. Bismarck's string of successes began with the knotty problem of Schleswig-Holstein, two provinces whose disposition had created tension between Germans and Danes for many years. In November 1863, Denmark effectively annexed Schleswig. Denmark's actions outraged the German states, and in December Austria and Prussia formed a partnership to resolve the Schleswig-Holstein question. Apparently Bismarck also saw this partnership as a way to involve Austria in a venture that sometime in the future might provide Prussia with an excuse to challenge Austria's control over the German-speaking lands. This is what Bismarck intended to do, since he had concluded that Austria stood in the way of Prussia's domination of Germany.

In January 1864, Austria and Prussia gave Denmark an ultimatum calling upon the Danes to relinquish Schleswig. Denmark rejected the ultimatum, and war broke out on February 1, 1864. Lacking support from any Great Power, Denmark was soon defeated and agreed to turn over Schleswig and Holstein to Austria and Prussia. In August 1865, Austria and Prussia signed the Treaty of Gastein, which stipulated how they were to rule Schleswig and Holstein. Bismarck intentionally made the treaty vague and complicated in order to use it to pick a fight with Austria on his terms whenever it suited his purposes.

However, before Bismarck could contest Austrian influence in Germany, he had to line up the other Great Powers so that when war with Austria occurred, the Habsburg state would be bereft of allies. In 1863 Bismarck earned favor with Russia by initiating the Alvensleben Convention directed against Polish rebels who were then challenging Russian rule in Poland.

Two years later, Bismarck met the French emperor Napoleon III at Biarritz, where he secured Napoleon's support in the event of war with

Austria. Bismarck accomplished this diplomatic triumph by promising Napoleon vague territorial compensation in the Rhineland, Belgium, or Luxembourg, areas where Prussia had little influence and owned no territory it could give to France. Astonishingly, Napoleon not only accepted the Prussian "offer" but also put on paper his demands for what came to be referred to as a "tip." Bismarck carefully preserved these demands for future use.

Bismarck also made overtures to the new Italian state. Knowing Italy's dislike of Austria and its desire to annex the Italian-speaking province of Venetia from Austria, Bismarck signed a treaty with Italy in April 1866 that called for Italy to join Prussia in war against Austria.

Bismarck's attempts to secure the support of the smaller German states were not so successful. These states feared Prussia and saw in Bismarck's maneuvers a threat to their continued independence.

During spring 1866, Bismarck prepared for war with Austria. Exploiting the Treaty of Gastein's ambiguity, Bismarck exasperated Austria. When he proposed to the German Confederation that a German parliament be summoned with delegates selected by universal male suffrage, the conservative Austrian state lost patience and mobilized its army. Prussia responded similarly, and war began on June 20, 1866. Italy joined Prussia, while several smaller German states sided with Austria.

Conventional wisdom anticipated a victory for the Austrians. Instead, Prussia routed Austria in seven weeks thanks to better equipment, better military leadership, and a modern rail network that allowed the Prussians to move their troops effectively. The key military engagement was the Battle of Sadowa (Königgrätz), where the Prussians smashed the main Austrian force and opened the road to Vienna.

Having ousted Austria from Germany, Bismarck moved to mollify the Austrians and to consolidate Prussia's position. In defiance of William I, who wanted to impose a harsh peace, Bismarck concluded the lenient Peace of Prague. By the treaty's terms, Austria lost no territory other than Venetia, which was ceded to Prussia's ally Italy. Austria agreed to the dissolution of the German Confederation and surrendered its rights in Schleswig and Holstein to Prussia, which then annexed those two provinces. Finally Austria recognized Bismarck's new creation, the North German Confederation, a Prussian-controlled union of the north German states.

Bismarck dealt more harshly with Austria's German allies. Hanover, Hesse-Cassel, Nassau, and Frankfurt were annexed to Prussia, thereby giving Prussia contiguous territory from Belgium and France to Russia.

All the remaining independent states north of the Main River were incorporated into the North German Confederation. Prussia did not seize the south German states; rather, Bismarck showed them Napoleon III's imprudent demands for a "tip" in the correct belief that this would alarm them and make them more inclined to view Prussia as a protector against a rapacious France. The victory over Austria also helped to quiet parliamentary opposition to Bismarck.

Only France stood in the way of Prussia's unification of Germany. Consequently, Bismarck waited for the opportunity to ensnare France. The wait proved to be a short one. In 1868 a coup deposed Queen Isabella of Spain. In their search for a new monarch, the Spanish approached Prince Leopold von Hohenzollern-Sigmaringen, a distant relative of William I. The thought of any Hohenzollern on the Spanish throne alarmed the French, who saw themselves being encircled by Hohenzollerns. It was this "Spanish Candidacy" that gave Bismarck the opportunity he needed.

At first Leopold refused the Spanish throne, but in June 1870, he changed his mind. The French were furious, and the Duke of Gramont, the French foreign minister, ordered the French envoy to Prussia, Vincent Benedetti, to protest vigorously to William I. The protests were heard, and William, who regarded the entire matter as a family affair rather than an affair of state, forced Leopold to retract his acceptance of the Spanish throne. The French, determined to push their advantage, then demanded that William agree never to allow Leopold to appear as a candidate again. William refused.

The conversations between William and Benedetti, which were polite if not cordial, took place at the Bad Ems resort. William sent a dispatch to Bismarck detailing the nature of these conversations, and this Ems Dispatch proved pivotal in bringing about war between France and Prussia. Bismarck, who had been angered because the king had excluded him from the "family affair," edited the Ems Dispatch to make it appear that the French representative and the Prussian king had traded insults. Occurring at a time of high tension, the release of the Ems Dispatch prompted France to declare war on Prussia on July 20, 1870.

While the rest of Europe stood by, Prussia convincingly defeated France. In early September the fortress city of Sedan fell with the surrender of 120,000 soldiers and Emperor Napoleon III himself. Strasbourg fell at the end of the month, and Metz, with 170,000 defenders, capitulated in October. In January 1871, Paris surrendered.

The Peace of Frankfurt, signed on May 10, 1871, officially ended the

Franco-Prussian War. Prussia did not treat France leniently. By the terms of the peace, Prussia annexed the province of Alsace and about two-fifths of the province of Lorraine. Moreover, France was forced to pay an indemnity of 5 billion francs, and a Prussian army of occupation remained until the indemnity was paid.

Meanwhile, several months earlier, on January 18, 1871, in the Hall of Mirrors at the Versailles palace, Bismarck had proclaimed the German Empire with William I as emperor. In a development that had great symbolic significance for Germany's future, Bismarck barred from William's coronation any representatives from popularly elected assemblies. Germany was now unified, but clearly Prussia ruled the roost.

INTERPRETIVE ESSAY
Eleanor L. Turk

On January 18, 1871, the crowned heads of the twenty-five German states met in the Hall of Mirrors at Versailles to proclaim the second German Empire. For the first time in over a millennium, there was a single German state. What made this event so remarkable was the new nation's immediate power. Even today, after losing two devastating world wars, a smaller and newly unified German state has once again changed the nature of Europe. What is it about this place, these people, this new nation that has exerted such a powerful impact on modern history?

In the twentieth century many new states have emerged in Africa and Asia, mainly as the result of achieving their independence from a former colonial overlord. Despite their *political* independence, however, many of the new states are economically weak and dependent on external guidance and aid for their survival. This was not the case with the German Empire: it unified one of the most rapidly developing economic regions of Europe; its educational system provided a work force capable of producing the most advanced industrial and military technology; its legacy of responsible administrative, military, and bureaucratic service by the aristocracy provided a trained core of leaders; its nationalism and pride in defeating Austria and France infused it with a sense of confidence and optimism. Even at its birth, therefore, the German Empire challenged the superiority of the long-established Great Powers.

Yet within fifty years the German Empire was gone. Germany's pride, power, and prosperity were smashed by a war and a peace treaty that reduced it to second-rate status. This essay will focus on the second German Empire's impact on the German people and on the European power structure, examining how a nation established with such marvelous assets could so fail in modern statecraft, and reflecting on that failure's implications for the German successor states: the Weimar Republic (1919–1933), the Third Reich (1933–1945), the dual republics of the post–World War II era (1945–1990), and the present German Federal Republic.

What was the political nature of the new empire? In the twentieth century, most new states gained their independence as the result of some popular movement. After having done so, they usually underwent a turbulent period of constitution-building during which they tried to find a balance between conflicting public interests and classes. Often there were periods of dictatorship under a charismatic leader, such as Fidel Castro, or militant factional struggles, as in Rwanda.

Germany had, in fact, had a brief period of popular upheaval in 1848. At that time middle-class liberals tried to use the Frankfurt Assembly to bring Germany's many states into a federal union with an elected national legislature and an executive branch headed by the king of Prussia. But that monarch refused to accept a crown "from the gutter," and in 1849 troops dispersed the assembly.

Not only was that popular effort a failure, but its collapse actually strengthened the hereditary rulers. It is important to remember that these were separate states which could shape their own political structures and make their own laws. In the 1850s most of the German rulers reacted to the Revolution of 1848 by dictating reactionary constitutions which countered liberalism's modernizing trends. They restricted the legislatures to merely advisory roles. The upper houses were hereditary or appointed, the lower houses often elected from only the wealthiest group of subjects, as in the case of Prussia, where its complex three-class voting system guaranteed that the wealthy upper class would dominate the electoral process.

Similarly, the German rulers limited the rights of their subjects to form political organizations or to discuss political issues in public. The press was also restrained. If a paper criticized the king or called for resistance to the government, its "responsible editor" could be jailed, all the offensive issues seized and destroyed, and the paper forced to pay a fine. Many of these regulations remained in effect until 1918. Naturally, under these circumstances the popular political movements that did emerge were very cautious.

During the 1860s, the economies of the German states began to modernize. Railroads linked them, and new industrial methods benefited from the region's wealth of coal. Industrialists and businessmen called for economic consolidation, demanding an end to the individual state regulations that restrained the growth of trade and industry. Many of them looked to Prussia to achieve this, since Prussia was the largest and most populous of the German states. Austria, which chaired the German Confederation, tried unsuccessfully to counter this north German rival.

In 1866 a seven-week war separated Prussia from Austria's nominal control. Prussia absorbed some of the German states that had supported Austria, and led the others north of the Main River into the North German Confederation in 1867. Established by treaty, this confederation was the prototype for the future empire. The kingdoms of Bavaria and Württemberg and the duchy of Baden remained outside the new confederation, but signed alliances to help defend it if it were attacked. In a second war of only three months' duration in 1870, the confederation and its south German allies defeated France. The meeting of the German rulers in Louis XIV's chateau at Versailles to proclaim their new state was an arrogant assertion of the old power elite.

The architect of unification was Prince Otto von Bismarck. Trained as a diplomat, he became president of the Prussian ministry (or cabinet) in 1862. He also was the principal author of the new state's constitution. It is important to realize that no constitutional convention of the people was held. Instead, Bismarck's constitution was essentially a treaty among the rulers that left their powers intact. Not surprisingly, it included no bill of rights; the definition of those freedoms was left to the individual states.

The federal government was, therefore, more like a United Nations than a United States. It had a bicameral legislature. The lower house, the Reichstag, consisted of 397 representatives elected through universal male suffrage; Prussia elected 235 of them. The upper house was a Federal Council (Bundesrat) of fifty-eight representatives appointed by the individual kings. They could act only on the instructions of their state government. Prussia had seventeen members, enough to insure that it could veto any measure it did not like. There was no cabinet, only a chancellor who reported to the emperor. Bismarck combined that role with his responsibilities as president of the Prussian ministry and foreign affairs minister in Prussia, and became the most powerful man in the empire. All federal laws had to be approved by both the Reichstag and the Bundesrat, and signed by both the chancellor and the emperor. In effect, the Reichstag had virtually no opportunity to initiate and pass a bill of its own. Clearly, the system was designed to preserve the traditional power elite. The national government was responsible mainly for foreign policy and military policy at first, although it expanded its activities into other areas of public policy. Here, too, the responsibilities emphasized the power of the executive rather than the legislature.

Latent in all this was the traditional elite's strong suspicion that the common man might prove dangerous to their control of the state. Interestingly, Bismarck's constitution also had the effect of conditioning the electorate to believe that the government was hostile and unresponsive. This was clearly so in the empire's early years. In Protestant Prussia, Bismarck launched a campaign against the Roman Catholic Church, the *Kulturkampf*, in an effort to eliminate its influence from education and politics. In 1878 he got the national Reichstag to outlaw the Social Democrat Party and to shut down its press.

Bismarck's campaigns were counterproductive. Although outlawed for twelve years, by 1890 the Social Democrats reemerged with the largest voter support of any German political party; the Catholic Center Party was second in size. However, it is illustrative of the Reichstag's futility that neither of these parties could exercise significant political leadership in the empire. Clearly, universal suffrage alone could not create democracy within that top-heavy German context.

Bismarck and his successors knew that they could not ignore the needs of the public at large, however. One of the curious aspects of this very conservative government was its paternalism, displayed in its willingness to grant some popular demands to limit the growth of political pressure which might threaten the executive's power. For example, in addition to being the first Great Power with universal male suffrage, the German Empire led the way in providing unemployment, accident, and pension insurance. These social advances in many ways compensated the electorate for its lack of any real political power. They did not, however, make the parties any less suspicious of the government.

Another characteristic of the German Empire was the political competition among the states, especially the major southern states and Prussia. This element, which is known as particularism, was reflected in the regional nature of most major political parties. Thus almost all of the Conservative Party's Reichstag delegates came from agricultural Prussia; the Catholic Center Party, whose major interest was protecting the Catholic Church in a Lutheran state, consistently elected delegates from the heavily Catholic Rhineland and Bavaria; and the Marxist Social Democrat Party was strong in the predominantly urban and industrial regions of Saxony and the Ruhr, where it agitated on behalf of the rapidly expanding working class. There were also small Polish and Danish parties representing ethnic minorities in the new state. Thus political parties acted as special interest groups, and since the association laws, until 1899, prohibited them from cooperating with similar parties across state lines, they found it very difficult to compromise on many aspects of national legislation.

Thus, while the German Empire looked like a modern state, with a national legislature and a written constitution, it was still very much a monarchy. Moreover, it was a monarchy at both the state and national level, since all the hereditary rulers remained in place. It is particularly important, therefore, to examine in more detail the responsibility of the king of Prussia, who also served as the German emperor.

When Bismarck created the North German Confederation in 1867, he deliberately cast his lot with the ruling dynasties. He had participated in the unsuccessful 1848 revolution and became convinced that publicists, revolutionaries, and parliamentarians were incapable of establishing a strong government. As the chief cabinet minister of the largest German state, he saw the empire as an extension of dynastic power, especially Prussian power. Thus the king of Prussia was the presiding officer of the Confederation and commander in chief of the Prussian army (and therefore the German army). He presided over the Prussian Military Cabinet, which had sole responsibility for determining military affairs. Even Bismarck was not a member of that body!

As a monarch, the king and emperor did not "belong" to any of the popular political parties; rather, he was "above the parties." So too was Bismarck, as the appointed president of the Prussian ministry and imperial chancellor (which also gave him oversight of diplomatic affairs). Thus none of the state or national political parties could exert any leverage over the executive branch of government. Appointed members of the national government were prohibited from serving in the Reichstag. As a result, the parties often were eager to compromise on principles in order to win specific concessions from the government.

From 1871 until 1888, the Prussian king and emperor, William I, worked comfortably with Bismarck, giving him a free hand in designing government policy. In 1888, William I died and was succeeded by his son, Frederick III, who was terminally ill of throat cancer. After reigning for only ninety-nine days, Frederick died. His successor was his son, William II, a headstrong, difficult young man, infatuated with Prussia's military tradition and determined to exercise royal authority through a "personal regime." He tolerated Bismarck's paternal guidance for only two years before accepting his resignation.

Before examining the reign of William II, however, it is necessary to look at the impact of German unification on the other Great Powers. Germany's lightning-quick victories over Austria and France were enormous shocks to the European power system, which had been in place since Napoleon's defeat in 1815. Prussia's defeat of Austria was so decisive, in fact, that William I wanted to march triumphantly into Vienna and to claim territory as well as victory. Bismarck argued that too great a victory would be dangerous, and that Germany would need Austrian friendship and diplomatic support in the future. Reluctantly, William agreed.

Unlike Germany, Austria was a multinational state, one composed of Germans, Hungarians, and Slavs, unified by the Habsburg dynasty. Following the defeat of Napoleon, the great Austrian statesman Clemens von Metternich designed the German Confederation to keep the smaller German states of central Europe under Habsburg control. This arrangement also helped to balance the relatively small German elite within the Austrian Empire with the large and mixed subject population of Hungarians and Slavs. With the end of the German Confederation, the ruling German minority was forced to grant concessions to the large Hungarian population. A new constitution was written in 1867 (the *Ausgleich*, or equalization) which gave the Hungarians greater autonomy in the regions they dominated. The name of the nation was changed to the Austro-Hungarian Empire as a sign of their new status.

Not surprisingly, the Slavs within Austria were disappointed at being excluded from power. Their exclusion was possible because the Austrian Slavs consisted of a number of cultures smaller and less homogeneous than either the German or the Hungarian. The Slavs were Poles, Bohemians, Ukrainians, and Slovaks in the northeast, Slovenes and Croatians in the southeast. They all wanted at least autonomy, like the Hungarians, but really hoped for independence like the Balkan Slavs, the Bulgarians and Serbs. They received support for their nationalistic aspirations from the growing Pan-Slavic movement, a sort of nationalistic assertion of Slavic greatness headed by the Russian Empire.

Thus the unification of Germany made the Habsburg dynasty vulnerable in its own homeland and forced Austria to orient itself toward the east in an effort to control the restive Slavic population. This brought Austria face to face with Russia, the champion of the Slavs. This was no longer the weak Russia of the Crimean War (1853–1856), but a new, militant Russia determined to modernize and expand.

Of course, any conflict between Austria-Hungary and Russia could spread to endanger the new German Empire. So Bismarck's diplomacy sought at first to emphasize the similarity of the three great empires, their secure conservatism (as contrasted with republican France and parliamentary Britain), and their mutual desire to maintain the status quo on the Continent. He hoped that by joining with his two eastern neighbors he could exercise a moderating influence. Bismarck's efforts culminated in the Three Emperors' League of 1873.

This association began to splinter when the Slavs in Bosnia and Herzegovina rose against Turkish rule in 1875. Russia supported the Slavs against Turkey. Bismarck negotiated some concessions from Turkey, but they were not enough for the unhappy Slavs. The insurrection spread to Bulgaria and Serbia, creating a major diplomatic crisis. In April 1877, in support of Pan-Slavic aspirations, Russia declared war on Turkey.

This changed the nature of the crisis decisively, as Great Britain wanted to preserve Turkey, and Austria certainly did not want any increase in Pan-Slavic agitation so close to its borders. The crisis also exposed the weakness of the Three Emperors' League. By March 1878, Turkey agreed to a devastating peace which so alarmed Britain and Austria that Bismarck intervened again. Assuming the role of disinterested and therefore "honest" broker, he invited representatives of the Great Powers to meet in Berlin in July 1878 to resolve the continuing controversy over the Balkans. The Congress of Berlin not only pushed Russia out of the Turkish regions it had taken, but also gave Austria-Hungary the right to occupy Bosnia and Herzegovina. Nominally a gain for Austria, it only increased the probability of further Slavic unrest.

As tension between Austria-Hungary and Russia grew, Bismarck tried another tack. He proposed a treaty with Austria in order to bolster Austrian foreign policy and, at the same time, warn Russia against stirring up the Slavs. Signed in 1879, the Dual Alliance between Germany and Austria-Hungary was a defensive arrangement. Germany promised to assist Austria-Hungary if it were attacked by Russia, and Austria-Hungary agreed to assist Germany if it were attacked by France. Neither was obligated to act if one of the partners started the war. This alliance inaugurated a whole new power structure in Europe, and eventually changed the nature of European diplomacy. Italy joined and converted the agreement to the Triple Alliance in 1882.

Bismarck also pursued a second strategy, that of projecting the interests of the other Great Powers away from the European continent. England, France, and Russia were eager to expand their imperial holdings; England and France in Africa, and Russia across northern Asia to Siberia. Despite the agitation of the Colonial Society in Germany, Bismarck limited German colonial claims. At the Berlin Conference (1884–1885), he encouraged the exploitation of the Congo and Niger River basins, hoping this adventure would keep his European neighbors, especially France, preoccupied.

France had also suffered from the unification of Germany. By the terms of the 1871 Peace of Frankfurt, which ended the Franco-Prussian War, France ceded Alsace and much of Lorraine, and accepted a German army of occupation in northern France until it paid an indemnity of 5 billion francs. Here, again, Bismarck had argued against territorial annexation, but he was overruled. Thereafter, as he had anticipated, French nationalists thought of nothing but the recovery of the lost territories and of *revanche*, revenge for the humiliating defeat.

In 1888 the last of the German emperors, William II, took power at age twenty-nine. In his youth he identified with his conservative grandfather, William I, and with the Prussian officer corps rather than with his liberal parents. He was a bright young man, quick to learn, eager to be liked, but lacking in common sense and exceptionally vain. As the royal heir he insisted on his way, and succeeding to the throne only increased this tendency. It was inevitable that he would clash with Bismarck, and did so over his royal prerogative to convene a meeting of the cabinet ministers without consulting the minister president. Bismarck, who had often used the threat of resignation to win his way, was shocked when the young monarch accepted it in 1890 and set about establishing a "personal regime."

It is at this point that the true weakness of Bismarck's approach to German unification appears. There were no checks and balances within either the Prussian or the imperial governments. As long as an astute figure like Bismarck exercised authority, there was a general policy of restraint. But young William resented any form of criticism or control. He wanted to bring Germany to its place in the sun. As the ruling emperor and the grandson of Queen Victoria of Great Britain, he was eager to claim his due place in the ranks of mighty rulers. Believing that his authority came from God, he saw no reason why he should not fully act the role of emperor and king. Eliminating Bismarck was just the first step: there was no way that either the Federal Council or the Reichstag could contain his energy and ambition.

William II's reign was productive yet turbulent. Thanks to unification, Germany's economy grew rapidly. Between 1871 and 1910, its population increased from 41 million to 64.9 million, its annual coal production from 29.4 million metric tons to 191.5 million, and its annual pig iron production from 2.7 million metric tons to 14.7 million.

At the beginning of his reign, William II hoped to win popular support as the "people's emperor." He called a conference to discuss ways of improving conditions for the working classes. But the political parties still agitated for more power in the Reichstag, and he soon became disillusioned with them. In 1894 he urged the government to introduce a law that would further restrict the rights of political parties and organizations. The Reichstag defeated the measure, and the distrust between the executive and the popularly elected legislature remained a significant feature of the reign.

There was no way to restrain this erratic, headstrong young ruler. Bismarck's successors tried various tactics. General Leo von Caprivi (1890–1894) tried to maneuver around the Prussian ministry and was fired. Prince Chlodwig Hohenlohe-Schillingsfürst (1894–1900) tried to stall implementation of the emperor's orders long enough to get him to change his mind. Prince Bernhard von Bülow (1900–1909) simply gave in, and wrote memoirs afterward shifting the blame for doing so. Criticism in the Reichstag and the press grew, but to no avail.

The closest they came to restraining William was in 1908, following the publication of an interview he gave to the British *Daily Telegraph*, claiming to have given Great Britain the military strategy for winning the Boer War (1899–1902). The British public generally laughed, but the German public was outraged. Criticism in the Reichstag was outspoken to the point of suggesting that William be deposed. William had a mild breakdown due to stress, and was somewhat inhibited thereafter; but his estrangement from the public only increased.

On the diplomatic scene, William II was determined to conduct a *Weltpolitik*, a "world policy" which would establish Germany as a global power. He reversed Bismarck's strategy of avoiding a challenge to the other powers. He launched a major building program to create a powerful, modern German navy. This immediately alarmed Britain and set off an arms race. He supported the demands of the Colonial Society and engaged in efforts to build a colonial empire. There he confronted France and Britain, driving them into a diplomatic partnership. He thought the Russians inferior and ended military and diplomatic arrangements with that empire, although he used personal correspondence to tell his cousin, Tsar Nicholas II, how to rule.

The image of the satisfied state, which Bismarck had so carefully constructed for the new empire, dissolved in a series of diplomatic crises. In 1896, without consulting his diplomats, William sent off the "Kruger Telegram" to congratulate the Boer (Dutch) president of the Transvaal on repulsing the Jameson Raid. The British, who had sponsored the raid, were outraged. In 1897 he sent forces to occupy Kiaochow on the China coast. The following year Germany secured the rights to build the Turkish railroads. Combined with the first major appropriation (1898) to build the German navy, these actions alarmed the other powers.

It is not surprising, therefore, that they combined in an effort to thwart further German expansion. France secured agreements with Russia to collaborate on military planning. This laid the foundation for the Dual Entente. France then settled its colonial differences with England, and in 1907 convinced Russia and England to agree on spheres of influence in Afghanistan and Persia. This facilitated the Triple Entente, which completed the division of Europe into two alliance systems. The Entente was tested in 1905 and again in 1911, when Germany attempted to use gunboat diplomacy to gain entry into Morocco. The conferences called to resolve the Moroccan crises resulted in resounding diplomatic defeats for Germany.

The final crisis occurred in Austria-Hungary, where Slavic nationalism led to the assassination of Archduke Franz Ferdinand, the heir to the throne, in Sarajevo in June 1914. Austria accused Serbia of setting the assassin to his task and wanted to declare war on its irritating little neighbor. Austria knew that Russia would act to protect its fellow Slavs, and therefore sent an inquiry to Germany to ask for its support. The inquiry went to William II, who, acting as commander in chief—and therefore not required to consult the civilian government—assured his ally that Germany was prepared to live up to its obligations. This "blank check" hastened the outbreak of World War I. In a matter of weeks Russia mobilized, and Germany invaded France in order to defeat it quickly and thereby avoid a two-front war.

Thus the way Germany was unified can be linked directly to the outbreak of World War I. The expulsion of Austria from central Europe made it vulnerable to Slavic nationalism on its eastern frontier. The preservation of monarchial independence from civilian control facilitated William's brash and abrasive diplomacy and opened the way for him to issue the "blank check".

In retrospect, it is clear that the German Empire of 1871–1918 was not so much a unification of Germany as a collection of the German states into one government. The monarchs were never fully unified with their subjects, at either the local or national level. That political reality, together with particularism and ineffective political parties, prevented the development of the democratic process in Germany. After the emperor abdicated and the Social Democrats proclaimed the German Republic in 1918, they inherited all the distrust the empire had generated. The German nation threatened to fall apart as communists rebelled in Berlin and Bavaria, and the Rhineland declared itself a separate republic. The situation was so turbulent that the newly elected National Assembly left Berlin for the city of Weimar in order to write a constitution for the new republic.

Even though the Weimar constitution was drawn up by popularly elected representatives and was one of the most democratic ever written, it could not teach the German people how to govern themselves. After nearly fifty years, the German Empire had accustomed the electorate to governmental paternalism, to political parties based on special interests, and to suspicion of popular democracy. By signing the draconic Treaty of Versailles, the Social Democrat government, rather than the general staff and the emperor, accepted blame for defeat in World War I. In fact, the many political disturbances following the defeat forced the Social Democrats to go hat in hand to the generals to ask their help in defending the infant republic.

Germany remained unified after World War I, but the war, which devastated its economy, the peace treaty, which humiliated its nationalism, and the Great Depression all engendered devastating national crises. The rise of Adolf Hitler and the establishment of the Nazi dictatorship must be analyzed against that background. Once in power, Hitler imposed an authoritarian regime infinitely more extreme than that created by either Bismarck or William II, and equally beyond the reach of the populace. His expansive diplomacy, absorbing the German-speaking peoples of Austria and Czechoslovakia, was a grotesque exaggeration of German nationalism. The Nazi defeat in World War II inevitably led to the end of "rule from above" in Germany.

Ironically, the victorious allies accomplished this by redividing Germany following World War II. Yet their own Great Power polarization during the Cold War forced them to reconsider the German question. The United States, Great Britain, and France used their occupation of western Germany to restrain and retrain Germans into a tradition of peaceful self-government.

The fall of the Berlin Wall on November 9, 1989, exactly seventy-one years to the day after Emperor William II's abdication, marked the beginning of Germany's reunification in the German Federal Republic. It was achieved, without a shot being fired, by the German people themselves. Only the future can tell whether this, at last, fulfills the high hopes of the 1848 revolutionaries for a peaceful union of the German-speaking peoples.

SELECTED BIBLIOGRAPHY

Bismarck, Otto von. *Reflections and Reminiscences*. Translated by A. J. Butler. 2 vols. New York: Howard Fertig, 1966. The history and analysis of German unification as Bismarck wanted us to understand it. Subsequent historians have not always agreed with him.

Böhme, Helmut, ed. *The Foundation of the German Empire: Select Documents*. Translated by Agatha Ramm. London: Oxford University Press, 1971. Primary source materials dealing with unification; particularly strong on economic matters.

Clapham, J. H. *The Economic Development of France and Germany, 1814–1914*. 4th ed. Cambridge: Cambridge University Press, 1936. This comparative study helps to explain why France lost the race to become the great continental power of the nineteenth century.

Craig, Gordon. *Germany, 1866–1945*. New York: Oxford University Press, 1978. A sweeping study of the impact of German unification on both the German people and the European continent.

———. *The Politics of the Prussian Army, 1640–1945*. New York: Oxford University Press, 1955. Careful examination of the Prussian military in its wider historical role, especially its importance in German unification.

Crankshaw, Edward. *Bismarck*. New York: Viking Press, 1981. Exceptionally well-written biography that concentrates on Bismarck's role in creating a unified Germany under Prussian control.

Eyck, Erich. *Bismarck and the German Empire*. 2nd ed. London: Allen and Unwin, 1958. A masterful one-volume analysis by a liberal German historian who grudgingly admired the Iron Chancellor.

Gall, Lothar. *Bismarck, the White Revolutionary*. Translated by J. A. Underwood. 2 vols. London: Allen and Unwin, 1986. Well-researched but controversial study argues that in pursuing personal power and ultra-conservative objectives Bismarck actually accelerated the process of change or modernization in Germany.

Hamerow, Theodore S. *Restoration, Revolution, Reaction: Economics and Politics in Germany, 1815–1871*. Princeton, NJ: Princeton University Press, 1958. An expert, thoughtful, and very readable classic by an outstanding American historian of Germany.

———. *The Social Foundations of German Unification, 1858–1871*. Princeton, NJ: Princeton University Press, 1969. A very careful analysis of the sociopolitical conditions in the German-speaking lands during the unification period.

Howard, Michael E. *The Franco-Prussian War.* New York: Macmillan, 1961. The definitive study of the war that brought German unification.

Langer, William L. *European Alliances and Alignments, 1871–1890.* 2nd ed. New York: Knopf, 1959. A prominent diplomatic historian details the complex web of diplomacy woven by Bismarck to reassure Europe that the new German Empire was peaceful and would not disturb the balance of power in Europe.

Medlicott, W. N. *Bismarck and Modern Germany.* New York: Harper and Row, 1965. A short, readable biography of Bismarck including an analysis of his political career.

Mosse, W. E. *The European Powers and the German Question, 1848–1871.* Cambridge: Cambridge University Press, 1958. A masterful analytic narrative by one of the top modern diplomatic historians.

Palmer, Alan. *Bismarck.* London: Weidenfeld and Nicolson, 1976. A popular, well-written biography of the Iron Chancellor.

Pflanze, Otto. *Bismarck and the Development of Germany.* 3 vols. Princeton, NJ: Princeton University Press, 1990. The definitive English-language biography of Bismarck, his life, and his times.

Simon, Walter M. *Germany in the Age of Bismarck.* New York: Barnes and Noble, 1968. The process of German unification is discussed in a thoughtful and clear manner.

Steefel, Lawrence D. *Bismarck, the Hohenzollern Candidacy, and the Origins of the Franco-German War of 1870.* Cambridge, MA: Harvard University Press, 1962. The best work on the complex issue that Bismarck ultimately used to complete his unification of Germany.

Stern, Fritz. *Gold and Iron: Bismarck, Bleichroder, and the Building of the German Empire.* New York: Knopf, 1977. This thick but readable work shows how Bismarck courted financial interest to build the economy of the new German Empire.

Sybel, Heinrich von. *The Founding of the German Empire by William I.* Translated by Marshall Livingston Perrin. 7 vols. New York: T. Y. Crowell, 1890–1898. An Austrian nationalist historian discusses German unification from the perspective of the losing side.

Taylor, A.J.P. *Bismarck: The Man and the Statesman.* New York: Knopf, 1955. Fascinating critical biography by an outstanding British historian who notes Bismarck's importance for Germany in the twentieth century as well as the nineteenth.

9

Marxism and the Rise of Socialism, 1848–1883

INTRODUCTION

Modern socialism greatly influenced the course of nineteenth- and twentieth-century history. Although modern socialism's precursors first appeared during the French Revolution, its real father was Karl Marx, who crafted a doctrinaire, allegedly scientific socialism that attracted numerous dedicated followers.

One of the earliest instances of the class-conscious behavior that came to characterize modern socialism occurred in 1796 when Gracchus Babeuf organized a conspiracy against the bourgeois government that ruled France. The plot was discovered and Babeuf was executed; but Philippe Buonarroti, one of the conspirators, escaped and spent the rest of his life agitating for a political revolution in order to solve the social problems inherent in capitalism.

Although less radical than either Babeuf or Buonarroti, Henri, the count of Saint-Simon, was another forerunner of Marx. Even though Saint-Simon was an aristocrat, he fought in the American Revolution and sympathized with some aspects of the French Revolution. Saint-Simon envisioned an economy and society that would be planned and directed by experts, or technocrats, who would stand above class conflict. The

Karl Marx (1818–1883), the "father of modern socialism." Although Marx was difficult to get along with, his critique of capitalism and the socialist solutions he proposed attracted a dedicated following. (Reproduced from the Collections of the Library of Congress)

objective would not be the accumulation of private wealth, but rather the creation of a high level of prosperity that would be shared by all. This prophet of a planned economy that would include public ownership of at least some of the means of production never directly condemned the institution of private property, even though he found it inefficient and a source of conflict. However, his followers were not so restrained; they attacked private property as the source of undeserved wealth for the lazy and recommended its abolition as a way to end man's exploitation of man.

Robert Owen was another early pioneer of at least semi-socialistic thought. Owen started as a worker in a textile factory that he later managed and owned. He was appalled by the prevailing conditions for factory workers, and converted his own holdings into model communities. He urged the establishment of additional model communities featuring a balance between agrarian and industrial production. Owen would place these communities in a rural setting and have them be self-sufficient. Those who worked and lived in the communities would jointly own and manage them. Owen founded his most important community at New Harmony, Indiana, in 1825, but it failed three years later.

The Frenchman Charles Fourier also anticipated Marx. Fourier concluded that a modern, urban, industrial society based on the pursuit of individual wealth destroyed the human spirit. Consequently, in order to allow man to achieve the greatest degree of happiness, he proposed that all society be divided into small units, or communities, called phalansteries. The typical phalanstery would be located in a rural area and would be virtually self-sufficient. All members of the phalanstery would work in harmony, shifting tasks frequently to avoid boredom. Fourier believed that mutual cooperation would result in the greatest good for the greatest number.

Although the precursors of Marxist socialism proposed different programs, they all believed that competition for private gain harmed society. Furthermore, they all believed that it was not only possible but also imperative for the good of mankind to reform society according to the principles of cooperation and harmony. However, it was Karl Marx who provided a more compelling analysis of the problem and suggested more practical measures to achieve the goals of the early socialists.

Karl Marx was born in 1818 in the Rhineland town of Trier. His family was Jewish, although Marx became a militant atheist. Marx studied at the universities of Bonn and Berlin, and while at the latter came under the influence of that era's most important philosopher, G.W.F. Hegel.

Unable to find an academic position after receiving his doctoral degree in 1841, Marx drifted into radical journalism. His sharp attacks on Prussian society disturbed the authorities, and in 1843 he was forced to move to Paris, where he met his lifelong collaborator, Friedrich Engels, the son of a German industrialist who owned several factories in England. France expelled Marx in 1847 for his radical activities, and he moved first to Brussels before settling permanently in London.

For many years, Marx and his family lived in poverty, surviving on the meager earnings his writings brought in and on handouts from Engels. Marx spent his days in the British Museum, gathering information for his nonstop attacks on capitalism. In January 1848, on the eve of that year's revolutions, he published *The Communist Manifesto*, a devastating critique of capitalism. In 1867, Marx published the first volume of his opus, *Capital*. Volumes 2 and 3, edited by Engels, appeared in 1885 and 1894, respectively. Ironically, as Marx's fame spread, the royalties he received for his publications increased. By the time of his death in 1883, he and his family had taken up a comfortable bourgeois existence.

Marx's philosophy clearly reflected Hegel's influence. Hegel had argued that history moves according to an eternal rhythm. The dominant institutions of an epoch or period constitute what Hegel called the thesis. As these institutions mature, they generate opposites, which Hegel called the antithesis. Conflict between the thesis and antithesis follows, but what finally emerges is a combination of the two that Hegel referred to as the synthesis. This synthesis then becomes the thesis, and the movement of antithesis, conflict, and synthesis starts all over again, thereby pushing history forward. The entire process is called the dialectic.

Hegel reasoned that God, reflected in the spirit of the age, or *zeitgeist*, controlled the dialectic; but Marx rejected God as the ruling force and instead proclaimed that "the mode of production in material life determines the general character of the social, political, and intellectual processes of life." Consequently, the foundation of Marx's thought is sometimes called dialectical materialism. It is also sometimes called economic determinism because, according to Marx, economics, or the prevailing mode of production, determines everything else in life.

Marx also wrote that "the history of all hitherto existing society is the history of class struggle." Those who do not own the means of production fight fiercely to free themselves from their oppressors, the owners of the means of production, who struggle to retain their dominant position. In ancient times this conflict featured slave against master. During the Middle Ages, serfs challenged lords of the land. In the modern epoch, the struggle pitted the proletariat, or working class, against the bourgeoisie, or the factory owners and their allies.

For Marx, this was an international struggle. Ignoring the strength of modern nationalism, he proclaimed that class divisions were paramount and that workers everywhere had more in common with each other than with their bosses. Marx ends *The Communist Manifesto* with the stirring declaration, "Workers of the world, unite!"

Marx was a keen observer of the Industrial Revolution then reaching maturity in Great Britain. By the mid-1840s, he had developed his concept of "alienation." He said that modern industrial society, with its regimentation, impersonalization, mechanization, and lack of a proprietary interest for the worker, alienated the worker from the workplace and the product he produced.

From the classical economists who preceded him, Marx appropriated the Iron Law of Wages, which said that employers, in order to maximize their profits, would pay their employees as little as possible. Consequently, under capitalism workers would be doomed to receive nothing more than subsistence wages in perpetuity.

Marx also took his theory of surplus value, or labor theory of value, from orthodox economists. According to this theory, a worker creates a product that sells for a greater price than the wage the worker receives for making that product. This difference between price and wage rightfully belongs to the worker. However, the capitalist lays claim to the difference in the form of profit. But the capitalist has done nothing to earn that profit; he has not produced any product through his labor. In short, the capitalist is robbing the worker!

Not only does the possessing class exploit the proletariat at the factory and in the marketplace, but according to Marx it also dominates all other human activity. Marx cited religion to make his point. He maintained that the dominant class created religions in order to pacify the exploited class. Those who controlled the means of production set the prevailing moral standards, hired the priests or pastors, and consciously enhanced the Church's influence for selfish reasons. Frequently, religion promised heavenly rewards for earthly passivity or threatened eternal damnation for the nonconformist. Marx called religion the "opiate of the people," a narcotic to keep the worker drugged and submissive in the face of bourgeois exploitation.

However, in true dialectical fashion Marx pointed out that capitalism contained the seeds of its own destruction. Industrial capitalism demanded that more and more goods be produced. Eventually, the marketplace will become flooded, prices will drop, and the weakest of the bourgeoisie will fail and fall into the ranks of the proletariat. As the ranks of the proletariat swell, there is increasing pressure on an ever smaller number of capitalists. The system itself, which features alternating periods of boom and bust commonly called the business cycle, heightens the pressure as it increases the misery of the proletariat. So too do the wars that result from increased economic competition since it is the children of the working class who will fight and die in these wars.

Marx argues that the misery will become so great that the desperate working class will rise up and overthrow the bourgeoisie. The workers' revolution will be violent, and blood will flow in the streets, but this is necessary for success. While the working class will provide the force for victory, the "vanguard of the proletariat," a group of dedicated socialists—but not necessarily from the working class—will have laid the revolution's groundwork. The vanguard of the proletariat will agitate among the workers and organize them, school them in basic socialist doctrine, indicate the myriad ways they are being exploited, and, finally, point the way to the proletarian revolution.

The revolution's ultimate objective is the destruction of the bourgeoisie and the creation of a classless society. Once this is achieved, the state, the ruling class's traditional instrument of power, will no longer have any reason to exist, and it will wither away. However, this transformation is a major task that cannot be accomplished overnight. During the transformation, it will be necessary to have a "dictatorship of the proletariat" to eradicate all vestiges of bourgeois society and to push the process forward.

Although Marx's strong suit was philosophy, he and Engels tried to move his work from the realm of theory to the realm of practice. In 1864 the First International Working Men's Association, or First International, an ambitious attempt to bring together workers and radicals of all hues from throughout Europe, was established. Although Marx did not create the First International, he delivered its inaugural address and soon dominated it. However, Marx was an incompetent leader. His intolerance and ruthlessness—as much as persecution from fearful governments—killed the International well before Marx's death in 1883. Nevertheless, Marxism gradually emerged as the most popular radical socialist doctrine.

INTERPRETIVE ESSAY
John K. Cox

Several basic observations should be made when discussing Marxism's impact on the nineteenth century. One is that Marxism merged with other radical movements to challenge the traditional European way of life based on church, village, family, and monarchy. Not only Marxism, but other forms of socialism, industrialism, liberalism, and nationalism (to name but a few) emerged to confound the status quo. Another basic observation is that revolutionary socialism's center of gravity gradually moved eastward over the course of the century. At first, most socialist-influenced reform movements appeared in Great Britain and France. After mid-century, Germany, with its well-organized socialist movement, led the way. However, by the end of the century Russia's socialist revolutionaries were poised to capitalize on their country's unaddressed problems and the growing level of discontent. A third general observation is that nineteenth-century socialism was simultaneously a description, or analysis, of social ills, *and* a prescription for social change. Marxism was at once a cry of protest from society's "have-nots" and those who saw themselves as their protectors and an organizing principle.

Although Karl Marx proved himself inept as a political leader, his ideas grew to be very important even during his lifetime. They became even more influential after his death in 1883. The secret of Marxism's importance was its tendency to link itself with various forms of social, political, and ethnic discontent. Thus, Marxism—and the modified versions that followed—played a significant role in many crises. It is important to stress that Marxism must be studied as a collection of various political theories and as an assembly of diverse political and social movements. Indeed, Marx's socialism fragmented almost as soon as it was born. The most famous split pitted "Orthodox" Marxists against "revisionist" Marxists; another key division separating Marxists turned out to be the very same national loyalties which, according to Marx, should have been subservient to the class interests of the international proletariat.

Sometimes gender hindered workers' cooperation. An early feminist who was active in France and England, Flora Tristan, raised important issues about the role of women in capitalist societies. Male workers would never be free, she said, until women were free too. Among other things, she demanded that women who work receive access to child care. In Europe, men sometimes feared women as a cheaper source of labor in a very competitive job market (just as in the United States racial or ethnic prejudice sometimes set workers against one another); but usually husbands in proletarian families encouraged their wives to work because the household needed the additional money to survive. Karl Marx and another German theoretician, August Bebel, wrote on the causes of capitalism's exploitation of women.

Throughout the nineteenth century, the plight of the working class attracted increased attention. The novels of Charles Dickens, Émile Zola, and Upton Sinclair painted a grim picture of industrial life. In Germany, Gerhard Hauptmann's naturalistic dramas confronted audiences with the issue of economic exploitation. In the United States, Jane Addams's *Twenty Years at Hull-House* and Jacob Riis's *How the Other Half Lives* exposed the seamy side of American cities.

Labor activists, socialists, and Marxists eventually banded together to become more effective. The International Working Men's Association, commonly referred to as the First International, existed from 1864 to 1872. Marx attempted to run this organization as an international coordinating body for socialists. After the failure of the Paris Commune in 1871, however, the movement broke up. When it reformed as the Second International in 1889, the participants were organized on a national basis; however, this form greatly handicapped the achievement of socialist objectives. World War I killed the movement because many socialists supported their countries in the war instead of heeding Marx's pronouncement that proletarians have no country. Other major problems resulted from disagreements between Orthodox Marxists and both revisionists and anarchists, sometimes referred to as "right opportunists" and "left opportunists," based on their relative unwillingness or overzealousness to employ violence to change society.

Germany provides a good model for the study of socialism's impact. Ferdinand Lassalle (1825–1864) is emblematic of the early types of socialism in Europe. Although he met both Marx and Engels in 1848, Lassalle remained in essence a gradualist and a romantic. After studying philosophy in Berlin, Lassalle published enough on law, politics, and economics to earn some recognition. In 1863 he founded one of the first unions, the Allgemeiner Deutscher Arbeiterverein (Universal German Workers' Association). The Prussian chancellor, Otto von Bismarck, tried unsuccessfully to use Lassalle to undermine the radical left. Lassalle's basic ideas—suffrage and workers' cooperative associations, which would replace individual competitive companies—did not win him much lasting support among German laborers or their leaders.

Another German who was influenced by Marx was August Bebel (1840–1913). Bebel was a veteran activist who helped lead the German socialist movement after Bismarck outlawed it in 1878. In 1869, he had been one of the co-founders of the Sozialistische Partei Deutschlands (Social Democratic Party). This party, commonly known as the SPD, is still a major force in German politics today. Bebel occupied an intriguing place on the spectrum of Marxist thought. One might classify him as orthodox but not actually revolutionary. That is, Bebel accepted most of the radical rhetoric of European Marxism. He spoke of "revolution" and distanced himself from liberal parties, with which some cooperation on specific issues would have been possible. Yet he devoted many of his efforts to trade union activism instead of forming an elite revolutionary underground. Bebel's followers differed from Lassalle's in being less nationalistic; their parliamentary delegates opposed the loans needed for the Franco-Prussian War, expressed their solidarity with the Communards in Paris, and urged their government not to annex any French territory at the conclusion of the war.

The third socialist who knew Marx and carried his work to the next generation of Germans was Karl Kautsky (1854–1938). Although he never officially led the party, Kautsky helped write the SPD's famous Erfurt Program with Wilhelm Liebknecht in 1891. Kautsky became most famous for opposing the revisionism (evolutionary, as opposed to revolutionary, socialism) of Eduard Bernstein. As editor of the theoretical journal *Die Neue Zeit* (The New Age), Kautsky defended orthodoxy, but he also differed in key ways from more militant activists such as Rosa Luxemburg, Karl Liebknecht (Wilhelm's son), and V. I. Lenin. Kautsky urged workers not to settle for less than a revolution; reforms would, in the final analysis, only serve to strengthen capitalism. But, he insisted, a revolution need not be violent to be thorough and effective. As long as the proletariat came to power by some means, bourgeois class hegemony could be ended.

Eduard Bernstein (1850–1932), more than any other European thinker, embodied the revisionist, or gradualist, Marxist position. Early in his career he was the London correspondent for the party organ, *Vorwärts*

(Forward). In 1898, however, he outlined his differences with Kautsky and other important leaders in a general letter to the SPD. He, of course, saw himself as a true follower of Marx; much of Marx's teaching he accepted whole. But he criticized Marx on issues of timing. In his work *Evolutionary Socialism,* Bernstein stated that the collapse of the capitalist system would not come as soon as Marx had predicted; furthermore, this delay held benefits for workers because, instead of being more and more isolated from wealth and political power, they were actually moving toward these things. Trade unionism, reforms, suffrage, and cooperation with other parties thus became the hallmarks of Marxist revisionism.

The revolutionary scene in France showed splits similar to those in Germany. The main dividing line separated factions led by Jules Guesde (1845–1922) and Jean Jaurès (1859–1914). They disagreed over cooperation with liberal parties, the use of strikes, and faith in voting as a means of changing the country's social system. Though Guesde represented the more orthodox program and opposed what he called the "dead letter" of reform, he was a member of parliament, and he supported France's government in World War I (unlike Lenin, Kautsky, and Luxemburg). Jaurès's followers were sometimes called "possibilists" because of their evolutionary goals. Jaurès, like the earlier Paris Communards, proudly ascribed much value to France's own revolutionary tradition dating back to the late eighteenth century; he regarded this tradition as distinct from—and sometimes in opposition to—Marx's set of revolutionary premises.

The two wings of the French socialist party split in 1879, but reconverged in 1905. Outside this party structure was the more radical figure of Georges Sorel (1847–1922), who favored huge strikes for the workers to seize control of the state and the economy. While this program, known as syndicalism, resembled anarchism, it was supposed to be led by a conspiratorial elite. Still, Sorel did not want to see unions co-opted by any one party because he loathed what he called the "dictatorship of the intellectuals."

Since the French government had strongly opposed the First International, labor unions grew to have considerable strength. Anarchism, whose chief advocate in France was Pierre-Joseph Proudhon, also played an important role. In 1895 the General Confederation of Labor was formed with the aim of preventing any political party from dominating the unions. Eventually this umbrella organization swallowed up many other unions, helping the notion of the mass strike as defined by Sorel to take on an almost mythical significance.

Great Britain found itself in an anomalous situation regarding socialist activism. On the one hand, it had the largest unions in Europe; yet its workers were in many ways the least radical. Britain's first major reformers were the Chartists. They were active from the late 1830s through the 1840s. Their goals did not include the transfer of ownership of the means of production; indeed, they were little concerned with working conditions. Questions of political process dominated their agenda. The Chartists regarded greater representation in Parliament as the first step toward bettering their lot. Thus they sought the introduction of universal male suffrage and the abolition of property criteria for officeholders. Even though many of the movement's leaders were persecuted, most of their desired political changes were eventually enacted. In addition, as Great Britain's industrial development proceeded, the Corn Laws (high tariffs on imported grain) fell in 1846 and the workers' level of physical well-being rose as cheap grain flooded the market.

In the 1890s, British activists not satisfied with the pace of industrial reform gathered in the Fabian Society. It had many famous members, such as the playwright George Bernard Shaw and influential intellectuals Sidney and Beatrice Webb; these thinkers clearly belonged to the evolutionary branch of socialism. The Fabians were gradualists in both their thinking and their tactics. They took their name from a Roman general of the third century B.C., Fabius, who was known as "the Delayer" due to his strategy of defeating the Carthaginians by attrition. The Fabians pressed their concerns on the level of humanitarianism and economic policy. The writings of Lassalle figured prominently in their thinking.

In 1900 Great Britain's Labour Party came into existence. It was a mixture of socialist, Fabian, and liberal elements. In one of its first Parliamentary battles, it overturned the Taff Vale Decision, which had enjoined unions to compensate employers for production losses during strikes.

From the late eighteenth century onward, tsarism in Russia engendered a great deal of opposition, much of it humanitarian or nationalist in nature. Socialism also had a well-developed legacy in Russia before the arrival of Marxism. The tone for many ideological debates in Russia was set by the Slavophile controversy in the first half of the nineteenth century. The Slavophiles saw a need for Russia to change, but they insisted that Russia had to change in specifically Russian ways. They placed great faith in the Russian peasant and eschewed the secular, materialistic, and overly rational ways of western European thinking. The Westerners, on the other hand, urged the adaptation of Western political and economic rights. Publicists and literary critics such as Vissarion Belinsky and Nikolai Chernyshevsky grew increasingly radical, calling for an instrumentalization of literature in the name of fomenting revolution. Meanwhile the émigré Russian intellectual Alexander Herzen, noting the failure of socialist causes in the Revolutions of 1848, advanced a romantic vision of Russia as the noble torchbearer for social progress.

Gradually the Russian radical movement coalesced into two groups: the Marxists, led at first from Switzerland by Georgi Plekhanov, and the Populists (later Socialist Revolutionaries). The former group organized itself into the Emancipation of Labor in 1884 and became the Marxist Social Democratic Labor Party fourteen years later. Plekhanov wrote treatises on the industrialization of the Russian economy and called for a continued increase in production and for an overthrow of tsarism in favor of a bourgeois democracy. These two planks of his platform were considered prerequisites for a second, socialist revolution. This was in many ways an orthodox communist vision; Lenin absorbed much of it, although he would hasten along the historical process and avoid some of Plekhanov's stages. The Populists, who often resorted to terror, and who killed Tsar Alexander II in 1881, thought that Russia could avoid many of the ills of capitalism by returning to its peasant roots in a way the Slavophiles had envisioned.

Also very important in the Russian revolutionary tradition were the anarchists. Very often, anarchists were former Marxists or socialists who had been driven from their parties by persecution or drawn away by the lure of more violent and direct action. The most famous Russian anarchist, Mikhail Bakunin, proved to be a thorn in the side of Marx at international socialist meetings. Anarchists not only rejected the notion of any type of government of the workers after the revolution, but also tended to engage in more indiscriminate violence than communists. Anarchists also wanted to destroy the old regimes of Europe totally, while Marxists wanted to build their new society upon the material foundations of capitalism. Sometimes anarchists are also called "nihilists," indicating that they believe in nothing, whether it be a Marxist's blueprint for a revolution or a liberal's laissez faire. Nonetheless, the conspiratorial tactics and fanatical dedication of revolutionaries like Sergei Nechaev and Petr Tkachev served as models for the Bolsheviks.

The most important Russian Marxist was Vladimir I. Lenin. He was the leader of the Bolshevik faction, which had split in 1903 over tactical questions with another group known as the Mensheviks. By 1905 Lenin's basic doctrinal and political ideas were in place. Lenin, more than any other revolutionary, engineered the Bolshevik Revolution of 1917. Lenin refined Marxism in several significant ways. His ideas not only inspired the Russian revolutionaries to decisive action, they also prepared the theoretical way for a socialist revolution in a country that was far from having the kind of industrial system that Marx himself had singled out for potential proletarian uprisings.

One of Lenin's most important ideas called for a "dictatorship of the proletariat" after the socialist revolution. This autocratic government would be of limited duration, but it was necessary to secure the gains of the revolution. Lenin also demanded the creation of a vanguard party composed of a revolutionary elite which would operate underground in a highly disciplined, conspiratorial, and almost certainly violent fashion, to raise the consciousness of the masses. Marx had been vague in his original writings on the nature of the transition from old regime to socialist rule; Lenin filled in the gaps by pinpointing the party as the agency of change.

Another key idea of Lenin's concerned the revolutionary nature of the peasantry. He grouped industrial workers and peasants together as "working people," thereby multiplying the number of potentially revolutionary individuals in Russia. Finally, at the level of global economics, Lenin defended the appearance of a socialist revolution in Russia by asserting that his country already was a capitalist country. Even though Russia did not have, proportionally, as large an industrial base or working class as Germany, France, and England, it was the "weak link" in the capitalist chain that had recently brought much of Africa and Asia into its imperialist orbit. The workers of western Europe were sharing in the spoils of the European exploitation of other continents; this imported wealth was gradually raising the workers' standard of living and preventing them from enacting truly revolutionary plans. Along with other radical Marxists such as Kautsky, Lenin asserted that settling for better working conditions and pay raises was just blind "opportunism," which ultimately would only strengthen the hand of the bourgeoisie. Russia, also a victim of foreign exploitation, was thus the logical choice for a revolution.

Lenin's ideas represent a crucial development in Marxist thought and the rise of socialism. They helped the Bolsheviks come to power in what was the first great socialist revolution. These ideas were also quite controversial among many other Marxists. Debate over their validity—and their often disastrous results—continues to this day.

The revolutionary movement in Russia culminated in triumph for Lenin's Bolsheviks. This stunning achievement—buttressed by the reunification of socialist Russia with the other lands of the former tsarist empire in the Union of Soviet Socialist Republics (USSR)—was made more concrete by the collectivization and industrialization campaigns of the next Soviet leader, Josef Stalin. Stalin considered himself a true disciple of Lenin, who in turn considered himself a true disciple of Marx. The result of this successful revolution, then, was the establishment of a claim to orthodoxy by one specific group of Marxists; after 1917, avowedly pro-Soviet communist parties formed in many countries. This stands in contrast to the earlier, mid-nineteenth-century appreciation of Marx as one of many important thinkers. The scope, duration, and perceived threat of the Soviet experiment led many in the West to associate Marxism only with Leninism. To do so, however, is to commit the intellectual disservice of ignoring the numerous competing strands of Marxist thought that influenced European society in a variety of ways.

In the world beyond the major industrialized states of Europe, Marxism had less of an impact in the nineteenth century than it would have in the twentieth. For example, the decolonization struggles that swept Africa and Asia after World War II were bound up with—though by no means determined by—Marxist movements of various kinds. In the United States, Marxism played a secondary role in the history of the late nineteenth-century labor movement. Various kinds of socialist thought, along with anarchism, only occasionally appeared in American labor's strikes, organizing actions, and petitions for decent working conditions. However, the American trade union movement suffered when it was tarred with the labels "communist" and "full of foreigners."

Although the United States was heavily industrialized by 1900, organized labor did not play a major role in its politics. The country's largest labor organization, the American Federation of Labor (AFL), founded by Samuel Gompers in 1886, never reached a membership comprising even 20 percent of the work force because it excluded unskilled workers. Not until 1935 did assembly-line workers from mass-production industries such as automotives and textiles form an effective organization in the Congress of Industrial Organizations (CIO). Racial tensions also harmed the labor movement.

Another handicap that American unions faced was a lack of agreement among both leaders and rank-and-file workers over whether or not to use strikes to achieve political ends. In the 1870s, unrest in northeastern Pennsylvania's coal mines had led to violent confrontations involving Irish workers known as the "Molly Maguires." Nineteen of the strikers were executed. In the following decade, the experience of the Knights of Labor, founded in 1869, is instructional. Although the union's leadership decried strikes, its members participated in some major work stoppages, causing the Knights to lose strength throughout the 1880s as concern grew that strikes lent too radical an image. The Chicago Haymarket Riot of 1886, in which several policemen and civilians were killed, added to the public fear of strikes. When the government discovered and executed anarchists and other radicals in the rioters' leadership, this fear intensified, and when some of the radicals were revealed to have belonged to the Knights, the union died.

Another radical American group, the International Workers of the World (IWW), or "Wobblies," was active in the years before World War I. The IWW generated a dramatic agenda, including workers' ownership of certain means of production, and it was involved in a series of confrontational strikes. The IWW included the unskilled workers that the AFL had rejected; it also opposed American participation in World War I, as did some European workers' groups. During and after the war, the U.S. government cracked down on the IWW, and the IWW's principal leader, William D. "Big Bill" Haywood, eventually fled to the Soviet Union.

Most groups, however, such as the AFL, disavowed any political objectives; their "pure and simple" goals had to do with working conditions and pay. The overwhelming majority of American unions were nonviolent, whether or not they endorsed a political agenda or the use of the strike. Famous figures such as Mother Jones (Mary Harris Jones, 1830–1930) agitated across the country, especially in coal-mining states like West Virginia, for better working conditions and for a more general appreciation of the dignity of working people.

In terms of organized socialist political activity, Daniel DeLeon (1852–1914) established the Socialist Labor Party in 1877. He stressed the importance of making common cause with labor unions, but warned against the false solution of mere cosmetic changes in working conditions. DeLeon's vision was in some ways more radical than that of the other famous American socialist, Eugene Victor Debs (1855–1926). Debs founded the Social Democratic Party in 1898 and ran five times for the presidency of the United States, finishing once with 6 percent of the vote.

Socialists won few elections in the United States, with the notable exception of the city of Milwaukee.

On a general level, the importance of Marxism cannot be denied. Among other things, Marxism functioned as a means of expression—in terms of analysis, critique, and political action—for persons concerned with the lives of workers in industrial societies. Marxism also served as a political ideology for various revolutionary groups. In this context, the impact of Marxism varied greatly from country to country, depending upon local conditions. Some Marxist groups disappeared or were suppressed, while others, such as the Bolsheviks in Russia, took power.

Marxism interacted with many other ideologies including feminism, anarchism, and nationalism. Even liberal capitalism, which endorsed a gradual amelioration of the workers' plight and provided for a rise in the overall standard of living by the end of the nineteenth century, was in part a response to Marxist and socialist criticism. This intellectual cross-fertilization created the modern political landscape in Europe and North America. Moreover, Marxism was never a unified movement or even a precise system of thought. Just as Marx's intellectual forebears such as the utopian socialists embraced a variety of views, so did the people who called themselves (or bore the label) Marxists. Although one may say that Marxism as a political philosophy is roughly synonymous with "scientific socialism" or "communism," this is a loose equation, and its terms represent only categories of thought from an earlier, changing Europe that was a maelstrom of conflicting social groups and competing ideas.

Finally, it is only with difficulty that one can reckon Marxism as successful in the nineteenth century, since no communist parties came to power until 1917. Marx certainly underestimated the endurance and adaptability of capitalist systems, which were themselves quite varied; other thinkers like Bernstein ultimately conceived of the political realities of western Europe more realistically than Marx. Cooperative movements among farmers and workers existed in France, England, Germany, and other countries well before Marxism became entrenched; and these movements sometimes had an impact on citizens' daily lives. Nevertheless, when one considers the vast amount of social reform, suffrage expansion, and worker protection legislation that was enacted over the century, it is apparent that the Marxists (along with other socialists, reformers, and union organizers) had a major impact on the face of European society.

Other important effects of Marxism would have to wait for the twentieth century. Ultimately some of them would be just as significant as the results of nineteenth-century Marxism: the growth of fascism in reaction to Marxism; the use of Marxism in the decolonizing world after World War II as a tool for state-building and economic development rather than as a redistributive measure in the European tradition; the extension of Marx's ideas on workers' alienation (being separated from finished products and profits) to the atomizing notion of "contestation," in which all forms of authority are challenged as "hegemonic."

SELECTED BIBLIOGRAPHY

Anderson, Thornton. *Masters of Russian Marxism.* New York: Appleton-Century-Crofts, 1963. A study of the writings of Plekhanov, Lenin, Martov, Kollontai, Trotsky, and other Russian communists.

Avrich, Paul. *Anarchist Portraits.* Princeton, NJ: Princeton University Press, 1988. Covers the prominent figures in this radical, often violent, movement running parallel to Marxism.

Bernstein, Eduard. *Evolutionary Socialism: A Criticism and Affirmation.* Translated by Edith C. Harvey. New York: Schocken, 1961. The manifesto of the European Marxists who were labeled "opportunists" by Kautsky and Lenin, but who placed their faith in peaceful political change as a route to a better society.

Burns, Emile, ed. *The Marxist Reader: The Most Significant and Enduring Works of Marxism.* New York: Avenel Books, 1982. A solid anthology, mostly of Marx and Engels's works, that includes long excerpts from *Das Kapital* and Lenin's *The Teachings of Karl Marx.*

Carr, E. H. *Studies in Revolution.* New York: Grosset and Dunlap, 1964. Essays on Russian thinkers such as Herzen, Plekhanov, and Lenin, as well as Marx and Lassalle.

Freedman, Robert, ed. *Marxist Social Thought.* New York: Harcourt, Brace and World, 1968. A first-rate exposition of Marx's ideas, from the materialist conception of history to the role of the state.

Fried, Albert, and Ronald Sanders, eds. *Socialist Thought: A Documentary History.* New York: Doubleday, 1964. A thorough anthology beginning with the political writings of Morelly and Rousseau, moving through the utopian socialists, anarchists, and German philosophers and revisionists to the Bolsheviks.

Gleason, Abbott. *Young Russia: The Genesis of Russian Radicalism in the 1860's.* New York: Viking, 1980. A well-written and lively discussion of Russian journalists, students, philosophers, and terrorists.

Gombin, Richard. *The Origins of Modern Leftism.* Translated by Michael K. Perl. Baltimore: Penguin Books, 1975. An intriguing study of the tumultuous expansion of Marxist thought.

Gorman, Robert A., ed. *Biographical Dictionary of Marxism.* Westport, CT: Greenwood Press, 1986. An excellent basic resource analyzing main Marxist ideas and providing background to key events.

Heer, Friedrich. *Europe, Mother of Revolutions.* Translated by Charles Kessler and Jennetta Adcock. New York: Praeger, 1972. A complex exposition of German, French, and Russian philosophy and political ideology in the nineteenth century.

Herzen, Alexander. *My Past and Thoughts: The Memoirs of Alexander Herzen.* Translated by Constance Garnett. Revised by Humphrey Higgins. Introduction by Isaiah Berlin. 4 vols. New York: Knopf, 1968. Traces the evolution of the thought of one of Russia's earliest non-Marxist socialists.

Hook, Sidney. *Marx and the Marxists: The Ambiguous Legacy.* Princeton, NJ: Van Nostrand, 1955. A handy summation of main trends and events. Includes an appendix of excerpts from key theoretical works.

Hughes, H. Stuart. *Consciousness and Society: The Reorientation of European Social Thought, 1890–1930.* New York: Random House, 1958. A classic study that places Marx, Sorel, and other thinkers in a broader intellectual context.

Judt, Tony. *Marxism and the French Left: Studies on Labour and Politics in France, 1830–1981.* Oxford: Oxford University Press, 1986. A wide-ranging selection of essays covering the interrelationship between labor movements and socialist and communist parties.

Kolakowski, Leszek. *Main Currents of Marxism: Its Rise, Growth, and Dissolution.* Translated by P. S. Falla. 3 vols. Oxford: Clarendon Press, 1978. A monumental work of intellectual history which covers both nineteenth- and twentieth-century currents.

Laidler, Harry W. *History of Socialism: A Comparative Survey of Socialism, Communism, Trade Unionism, Cooperation, Utopianism, and Other Systems of Reform and Reconstruction.* New York: Thomas Y. Crowell, 1968. A massive work that includes synopses of dozens of famous theoretical works as well as election results and biographical information.

Landauer, Carl. *European Socialism: A History of Ideas and Movements from the Industrial Revolution to Hitler's Seizure of Power.* In collaboration with Elizabeth Kridl Valkenier and Hilde Stein Landauer. 2 vols. Berkeley: University of California Press, 1960. Volume 1 covers the socialist world up until World War I.

Lichtheim, George. *Marxism: An Historical and Critical Study.* New York: Columbia University Press, 1982. Covers the growth of revisionism and Marx's critiques of bourgeois society.

MacKenzie, Norman, and Jeanne MacKenzie. *The Fabians.* New York: Simon and Schuster, 1977. One of the standard works on this British socialist movement.

McClellan, David. *Marxism after Marx: An Introduction.* Boston: Houghton Mifflin, 1979. An excellent survey with important chapters on early Marxism, Engels's contribution, and revisionism. Includes a number of first-rate bibliographies.

Mendel, Arthur P. *Essential Works of Marxism.* New York: Bantam, 1961. A valuable classroom edition containing the complete *Communist Manifesto* and other works by Engels and Lenin.

Pomper, Philip. *The Russian Revolutionary Intelligentsia*. Arlington Heights, IL: Harlan Davidson, 1970. A solid study of the origins and development of the Russian underground.

Schapiro, J. Salwyn. *Movements of Social Dissent in Modern Europe*. Princeton, NJ: D. Van Nostrand, 1962. Readings and commentaries on non-Marxist reformers and revolutionaries from William Godwin to Mikhail Bakunin.

Tucker, Robert C., ed. *The Marx-Engels Reader*. New York: W. W. Norton, 1972. A thorough anthology of writings that includes several specific commentaries on events in Europe, such as Napoleon III's accession to power and imperialism in India.

THE REAL TROUBLE WILL COME WITH THE "WAKE."

The imperial countries fight over the carcass of China. After 1870, the Western states engaged in a wild scramble to build empires throughout the globe. (Reproduced from the Collections of the Library of Congress)

10

Imperialism, 1870–1900

INTRODUCTION

Imperialism is the policy of extending a nation's authority by territorial acquisition or by the establishment of economic and political hegemony over other nations. Since at least the middle of the fifteenth century, the Western world has been expanding; but beginning in the late nineteenth century it went on an imperialistic binge that brought virtually the entire globe under its control.

During the early centuries of Western expansion, explorers, merchants, and priests traversed the globe. In the Americas, they established huge colonial empires at the expense of the native inhabitants. Spain, Portugal, England, and France became Europe's leading colonial powers. However, by the end of the third decade of the nineteenth century, European empires in America had practically disappeared after colonists transplanted to the New World successfully rose in rebellion against their mother countries. Only Great Britain retained an American empire worthy of the name, despite losing its most important North American colony.

However, one should keep in mind that except in the New World, the Europeans were not determined to build empires; rather, they concentrated on commerce. They were quite content simply to trade profitably with the natives. The attraction for Europeans was in securing native products, not in possessing the natives and their lands.

For much of the nineteenth century, Europe focused its energies on nation-building, the Industrial Revolution, and the conflict between liberalism and conservatism. For many nations, colonial expansion was little more than an afterthought, although at this time France moved into Algeria, the Netherlands extended its influence over Java to other Indonesian islands, Britain tightened its grip on India, and several Western states "opened" Japan and began to penetrate China.

However, after 1870 the Western world once again expanded, this time swooping down upon the globe and figuratively devouring it. Mere trading agreements no longer sufficed; the West had to possess, or at the very least dominate, every earthly nook and cranny whether it held any real value or not. Westerners moved in and took over. They invested heavily in their colonies; they occasionally built an impressive infrastructure ranging from schools to railroads; in some instances, they came to live there; and they imposed their ideas, values, and systems (and tried to impose their religion) without any regard for the sensibilities of the native peoples. They ruled either directly or through the native elite, who were either coerced or co-opted into acting on behalf of the white man.

What explains this sudden and unexpected development? Several factors coalesced to provide the impetus for imperialism, but certainly economic considerations figured prominently. In an era of rapid industrialization, colonies promised inexpensive raw materials, cheap labor, and guaranteed markets. Political considerations also counted. As rivalries among European states intensified, many countries acquired colonies to validate their claims to greatness. Christianity, an aggressive religion in that it actively seeks converts, spurred on colonial conquest. Finally, many in the Western world were convinced of Western Civilization's superiority and were determined to bring its benefits to the peoples of the non-Western world.

Whatever imperialism's motives, its success rested on the Western world's technological and organizational predominance, particularly its efficient military formations, which included gunboats, modern rifles, and Maxim, or machine, guns. Against these armaments, the nonwhites of the world could not hope to prevail. At the Battle of Omdurman, fought in the Sudan in 1898, the British slaughtered approximately 11,000 Muslim tribesmen while losing 28 of their own soldiers.

Late nineteenth-century imperialism was a global phenomenon. In

Latin America, widespread economic penetration, especially by the United States, undercut the political independence of that region's nations. In 1898 the United States made war on Spain and seized what remained of that country's American empire. The United States annexed Puerto Rico and controlled a nominally independent Cuba. A few years later, the United States instigated a successful revolution in Panama, a province of Colombia. Subsequently, the United States built a transoceanic canal there and effectively established a protectorate over Panama.

In the Middle East, Europe's imperial powers greedily eyed the declining Ottoman Empire. While Russia and Austria-Hungary nibbled away at Turkey in Europe, Great Britain and France concentrated on the Mediterranean, where Egypt proved to be the most inviting target. Earlier in the century, both Britain and France had encouraged the pasha of Egypt, who was subordinate to Turkish rule, to act independently; after mid-century, the Egyptian ruler virtually ignored Constantinople. Borrowing heavily to modernize Egypt, the pasha Ismail fell into debt to the Europeans. In order to meet his obligations, Ismail sold his shares in the Suez Canal to Great Britain in 1875. Nevertheless, by 1879 Ismail was bankrupt, and a consortium of European creditors assumed control of Egypt's finances. When angry Egyptian army officers threatened to repudiate Egypt's debt, Britain bombarded Alexandria and occupied the country, leaving only after World War II. At about the same time, France followed a similar pattern to gain control over Tunisia.

Imperialism's most spectacular triumph occurred in black Africa, or that portion of the continent situated south of the Sahara Desert. In 1875 only about 10 percent of sub-Saharan Africa was subject to European rule; by 1895 almost all of black Africa had succumbed to the imperialists. Great Britain, France, and Germany led the imperial charge.

Beginning in the 1870s, Europeans moved inland from their coastal trading facilities. France seized much of West Africa and then moved eastward in order to create a huge French empire stretching from the Atlantic to the Indian Ocean. The British moved south from their stronghold in Egypt and north from the Cape Colony, seeking a belt of colonies running north-south that would enable them to construct a Cape to Cairo railroad. Germany showed little interest in colonies until the mid-1880s; but from that time forward it became very active in Africa, adding Togo, the Cameroons, Southwest Africa, and East Africa to its empire.

A decade earlier, Leopold II, the king of Belgium, acting as a private individual, formed the International Association for the Exploration and Civilization of Central Africa. Assisted by the newspaperman and adventurer Henry M. Stanley, Leopold carved out for himself a huge colony in the heart of Africa. Exercising ownership rights over what became the Congo (now Zaire), Leopold exploited the natives mercilessly. Not to be outdone, France sent out Pierre de Brazza in 1880 to lay claim to central African territory.

In 1884–1885, a conference was held in Berlin in order to bring some order to the chaotic colonial scramble. Organized by French president Jules Ferry, an ardent imperialist, and the German chancellor, Otto von Bismarck, the Berlin Conference set down important ground rules for the contending imperial powers. It established the principle that a European country's coastal claim would give that country the right to claim the interior beyond the coast. It also required that any country making a claim had to exercise "effective occupation" in order to achieve recognition for that claim. The Berlin Conference also agreed to eliminate slavery and to restrict the sale of alcohol and firearms to the natives.

Despite these attempts to regulate the imperial scramble for Africa, clashes took place. One of the most important occurred in 1898 when Britain and France collided at Fashoda in the Sudan. Beset by domestic difficulties, France reluctantly backed down and thereby abandoned its dream of a contiguous east-west empire. The clash between Great Britain and the Dutch settlers of southern Africa was even more spectacular. It led to the Boer War (1899–1902), a struggle that proved longer and more costly than Great Britain had ever imagined.

The stampede for empire also affected Asia. Great Britain and Russia struggled for control of Persia, finally dividing that country into spheres of influence in 1907. Afghanistan was also the scene of Anglo-Russian rivalry. In 1886 Britain laid claim to Burma, and ten years later it claimed Malaya. Meanwhile, the Dutch expanded from their base in Java to bring under their control most of the 3,000-mile-long Indonesian archipelago. At the same time, France gained a large empire in Indochina. In 1898, in the wake of the Spanish-American War, the United States established an imperial presence in the Philippines.

The three most important Asian countries were India, Japan, and China, and each figured prominently during the "Age of Imperial Expansion." India had been a British colony for many years before the Great Rebellion broke out in 1857. After defeating the rebels, Britain imposed direct rule on India. The British Parliament in London directed Indian affairs through an all-white colonial administration, and in 1876 Queen Victoria was proclaimed empress of India. In many ways, strong

British rule benefited India. The British were competent and generally sympathetic to the Indians. They established schools, promoted economic development, and did much to make India a unified and viable state. Yet, they rejected Indian culture, practiced an insidious form of racism, and frequently treated individual Indians with the utmost disdain.

Until 1853 Japan lived in isolation. Then U.S. commodore Matthew Perry arrived with a naval squadron and forced the Japanese to open their ports to American traders. Shocked and humiliated, Japan underwent a revolution in 1867 that brought to power energetic reformers. Determined not to fall victim to the white man, these reformers decided to remake Japan in the image of the West in order to avoid conquest by the West. They tried to achieve this while retaining as much of traditional Japanese culture as they could. In the long run, they overachieved. Japan not only grew strong enough to ward off the Europeans, it even began to manifest some of the white man's more odious characteristics, especially an imperial lust. In 1876 Japan employed gunboat diplomacy to open Korea (and in 1910 formally annexed the hapless Korean kingdom). In 1894–1895, Japan attacked China and seized Formosa. A few years later it joined the other imperialist countries in the mad scramble for influence and territory on the Chinese mainland.

China itself deserves special mention. This rich prize caught Great Britain's attention earlier in the nineteenth century, and the subsequent Opium War (1839–1842) and gunboat diplomacy opened China's markets to the West. The decrepit Manchu (Qing) dynasty that ruled China half-heartedly initiated reforms designed to preserve Chinese independence, but Japan's victory in the 1894–1895 war revealed China's weakness. Before long, Great Britain, France, Russia, Germany, and Japan all made claims on China. The United States urged an "Open Door" policy that would give all countries equal access to China. The American position won out, and China retained its nominal independence. In fact, China survived only because of the intense jealousy among the imperial powers, who preferred the fiction of an independent China to seeing one competitor or another gain an advantage.

Nevertheless, China was the site of a fitting climax to the era of imperialism. In 1904 two imperial powers, Russia and Japan, came to blows over Manchuria, a Chinese province. The Russo-Japanese War (1904–1905) saw Japan, itself only a few years earlier a potential victim of imperialism, soundly defeat the European imperialists.

INTERPRETIVE ESSAY
T. K. Welliver

The great imperial scramble of the late nineteenth century is one of the most dramatic episodes in modern history. In the decades before World War I, the European powers brought dozens of African, Asian, and Pacific territories under colonial rule for the first time. Those countries that were not conquered, such as China, Persia (Iran), Siam (Thailand), and Ethiopia, were dominated by the Europeans in other ways. In the process, imperialism transformed the lives—for good or ill—of hundreds of millions of people worldwide. Old systems of government were swept away; European settlers, administrators, merchants, and missionaries fanned out in the colonies to seek profit, educate, convert, govern, and trade. Africans and Asians could and did adapt to these new circumstances, but they did not have the luxury of doing so at their own pace.

The process of imperial conquest illustrates the stunning technological gap that had opened between the West (and Japan) and the rest of the world. In fact, it was nineteenth-century European technological advances that made the conquest possible. Before the mid-nineteenth century, conquering tropical Africa and Asia would have been an extremely costly undertaking in lives and resources. West Africa, during the four centuries of the slave trade, had become known as "the white man's grave." For new arrivals from Europe, susceptible to tropical diseases such as yellow fever and malaria, the odds were against surviving more than a year. This began to change with the adoption of quinine as a remedy for malaria in the 1830s and 1840s. With quinine, mortality rates for Europeans in the tropics dropped dramatically. Without it, conquest and colonization would have been well-nigh impossible.

The telegraph, with the laying of underwater cables in the 1860s and 1870s, was an obvious aid in ruling far-flung empires. Steamboats—both oceangoing vessels and riverboats—were decisive in reducing the cost of communications and transportation and in opening up the interior of Asia and Africa to European penetration. Without the steamboat and the railroad, the conquest and economic exploitation of many areas would hardly have been worth the effort. The first step in opening up both the Niger and the Congo Rivers to European penetration was to put steamboats on them. The conquest of the upper Nile valley by the British involved both steamboats and a railroad, as well as an underwater telegraph cable in the Nile. The French used a railroad line linking the Senegal and Niger Rivers to assist their conquest of the western Sudan. Steamboats, railroads, and telegraphy made virtually any part of the world accessible to the merchant, the entrepreneur, the soldier, the planter, the administrator, and the missionary.

New military technologies had also given the Europeans a lopsided advantage over their adversaries. By the 1870s breechloading rifles were common and were soon joined by repeating rifles and machine guns. Many of the "battles" against African or Asian armies were simply massacres. The occasional defeat could often be attributed to Africans or Asians obtaining European weapons themselves. In the worst such defeat—that of the Italian army by the Ethiopian emperor Menelik II at Adowa in 1896—it was the French, and the Italians themselves, who had supplied Menelik with his modern weapons.

The technological superiority of the Europeans helped to fuel another trend—racism. The belief in the inferiority of nonwhite races was nothing new among Europeans, but it now reached new heights, even developing into a "science." Taking their inspiration from Charles Darwin's theories, many Western thinkers came to believe that racial inequality (which was self-evident to most Europeans) was the product of differing evolutionary paths. Each race therefore had differing characteristics and abilities, which could be scientifically measured and explained. What the theory boiled down to was that the whiter one was, the more "highly evolved" one was. Those from northwest Europe— British, Germans, French, Dutch—therefore stood at the apex of evolution and civilization. As it so happened, these nations (and the Americans) were also the most economically and technologically developed at the time. It also happened that these countries had the biggest overseas empires (although the Russians did have the largest continental empire).

This unshakable belief in their own superiority was not only the product of the Europeans' domination of the world, but also a convenient justification for it. The doctrine of racial superiority resulted in at least two distinct policies toward other races. On one hand, it was used to justify removing or exterminating "inferior" races (such as the North American Indians or the Herero in German South West Africa) who stood in the way of progress and white settlement. Fortunately, this approach was relatively rare. On the other hand, racist thought developed into the concept of "trusteeship," whereby it was held to be the role—

even the duty—of European societies to rescue the brown and black races from violence and squalor, and to bestow upon them the benefits of peace, Western culture, and economic development. The famous missionary David Livingstone called for "commerce and Christianity" to be introduced into Africa to counteract the ravages of the slave trade. With the benefit of Western Civilization, others could begin to progress toward higher stages of evolution and perhaps, centuries down the road, take care of themselves. To this way of thinking, colonial conquest was not a matter of increasing European might, but rather a noble *sacrifice* on the part of Europeans in the cause of civilization. This concept— also known as the White Man's Burden—helped to justify the fact that while Europeans were becoming more democratic at home, they were establishing authoritarian governments abroad. And although it was extremely paternalistic, hypocritical, and racist, its appeal for the humanitarian sentiments of the European public was enormous.

The European public itself was caught up in the excitement and drama surrounding the exploration and conquest of exotic lands. Famous missionaries, explorers, and military heroes often had greater influence on public attitudes toward colonization than did politicians. Thus much public scorn was heaped upon William Gladstone's government in Britain for its "failure" to rescue a trapped British expeditionary force under General Charles Gordon at Khartoum in 1885, or at least to avenge his death at the hands of Sudanese insurgents.

Imperial policy could and did become an important issue in European politics. Otto von Bismarck, chancellor of Germany until 1890, regarded colonies as a waste of time but exploited imperialist sentiments anyway. Colonial matters figured prominently in Gladstone's 1880 "Midlothian Campaign" when he successfully attacked his opponent, Prime Minister Benjamin Disraeli, and his colonial policy. In the 1907 "Hottentot Election" in Germany, a major issue was Germany's colonial policy, especially its brutal suppression of a native rebellion in South West Africa. A military defeat in Indochina brought down the French cabinet in 1885 (and problems in Algeria brought about the end of the French Fourth Republic in 1958). However, for the most part it was only when things went badly in the colonies that imperial policy became a major subject of debate.

Politicians in Europe (at least in the more democratic states) were in fact trapped between the public's expansionist mood when national "honor" was at stake, and the public's opposition to the vast expenditures needed to conquer and administer the new territories. One favored solution to this problem was to place the burden of conquest and exploitation in the hands of chartered companies. Most of these companies failed to turn a profit, however, and when faced with serious armed opposition they had to be bailed out and taken over by their respective governments. Each colonial power then had to shoulder the financial burden of its own empire. They therefore insisted that the colonies pay for their own administration, and, to some extent, their own defense.

In the early twentieth century, once the scramble was over and the financial reckoning came, serious opposition to imperialism developed in Europe. The Boer War provoked loud criticism of the British government, the German government was rocked by a series of scandals involving colonial officials, and the campaign against Belgian King Leopold II's policies in the Congo—which he held as virtually a personal possession—reached fever pitch. John A. Hobson published his influential critique of British imperialism in 1902, after the scramble was largely over. It was at this point that politicians were forced to justify the huge territorial acquisitions of the previous twenty years. Colonies are valuable fields for trade and investment, they argued, and therefore good for the economy. At the same time, European workers had no need to fear losing jobs to the colonies, for the brown and black peoples of the colonies were to become consumers of European manufactures as well as suppliers of raw materials to European industry. It was argued that these colonies could be crucial for the country's survival if other empires began to close their own colonies to foreign trade and investment. In fact, it was becoming increasingly clear that European workers were not threatened by the colonies because—despite the advance billing by missionaries, explorers, and soldiers—most of them remained grievously undeveloped and unattractive to European capital. Economic self-interest, nationalism, and humanitarianism—this was a potent combination of forces, and soon the criticism subsided. Although socialists and some liberals continued to criticize particular colonial policies, even these groups came to accept colonial rule as necessary for the time being, and perhaps even a good thing for the colonized peoples.

Did Europe actually profit from imperialism? Certainly many individuals became wealthy from the colonies, but not all the colonies acquired in the scramble were attractive to investors. The colonies did provide raw materials for European industry and secure markets for manufactured goods. But these sources and markets were often disappointingly small, and direct European control may not have been necessary to exploit them. The systems of "imperial preference," developed to encourage trade within each empire, probably introduced extra costs to consumers. And taxpayers had to pay for the huge armies and navies needed to defend far-flung possessions. On the other hand, why would these countries undertake conquest if it were not lucrative?

One possible answer to this question lies in the diplomatic tensions developing in Europe. The 1880s and 1890s were years of intense diplomatic rivalry between European nations, and much of this competition was played out in the colonial scramble. Of the Great Powers, only the Russian and Austrian empires were not involved in the African scramble, although Russia was heavily involved in Asian expansion. Having colonies seems to have bolstered national pride, especially in the case of France, humiliated by the Prussians in the 1870–1871 Franco-Prussian War. Certainly it was a common belief that in order to be a Great Power, one had to possess a great empire. Britain, the largest imperial power, was the envy of the other European countries. France, angered by the British occupation of Egypt in 1882, deliberately competed with the British for colonies in West Africa, southeast Asia, and the Nile valley. Though less enthusiastic, Germany also pursued a colonial policy designed to irritate the British. Meanwhile Italy, Germany's ally, cooperated closely with the British, as did the Portuguese. All of the Powers were worried about King Leopold's activities in the Congo, fearing that they might be prevented from using that river for access to central Africa.

Of course many of these same countries would be at war in 1914. Did the colonial scramble help cause World War I? Probably not much; some have even argued that it actually delayed a European conflict, as the Great Powers released their aggressive urges overseas. But there are many links between the two events. The Boer War led to condemnation of Britain by the other Powers and seriously damaged Anglo-German relations. Soon thereafter the British and French patched up their differences. The Anglo-French Entente of 1904 depended on French acceptance of the British occupation of Egypt in exchange for a free hand in Morocco. French activities in Morocco provoked German hostility, leading to the Algeciras Conference (1906) that validated France's domination of Morocco and humiliated Germany, and later the Agadir Crisis (1911) that confirmed the Algeciras Conference's verdict. The Italian invasion of Libya in 1911 led indirectly to the outbreak of the First Balkan War of 1912, which itself set the stage for the conflict between Austria and Serbia that touched off World War I. It must be kept in mind, however, that colonial competition never resulted in armed conflicts between European states. There were several close calls, such as the 1898–1899 Fashoda

Incident and the Agadir Crisis; but despite the occasional saber rattling, European nations were reluctant to fight each other over colonies.

If imperialism was not a major cause of the war as such, it may well have affected the way the war was fought. More than one historian has suggested that the years of colonial wars against poorly armed opponents had made European generals overconfident. The colonial experience therefore could have contributed to the unspeakable and pointless slaughter of the Western Front. Imperialism also played a role in the peace settlement. The collapse of the German and Ottoman empires during the war gave the victors the opportunity to acquire even more overseas colonies. A kind of mini-scramble took place in 1919 as the French, British, Italians, Japanese, and others sought to divide the spoils. But times had changed: these new colonies were actually designated as "mandates" to be ruled under the supervision of the League of Nations. The stated goal was now to prepare these countries for independence. The Allies' (and especially President Woodrow Wilson's) own wartime rhetoric about freedom and self-determination had put old-fashioned imperialism on the defensive.

When viewed globally, the effects of imperialism varied tremendously. Each imperial power had a different purpose for, and relationship to, its colonies. Britain's long imperial tradition and huge empire put it in a category of its own. France's zest for colonial expansion is in stark contrast to Belgium's reluctant annexation of the Congo. Portugal's colonies were used as outlets for excess population; Germany's were used as diplomatic counters. Given its own history, acquiring colonies proved rather awkward for the United States, resulting in convoluted justifications and confused policies. For some countries, colonies were of great economic benefit; for others, they constituted a drain on resources. In the colonies themselves, the character of colonial rule was shaped by local political, cultural, social, and economic conditions, the circumstances of conquest, and the shifting policies of the colonizing powers. Even within a single colony the impact of colonial rule could vary widely from district to district.

For many Asians and Africans, their first view of a white man was over the barrel of a gun. This is ironic, because the imperialists maintained that they were bringing peace to the rest of the world. While the staking of territorial claims went very quickly, the actual conquest turned out to be long and bloody. In one extreme case, it took the Dutch more than thirty years (1873–1908) to gain complete control of northern Sumatra. Colonial conquest was usually accomplished with minimal military forces, and (as a consequence) a great deal of violence. On one hand, there were the great pitched battles, where African or Asian forces, armed with antiquated weapons, charged European repeaters, artillery, and machine guns. On the other hand, there was also a great deal of small-scale violence: villages and crops burned, old and young alike slaughtered. The violence continued even after the conquest was supposedly complete. Unable or unwilling to pay for a thorough administrative or military presence in their huge new colonies, the Europeans relied on the threat of force to maintain their authority. "Pacification" and "punitive expeditions" continued for decades. Two of the worst cases of violence were the German operations against a rebellion in South West Africa in 1904, and the activities of soldiers and officials in Leopold's Congo.

The violence was merely a precursor to much more fundamental changes. Old ways of life, systems of government, laws, customs, and social structures were undermined or altered in various ways. Traditional rulers often were deposed when they resisted colonial rule. When they collaborated, they had to implement the government's orders, refrain from warring with one another, collect taxes, halt the slave trade, and administer new laws. In several colonies, the British implemented a policy of "indirect rule" or rule through already existing authorities. The main reason for this policy was that it was cost-effective, saving the salaries of white administrators and soldiers. Other imperial powers tended to rule more directly, but all used the kings or chiefs to some extent. In some parts of Africa, colonial authorities even created chiefs where none had existed before.

Rulers who had regarded their kingdoms as personal possessions were now introduced to the concept of the state as an institution. Tax-farming was eliminated and corruption attacked. Rulers were placed on fixed salaries and no longer had access to revenues. Europeans controlled the appointments of chiefs, lesser officials, and judges. They gradually eliminated the systems of slavery, concubinage, and debt bondage, all of which had been widespread in Africa and Asia. Europeans also interfered in the disposition of land and other wealth (in the process managing to confiscate valuable lands for white settlers or for mining interests). These actions all served to weaken the old authorities. The introduction of Western-style schools produced a new class of educated Asians and Africans who could—and would—challenge the chiefs. Meanwhile, the weight of the colonial state was used to preserve the rulers on their thrones, accompanied by much pomp and circumstance. Thus it is not surprising that most of these chiefs, kings, sultans, and so forth emerged from the colonial period with considerable prestige but with little actual power.

Things were, if anything, worse for those who lived in "settler" colonies. In this handful of African territories—Algeria, Tunisia, Kenya, Mozambique, Angola, South Africa, Northern and Southern Rhodesia, South West Africa—white settlers sought influence over the colonial government, to the detriment of the African inhabitants. Lands were confiscated for the settlers, and Africans were relegated to crowded reserves and forced in various ways to provide labor for the white community. Vociferous settlers also delayed the granting of independence to these countries, and in many cases their actions provoked bloody uprisings or liberation struggles by the Africans.

Where the Europeans did not conquer, they still undermined old political structures. Even if they were able to resist Western armies, few countries were able resist the onslaught of Western ideas. One after another, traditional monarchs were forced to grant constitutions, establish parliaments, modernize administrations, reform their legal systems, and establish Western-style educational systems. In the case of China, the pressure to reform the government and the economy along European lines reached a crescendo in the late nineteenth century. But repeated humiliations at the hands of the Europeans (and the Japanese in 1894) actually slowed reforms and further weakened the imperial system. In the 1880s and 1890s Europeans demanded and received valuable concessions from the Chinese government, and it appeared that the entire country would be partitioned in much the same way as Africa. In 1900 the Boxer Rebellion erupted with attacks on foreigners, resulting in armed European and Japanese intervention and a further humiliation of China. Though neither conquered nor partitioned, China could not escape the tremendous forces of change unleashed by European ideas, technology, and industrial might. In 1911 a group of Chinese revolutionaries led by Dr. Sun Yat-sen overthrew the Qing dynasty and declared China a republic.

One of the most dramatic changes the Europeans brought about was the drawing of new boundaries. The colonial partition consolidated peoples from various (and sometimes antagonistic) ethnic groups into single colonies, which later became independent "nations." Furthermore, members of a single ethnic group sometimes found themselves divided by a new international boundary. These borders reflected the interests of the colonizing powers, not the viability or cultural coherence of the colonies themselves. When independence came, these rather artificial creations were expected to function as nation-states. In other words, the modern nation-state system was imposed from outside. A complex arrangement that had evolved in Europe over centuries was applied to Africa and Asia in a matter of decades. Small wonder that political instability has been one of the hallmarks of the former colonies in recent years; the task of "nation-building" has only just begun in these countries. To make the process of nation-building even harder, many of the new states, particularly in sub-Saharan Africa, have been forced to adopt the language of the relevant colonial power as the "national" language. In a multi-ethnic society, to adopt the language of one group would provoke jealousy among other groups; but to use several languages would be inefficient and might prevent the creation of a common identity. Therefore in some African countries the national language is English, French, or Portuguese. In many countries, primary education is conducted in the local languages, while later studies are conducted in a European language. Ethiopia adopted English as the language of higher education, even though it was never actually ruled by the British.

If the colonies proved to be politically fragile, they were in many cases impoverished as well. Even though the promise of wealth was one motivating factor in the scramble, many of the colonies proved to be highly disappointing to the Europeans. Trade and therefore tax revenues were at such a rudimentary level that it was often difficult for the colonial administration to support even itself. There were exceptions, of course: South Africa's fabulous wealth in gold and diamonds, Malaya's rubber plantations and tin mines, Egypt's cotton, Burma's rice, the Gold Coast's cocoa, Zanzibar's cloves. But many colonies could only be made to pay through crass exploitation and forced labor. King Leopold's Congo turned a tidy profit from wild rubber, but only by using extremely brutal methods. Those colonies that became prosperous were usually reliant on one or two crops or minerals for export revenue. This "monoculture" made them vulnerable to fluctuations in world markets that often produced boom-and-bust cycles. This is still the situation today, at least in Africa. Little or no industrialization occurred in the colonies; they were suppliers of raw materials to European industries. Infrastructural improvements were made, often at government expense and using forced labor, in an attempt to make the colonies more profitable. These harbors, roads, railroads, and other facilities were designed to ease the export of cash crops and minerals to Europe, or to facilitate administration, rather than to encourage trade internally or with neighboring countries. This policy left most countries with deficient communications networks at independence (for years after independence, telephone calls between neighboring African countries would still be routed through Europe). At the same time, roads and railroads brought manufactured consumer goods from the outside world. Local industries, such as textiles, pottery, or metal-working, were destroyed or marginalized by cheap factory-produced goods. Even after independence, the former colonies tended to remain economically dependent on, but marginal to, the world economy.

The building of roads, railroads, and port facilities opened up vast territories to the world economy. The economies of entire regions changed as mining or cash crops replaced subsistence farming. New migration patterns unfolded as people were attracted to (or were forced into) work in the new ports, plantations, or mines. These laborers were usually men, who often left their families in the villages for extended periods of time. Population movement and urbanization also accelerated the spread of diseases (especially in the early colonial period) and the rise of new social ills such as prostitution. On the other hand, improving health care and sanitation resulted in increasing population growth. In the urban areas, migrants were forced to change their customs, residential patterns, and work habits. For those remaining in the countryside, families now faced taxation in cash, and the temptations (and competition) of imported consumer goods. To pay for these, peasants needed either to produce marketable crops or to work for wages. New opportunities for wealth (such as control over scarce land or access to education) led to greater inequalities in society. Furthermore, the European emphasis on individual rights and responsibilities tended to erode communal life.

Africans and Asians also experienced cultural change as the result of colonial rule. Officials, settlers, and missionaries tried to impose their own norms. Certain practices such as slavery, human sacrifice, ritual cannibalism, and infanticide were so abhorrent to the Europeans that they were banned outright. Other practices were actively discouraged. These included witchcraft, traditional religious practices, nudity, scarification, polygamy, bridewealth, and clitoridectomy and other forms of female circumcision. Efforts to suppress these practices often encountered fierce resistance, striking as they did at the heart of family life and social cohesion.

Along with settlers and missionaries, colonial rule brought large numbers of Indian merchants and laborers to eastern and southern Africa, the West Indies, and the Pacific islands, Chinese merchants and laborers to southeast Asia and southern Africa, and Lebanese merchants to West Africa. Within a generation or two, these immigrants became more prosperous than the native populations among whom they lived (often causing envy). They brought with them the cultures of their homelands, contributing to the interaction taking place in the colonies. But these immigrants tended to pick up the racist attitudes of the white rulers, reinforcing the sense of inferiority among native peoples. Some of the latter internalized these feelings, others reacted with hostility and rejection, while still others tried hard to become "European" in all but color.

Colonial rule also brought with it new systems of education. Schools providing Western-style education were founded either by missionaries or by the colonial governments themselves. Access to education could lead to employment with the government or European business, resulting in a dramatic rise in social status. Even though educational opportunities tended to be limited—it being felt that colonial peoples could not benefit from advanced studies—the spread of literacy was one of the most important consequences of imperialism. The introduction of newspapers and radio accelerated the spread of new ideas and attitudes. These ideas often undermined traditional practices and beliefs, but they also provided the ammunition needed to begin the fight for independence. It was Western ideas—individual dignity and freedom, nationalism, liberalism, and socialism—that Africans and Asians used to unite themselves and free themselves from European rule. It was the Western-educated elites, not the traditional rulers, who led these countries to independence and have dominated them ever since.

Missionaries, newspapers, and schools spread Western ideas and values throughout the world, but cultural influence is a two-way street. The West has over the years borrowed heavily from Africa and Asia. Hundreds of words from African and Asian languages have entered European languages. Finding Western culture tired or bankrupt, many artists, composers, and thinkers have turned to other cultures for inspiration and revival. Pablo Picasso and other innovators of modern art borrowed consciously from the "primitive" art of Africa and the Pacific. Varieties of Islam, Buddhism, and Hinduism have attracted European converts. The twentieth-century West continues to be heavily influenced by African music and Asian foods. Not all of this influence is entirely attributable to imperialism, but the imperial experience has no doubt helped accelerate this cultural exchange. In recent decades it has become even more intense. Where once Europeans migrated to the far-flung corners of their empires, now millions of people from the colonies and former colonies have migrated to Europe. France has a large Algerian and West African population, Britain a large Indian and West Indian population, and so forth. It seems likely that such population migrations will continue to shape European society in the future.

Had the colonial scramble never happened, many of the changes described above would have occurred anyway. Many of them were taking place before the scramble began, the case of Japan being a dramatic example. European civilization exerted enormous influence around the world due to its technological, economic, and military power, regardless of whether or not the Europeans engaged in actual conquest. One can easily find similar processes at work both in countries that were conquered and in those that remained independent. But the colonial scramble certainly intensified these effects, and, crucially, took much of the initiative away from Asian and African peoples. As the colonial era recedes into the past, our estimate of its significance also tends to recede. But for several generations of Europeans, Asians, and Africans, the era of colonial rule was the crucible in which the modern world was forged.

SELECTED BIBLIOGRAPHY

Baumgart, Winfried. *Imperialism: The Idea and Reality of British and French Colonial Expansion, 1880–1914.* New York: Oxford University Press, 1982. This book provides a concise introduction to, and assessment of, the different theories of the causes of the colonial scramble.

Brewer, Anthony. *Marxist Theories of Imperialism: A Critical Survey.* 2nd ed. London: Routledge and Kegan Paul, 1990. This is a readable summary and critique, from a Marxist perspective, of a number of prominent theories, including underdevelopment theories.

Doyle, Michael W. *Empires.* Ithaca, NY: Cornell University Press, 1986. Doyle attempts to construct a universal theoretical framework for the types and stages of imperial rule, incorporating examples (both Western and non-Western) from the ancient world to the present.

Edwardes, Michael. *The West in Asia, 1850–1914.* New York: Putnam, 1967. Edwardes gives an excellent, concise, and comprehensive (if somewhat dated) survey of the Asian theater of imperial rivalry, including a discussion of whether or not imperialism was "profitable."

Fieldhouse, D. K. *Economics and Empire, 1830–1914.* London: Macmillan, 1984. Fieldhouse provides a continent-by-continent analysis of the economic aspects of colonial expansion, with a brief but elegant conclusion which in some ways reinforces the Robinson and Gallagher thesis (see below).

Frank, Andre Gunder. *Capitalism and Underdevelopment in Latin America.* New

York: Monthly Review Press, 1967. In this seminal work of the quasi-Marxist "underdevelopment" genre, Frank argues that European capitalism fostered economic dependency and inequality in Latin America.

Gann, Lewis H., and Peter Duignan, eds. *Colonialism in Africa, 1870–1960.* 5 vols. London: Cambridge University Press, 1969–1975. The most thorough collection available concerning conquest and colonial rule in Africa.

Headrick, Daniel R. *The Tools of Empire: Technology and European Imperialism in the Nineteenth Century.* New York: Oxford University Press, 1981. Headrick provides a fascinating account of the technologies (in communications, medicine, and warfare) that enabled the European conquest of the tropics.

Hobson, John A. *Imperialism: A Study.* 3rd ed. London: Allen and Unwin, 1938. In this influential work, Hobson argued that powerful financial interests lay behind the policies of British colonial expansion.

Kiernan, V. G. *From Conquest to Collapse: European Empires from 1815 to 1960.* New York: Pantheon, 1982. A brief military history of European imperialism.

———. *The Lords of Human Kind: Black Man, Yellow Man, and White Man in an Age of Empire.* Boston: Little, Brown, 1969. This is a somewhat superficial but still interesting study of European attitudes toward other peoples (and these peoples' attitudes toward Europeans) in the age of imperialism.

Langer, William L. *The Diplomacy of Imperialism, 1890–1902.* 2nd ed. New York: Knopf, 1951. Detailed and thorough, this is a classic work in diplomatic history, and much of it has held up well over the years.

Lenin, V. I. *Imperialism: The Highest Stage of Capitalism.* New York: International Publishers, 1939. Lenin draws on Hobson's data and conclusions (see above) to argue that imperialism is a sign of the impending collapse of the capitalist system.

Lugard, Frederick. *The Dual Mandate in British Tropical Africa.* 5th ed. London: Frank Cass, 1965. This work was used as a blueprint by a generation of British colonial administrators in Africa; in it Lugard attempts to reconcile economic exploitation of colonies with the humanitarian duty of the colonizers.

Mannoni, Otare. *Prospero and Caliban: The Psychology of Colonization.* Translated by Pamela Powesland. London: Methuen, 1956. Mannoni introduces the concept of a "dependency complex" as he outlines a progression of psychological stages among colonized peoples.

Mommsen, Wolfgang J. *Theories of Imperialism.* Translated by P. S. Falla. New York: Random House, 1980. Mommsen presents a clear, concise summary of the various theories concerning the causes of imperialism.

Pakenham, Thomas. *The Scramble for Africa, 1876–1912.* New York: Random House, 1991. An exuberant account of the African scramble, mostly from the perspective of the conquerors.

Pierce, Richard A. *Russian Central Asia, 1867–1917: A Study in Colonial Rule.* Berkeley: University of California Press, 1960. An important work on an oft-neglected aspect of European imperialism.

Robinson, Ronald, and John Gallagher, with Alice Denny. *Africa and the Victorians: The Climax of Imperialism in the Dark Continent.* New York: St. Martin's Press, 1961. This work was the first to argue that conditions on the "periphery" were more important than European trends in triggering the scramble; it has generated considerable debate over the years.

Rodney, Walter. *How Europe Underdeveloped Africa.* Washington, DC: Howard University Press, 1974. Though controversial in its application of "underdevelopment" theory to Africa, this book has been very influential among African intellectuals.

Said, Edward. *Culture and Imperialism.* New York: Knopf, 1993. Using the techniques of literary criticism, Said examines the complex relationship between Western politics and Western culture from the age of imperialism down to the present.

de Schweinitz, Karl, Jr. *The Rise and Fall of British India: Imperialism as Inequality.* New York: Methuen, 1983. A short, incisive look at the political economy of three centuries of British involvement in India.

Smith, Tony. *The Pattern of Imperialism: The United States, Great Britain, and the Late-Industrializing World since 1815.* Cambridge: Cambridge University Press, 1981. Smith compares British imperialism with later U.S. imperialism, focusing on relations between these powers and the nations of Asia and Africa.

Stoecker, Helmuth, ed. *German Imperialism in Africa: From the Beginnings until the Second World War.* Translated by Bernd Zöllner. Atlantic Highlands, NJ: Humanities Press International, 1986. This collection of essays, mostly written by Stoecker, presents a comprehensive account of German colonization in Africa, and even carries the story beyond Germany's loss of empire in World War I.

Suret-Canale, Jean. *French Colonialism in Tropical Africa, 1900–1945.* Translated by Till Gottheiner. New York: Pica Press, 1971. This is the standard work on France's policies in its sub-Saharan African colonies.

Appendix A

Glossary

Anarchism. Anarchism was a violent political movement that became popular with radicals in the second half of the nineteenth century. Anarchists rejected the state and all other organizations such as the church and the military which seemed to limit unfettered individual liberty.

Balance of Power. One of the dominant concepts of international relations, the balance of power holds that preventing the dangerous growth of power in one nation or a combination of nations is desirable. An effective distribution of power among nations often can be accomplished through alliance and counteralliance.

Berlin Wall. Erected in 1961 to halt the exodus of people from East Germany, the Berlin Wall separated East Berlin from West Berlin. The wall came to represent the post–World War II division of Europe in general and Germany specifically. The Berlin Wall fell in 1989, thereby signaling the end of the East German regime and clearing the way for German reunification.

Boer War (1899–1902). This war pitted British troops against Afrikaaner, or Dutch, settlers in southern Africa and represented an effort to bring the Boer Republics of Transvaal and the Orange Free State into the British Empire.

Bourbons. The Bourbons were the ruling house of France from 1589 until 1793. After Napoleon's downfall, they regained the French throne in 1814, but they were ousted once again in 1830.

Canning, George (1770–1827). Canning was Great Britain's foreign secretary (1807–1809, 1822–1827) and prime minister (1827). He opposed Metternich's Concert of Europe and guided Britain along an independent course. He also supported independence for Spain's American colonies, seeing in this a golden opportunity for British commercial and political interests.

Carlsbad Decrees (1819). Alarmed by signs of rising German nationalism, Clemens von Metternich assembled the principal German states at Carlsbad, where he persuaded them to issue a set of decrees suppressing the German press and universities. The Carlsbad Decrees retarded liberalism and nationalism in Germany for many years.

Classic liberalism. Classic liberalism is a set of ideas made popular during the eighteenth and early nineteenth centuries that called for the rule of law, constitutionalism, freedom of religion, civil liberties, and a market economy free of governmental interference.

Classical economists. Classical economists shaped economic thought in the late eighteenth and early nineteenth centuries. They embraced laissez faire economic doctrine and frequently were disciples of Adam Smith.

Colonial Society. The Colonial Society, or *Kolonialverein*, was a German lobbying group formed in 1882 in order to push for the creation of a German overseas empire.

Commercial Revolution. Beginning in the late Middle Ages, capitalism began to supersede manorialism as the dominant economic system in western Europe. The changing nature of Europe's economy, with increased trade and commerce as well as the use of free as opposed to serf labor, was called the Commercial Revolution.

Confederation of the Rhine. Established by Napoleon I in 1806, the Confederation of the Rhine, which included most of the German states, was a puppet state controlled by Paris. With Napoleon's defeat at the Battle of Leipzig (1813), the confederation broke up and most of its members joined the coalition against Napoleon.

Confucius (551–479 B.C.). Confucius was a Chinese teacher and philosopher whose precepts not only dominated Chinese life but also greatly influenced Japan's culture.

Crimean War (1853–1856). This almost accidental war featured Great Britain and France fighting Russia over the question of influence in the declining Ottoman Empire. The war concluded in defeat for Russia, but it failed to end either that state's ambitions in the Balkans or its desire to dominate the Ottoman Empire.

Darwin, Charles (1809–1882). Perhaps the nineteenth century's most outstanding intellectual, Darwin was a British naturalist who hypothesized that all life develops in an evolutionary manner. His writings gave rise to the belief that some races had evolved more successfully than others.

Erfurt Program (1891). Adopted by the German Social Democratic Party at its 1891 conference held at Erfurt, the Erfurt Program established orthodox Marxism as the party's doctrinal foundation.

Franco-Prussian War (1870–1871). This war between Emperor Napoleon III's France and a combination of German-speaking states led by Chancellor Otto von Bismarck's Prussia resulted in a decisive victory for the latter and led to the formation of the German Empire in January 1871.

Frankfurt Assembly. Often referred to as the Frankfurt Parliament, the Frankfurt Assembly resulted from the Revolutions of 1848 in the German-speaking lands. The Assembly tried to construct a unified, liberal state, but its delegates fell to endless debating and the Assembly failed to achieve its goal.

German Confederation. Created in 1815 by Clemens von Metternich in the wake of Napoleon's defeat, the German Confederation was a loose union of thirty-nine German states dominated by Austria, with Prussia also playing a major supporting role.

Gladstone, William E. (1809–1898). Prime Minister of Great Britain on four separate occasions, Gladstone reflected the sentiment of the "Little Englanders," who believed that Britain's empire was too costly to maintain.

Gordon, General Charles "Chinese" (1833–1885). A British military officer, Gordon first gained fame leading Chinese troops in putting down the Taiping Rebellion. Later he was sent to the Sudan, where he and his small contingent of Egyptian troops were massacred by the natives at Khartoum.

Great Powers. This term describes several European states including Great Britain, France, Austria, Prussia (Germany), and Russia that controlled international relations in Europe during the nineteenth century.

Gunboat diplomacy. This phrase describes a diplomatic policy employed by strong naval powers, especially Great Britain and the United States, during the nineteenth and early twentieth centuries. Under this policy, naval vessels were stationed near harbors of countries experiencing internal political instability. The display of naval power was presumed to be sufficient to ameliorate a bad situation and to avert military intervention, although in practice there were numerous examples of direct intervention.

Habsburgs. The Habsburgs were the ruling house of Austria from 1267 until 1918. They also served as Holy Roman Emperors from 1438 to 1806.

Hobson, John A. (1858–1940). An English socialist. Hobson's 1902 book, *Imperialism: A Study,* argued that imperialism resulted from capitalism's desire for ever greater profits.

Holy Roman Empire. Formally established in 962, the Holy Roman Empire included a large number of German-speaking states. Although a Habsburg usually served as emperor, real power rested with the empire's princes, who ruled over the state's component parts. Napoleon dissolved the Holy Roman Empire in 1806.

Jameson Raid. The Jameson Raid was a failed attempt by Cecil Rhodes, head of Great Britain's Cape Colony, to foment revolution in the neighboring Transvaal, which was controlled by the Boers, or Dutch settlers. The raid not only prompted a controversial telegram from Germany's Kaiser William II congratulating the Boers, but it also helped to lead to the outbreak of the Boer War in 1899.

July Monarchy. This term was applied to the reign of Louis Philippe, who became king of France after the July Revolution (1830).

July Revolution (1830). This revolution, engineered chiefly by the French bourgeoisie, replaced the last Bourbon monarch, the ultra-conservative Charles X, with his more moderate cousin, Louis Philippe from the house of Orleans.

Laissez faire. In economics, the theory of laissez faire postulates that the economy will perform most effectively when the state refrains from interfering in economic life.

League of Nations. Created at the end of World War I, the League of Nations was an international body composed of sovereign states committed to the settlement of international disputes in a peaceful manner.

Mazzini, Giuseppe (1805–1872). One of the foremost theoreticians of modern nationalism, Mazzini believed that every national group possessed intrinsic value and should have the right to determine its own fate.

M.P. This is the common abbreviation for Member of Parliament.

Old regime. The old regime, or *ancien regime,* refers to the political and social system existing in France before the Revolution of 1789. It also refers to any defunct system.

Palmerston, Viscount (1784–1865). Palmerston was Great Britain's foreign secretary (1830–1841) and twice prime minister (1855–1858, 1859–1865). He ignored Metternich's Concert of Europe, choosing instead to pursue Britain's diplomatic objectives independently.

Paris Commune (1871). In the wake of France's defeat in the Franco-Prussian War (1870–1871), France fell into a state resembling civil war. Radicals, some of whom were inclined to support socialist ideas, seized control of Paris and established the Paris Commune. The Commune was finally defeated in fighting famous for its barbarism and brutality.

Partitions of Poland (1772, 1793, 1795). Seizing on the ingrained weaknesses of the dilapidated Polish state, its three neighbors (Austria, Prussia, and Russia) on three occasions at the end of the eighteenth century partitioned Poland. The third and final partition erased Poland from the map.

Polish Question. The Poles did not take kindly to the partition and elimination of their state at the end of the eighteenth century. Their discontent and determination to resurrect Poland gave rise to the Polish Question, which plagued European diplomacy in the nineteenth century.

Pugachev Revolt (1773–1774). Led by the charismatic peasant Emilian Pugachev, Russia's serfs staged a major insurrection that threatened to topple Catherine the Great. Seeking the end of serfdom, Pugachev's followers made considerable headway until defeated and dispersed by regular army units.

Reason of state. A phrase frequently expressed in the French (*raison d'etat*), reason of state served as a blanket excuse for a state to act in any manner it wished, both domestically and in international matters.

Risorgimento. Appearing in the latter part of the eighteenth century, the Risorgimento was a movement for the liberation, reform, and unification of the Italian peninsula. Greatly stimulated by the French Revolution and Napoleon I, the Risorgimento achieved its objectives shortly after the middle of the nineteenth century.

Russell, Lord John (1792–1878). Russell was a leading Whig politician and reformer who played an important role in drafting and passing the Reform Bill of 1832. On two separate occasions (1846–1852, 1865–1866), he served as prime minister.

Shinto. One of Japan's major religions, Shinto regards the Japanese emperor as a divine being.

Slavs. The Slavs are kindred peoples who live in eastern, east central, and southeastern Europe. They include the Russians, Ukrainians, Poles, Czechs, Slovaks, Slovenes, Croats, Serbs, and Bulgarians.

Smith, Adam (1723–1790). Adam Smith was a Scottish professor who embraced the ideas of the Enlightenment. In 1776 he wrote an influential book on economics, *The Wealth of Nations,* and he is generally regarded as the father of laissez faire economic theory.

Social Darwinism. Derived from Charles Darwin's pioneering nineteenth-century work on evolution, Social Darwinsim concluded that the struggle for existence and survival of the fittest applied to individuals and nations as well as plants and lesser animals. This concept both justified and encouraged belligerent, aggressive nationalism and racism.

Status quo ante bellum. From the Latin, status quo ante bellum means the existing condition or state of affairs before the outbreak of war.

Treaty of Versailles. The Treaty of Versailles was signed in June 1919, the final product of the Paris Peace Conference following World War I. Germans despised the treaty because of its perceived harsh treatment of Germany.

Western Front. The Western Front was the site of extensive military operations during World War I that took the lives of millions of combatants. It stretched from the English Channel through Belgium and France to the Swiss border.

White Revolutionaries. White Revolutionary is a term applied to statesmen who superficially appear to be quite conservative but whose policies represent a radical, revolutionary departure from the status quo.

Appendix B

Timeline

1801	Concordat settles church-state relations in France
1802	Peace of Amiens
1803–1805	War of the Third Coalition
1804	Napoleon crowned emperor
	Code Napoléon introduced
1805	Battle of Trafalgar
	Battle of Austerlitz
1806–1825	Latin American Wars of Independence
1806	Holy Roman Empire disbanded
	Berlin Decree issued
1807	Robert Fulton invents the steamboat
	Peace of Tilsit
	British slave trade abolished
1808	Spanish commence guerrilla war against French invaders

1810	Napoleon marries the Austrian archduchess Maria Louise
1812	Napoleon invades Russia
	United States declares war on Great Britain
1813	Battle of Leipzig
1814	Napoleon exiled to Elba
	Congress of Vienna convenes
	George Stephenson invents the locomotive
1815	Napoleon's Hundred Days
	Battle of Waterloo
	Napoleon exiled to St. Helena
	Quadruple Alliance
	Corn Laws enacted in Great Britain
1818	Congress of Aix-la-Chapelle
1819	Peterloo massacre
	Carlsbad Decrees
	British establish Singapore
1820	Revolutions in Italy and Spain
	Congress of Troppau
1821	Congress of Laibach
	Greek war of independence begins
1822	Congress of Verona
1823	Monroe Doctrine
1825	Decembrist revolt in Russia
1829	Independence for Greece
1830	Revolutions in France, Belgium, and Poland
1832	First Reform Act in Great Britain
1833	Great Britain outlaws slavery in its colonies
1834	Zollverein, or German customs union, formed
1839–1842	"Opium" War between Great Britain and China
1842	Treaty of Nanking marks beginning of "treaty system" in China

	British establish Hong Kong
1846	Corn Laws repealed in Great Britain
1848	Revolutions in France, Italy, Austria, and Germany
	Second Republic declared in France
	Karl Marx and Friedrich Engels publish *The Communist Manifesto*
1850	Taiping Revolution begins in China
1851	Crystal Palace exhibition held in London
1852	Louis Napoleon establishes the Second Empire in France
1853–1854	Commodore Matthew Perry "opens" Japan
1853–1856	Crimean War
1856–1860	Anglo-Chinese War
1856	Henry Bessemer invents the blast furnace
1857–1858	Sepoy rebellion in India
1858	Formation of Romania
1859	Austro-Italian War
	Charles Darwin publishes *On the Origin of Species*
1860	Kingdom of Italy established
1861–1865	U.S. Civil War
1861	Emancipation of the Russian serfs
1862–1882	France conquers Indochina
1863	Poles rebel against Russian overlordship
1864	First International Working Men's Association established
1865	Transatlantic telegraph cable laid
1866	Austro-Prussian War
1867	Creation of the Austro-Hungarian monarchy
	Second Reform Act in Great Britain
	Karl Marx publishes *Capital*
	Emperor Maximilian of Mexico executed
1868	Meiji Restoration in Japan

1869	Suez Canal opened
1870–1871	Franco-Prussian War
1870	Doctrine of papal infallibility proclaimed
	Third Republic declared in France
1871	German Empire proclaimed
	Paris Commune
	Charles Darwin publishes *The Descent of Man*
1873	Dreikaiserbund, or Three Emperors' League
1876	Queen Victoria proclaimed Empress of India
1877–1878	Russo-Turkish War
1878	Congress of Berlin
	Independence for Serbia
	International Congo Association founded
1879	Dual Alliance formed
1881	Emperor Alexander II of Russia assassinated
1882	Triple Alliance formed
1884	Third Reform Act in Great Britain
1885	Berlin Conference on Africa
	Indian National Congress founded
1889	Second International Working Men's Association established
	Japanese constitution promulgated
1890	Bismarck dismissed as German chancellor
	Construction of Trans-Siberian railway undertaken
1893	Right to vote extended to women in New Zealand
1894–1895	Sino-Japanese War
1894–1906	Dreyfus Affair in France
1894	Alliance between France and Russia
1896	Zionism founded
	Ethiopians defeat Italians at Adowa
1898	Spanish-American War
	Battle of Omdurman

1899–1900	United States declares "Open Door" policy
1899–1901	Boxer Uprising in China
1899–1902	Boer War
1900	Universal Exposition in Paris celebrates end of century

Appendix C

Population of Selected Countries (in Millions)

	1800	1850	1900
Argentina	0.9	1.1	4.7
Austria-Hungary	26.0	35.0	45.0
Brazil	—	7.2	17.9
China	295.0	430.0	450.0
Egypt	2.5	5.0	10.0
France	27.0	34.2	38.5
Germany (including Prussia)	25.0	33.8	56.3
India	130.0	206.0	294.0
Italy	17.2	24.3	33.6
Japan	29.0	30.0	45.0
Mexico	6.0	7.7	13.6
Russia	30.0	68.5	146.0
Spain	10.5	16.0	19.1
United Kingdom	15.7	27.3	41.5
United States	5.3	23.2	76.0

Appendix D

Countries Colonized During the "Imperial Scramble" (1870–1914)

Name of Country at Time of Annexation	Name of Country at Time of Independence	Colonizing Power
Afars and Issas	Djibouti	France
Bechuanaland	Botswana	United Kingdom
Belgian Congo	Zaire	Belgium
Bhutan	Bhutan	United Kingdom
Brunei	Brunei	United Kingdom
Burundi	Burundi	Germany
Chad	Chad	France
Cochin-China	Vietnam, South	France
Comoros	Comoros	France
Congo	Congo	France
Dahomey	Benin	France
Ellice Islands	Tuvalu	United Kingdom
Eritrea	Eritrea	Italy
Fiji	Fiji	United Kingdom
Gabon	Gabon	France
German East Africa	Tanganyika	Germany
Gilbert Islands	Kiribati	United Kingdom
Guinea	Guinea	France
Korea (Chosen)	Korea, North	Japan
Korean (Chosen)	Korea, South	Japan

Name of Country at Time of Annexation	Name of Country at Time of Independence	Colonizing Power
Laos	Laos	France
Libya	Libya	Italy
Madagascar	Madagascar	France
Maldives	Maldives	United Kingdom
Mali	Mali	France
Marshall Islands	Marshall Islands	Germany
Mauritania	Mauritania	France
Morocco	Morocco	France
Nauru	Nauru	Germany
New Hebrides	Vanuatu	France and United Kingdom
Niger	Niger	France
Nyasaland	Malawi	United Kingdom
Papua New Guinea	Papua New Guinea	Germany and United Kingdom
Philippines	Philippines	United States*
Rhodesia, Northern	Zambia	United Kingdom
Rhodesia, Southern	Zimbabwe	United Kingdom
Russian Turkistan	Turkmenistan	Russia
Rwanda	Rwanda	Germany
Senegal	Senegal	France
Solomon Islands	Solomon Islands	United Kingdom
Swaziland	Swaziland	United Kingdom
Togoland	Togo	Germany
Tonkin Annam	Vietnam, North	France
Tunisia	Tunisia	France
Ubangi-Shari	Central African Republic	France
Uganda	Uganda	United Kingdom
Upper Volta	Burkino Faso	France
Zanzibar	Zanzibar	United Kingdom

*After the 1898 Spanish-American War, the United States seized Spain's colonies.

Index

About the Editors and Contributors

BRUCE F. ADAMS is professor of history and chairman of the department at the University of Louisville. He received his Ph.D. from the University of Maryland. He is the author of *The Politics of Punishment: Prison Reform in Russia, 1863–1917* (1996), and the translator and editor of V. V. Shulgin's *Days of the Russian Revolution: Memoirs from the Right, 1905–1917* (1990).

ROBERT D. BILLINGER, JR. is professor of history at Wingate University. He received his Ph.D. from the University of North Carolina at Chapel Hill. He is the author of *Metternich and the German Question: States' Rights and Federal Duties, 1820–1834* (1991), and has contributed articles to *Statesmen Who Changed the World* (1993), and *Central European History*. Professor Billinger is a former Fulbright Scholar to Vienna.

M. B. BISKUPSKI is professor of history at St. John Fisher College. He received his Ph.D. from Yale University. He is the editor of *Polish Democratic Thought from the Renaissance to the Great Emigration* (1990), and has contributed articles to *The Polish Review* and *Polish American Studies*.

JOHN K. COX is assistant professor of history at Wheeling Jesuit College. He received his Ph.D. from Indiana University and has contributed to

Statesmen Who Changed the World (1993). He has traveled extensively in the former Yugoslavia and is currently secretary-treasurer of the Society for Slovene Studies.

JOHN E. FINDLING is professor of history at Indiana University Southeast. He received his Ph.D. from the University of Texas and is the author of *Dictionary of American Diplomatic History* (1980; 1989), *Close Neighbors, Distant Friends: United States–Central American Relations* (1987), and *Chicago's Great World's Fairs* (1994). He is the editor of *Historical Dictionary of World's Fairs and Expositions, 1851–1988* (1990) and, with Frank W. Thackeray, *Statesmen Who Changed the World* (1993), *Events That Changed the World in the Twentieth Century* (1995), and *Events That Changed America in the Twentieth Century* (1996). With Kimberly Pelle, Professor Findling edited *Historical Dictionary of the Modern Olympic Movement* (1996).

DANIEL W. HOLLIS, III is professor of history at Jacksonville State University. He received his Ph.D. from Vanderbilt University. He has contributed articles to *Encyclopedia of Twentieth Century Britain* (1995), *Dictionary of Literary Biography* (1995), *Albion* (1994), *Statesmen Who Changed the World* (1993), and *Historical Dictionary of Tudor England, 1485–1603* (1991).

J. BURTON KIRKWOOD is assistant professor of history at the University of Evansville. He received his Ph.D. from Florida State University in 1995. He is the editor of *The Urban History Workshop Review*. He has traveled extensively in Mexico, which is the area of his historical specialization.

PAUL D. LENSINK recently received his Ph.D. from Indiana University. He is the author of several articles on Eastern Europe for the *Encyclopedia of Modern East Europe* (forthcoming). He is a former Fulbright scholar to Slovenia and is currently researching the development of Slovene nationalism.

FRANK W. THACKERAY is professor of history at Indiana University Southeast. He received his Ph.D. from Temple University. He is the author of *Antecedents of Revolution: Tsar Alexander I and the Polish Congress Kingdom* (1980). He has contributed articles to *The Polish Review* and *East Central Europe*, and written chapters for *Eastern Europe and the West* (1992), and *Imperial Power and Development* (1990). With John E. Findling, he is editor of *Statesmen Who Changed the World* (1993), *Events That Changed the World in the Twentieth Century* (1995), and *Events That Changed America in the Twentieth Century* (1996). Professor Thackeray is a former Fulbright scholar to Poland.

ELEANOR L. TURK is professor of history and assistant vice chancellor at Indiana University East. She received her Ph.D. from the University of Wisconsin. She has contributed articles to *Great Leaders, Great Tyrants* (1995), *Reconsideration of the Imperial Era* (1988), and *Central European History*. Professor Turk is currently researching the question of civil liberties in imperial Germany.

T. K. WELLIVER is associate professor of history at Bellarmine College. He received his Ph.D. from Northwestern University. He is the editor of *African Nationalism and Independence* (1993) and a specialist in the history of modern Zanzibar.

GEORGE M. WILSON is professor of history and East Asian languages and culture at Indiana University. He is also director of Indiana's East Asia Studies Center. He received his Ph.D. from Harvard University. He is the author of *Patriots and Redeemers in Japan: Motives in the Meiji Restoration* (1992) and *Radical Nationalist in Japan: Kita Ikka, 1883–1937* (1969).